P9-DZN-342

"I often say the fundamental problem with our bilateral relationship is one of assumptions: Canadians think they know *everything* about the United States, and Americans think they know *enough* about Canada. And of course, we all could do a whole lot better learning a whole lot more about one another.

The Canadian Century offers the perfect tutorial for folks on both sides of the border.

Thoughtful, clear-eyed and provocative, *The Canadian Century* explains why the US ignores our dynamic neighbors to the north at our own peril. Canada has been building a safe and stable fiscal house for decades, proving itself a powerhouse on the global stage and a most vital economic, energy and military partner to the United States.

The authors provide a compelling—and optimistic—analysis of both the challenges and the triumphs the future offers our two dynamic democracies and make the case why the US–Canada partnership is so worthy of our leaders' time and attention."

—**DAVID H. WILKINS**, former US Ambassador to Canada, 2005–2009

"*The Canadian Century* reminds us that the temptation for governments to solve all our problems with higher spending always ends in grief—a lesson the US will soon learn. It's a reminder that prosperity can be ours if we remember Wilfrid Laurier's legacy of liberty, lower taxes and smaller government."

—**PATRICK LUCIANI**, author of *Economic Myths*

"Crowley, Clemens and Veldhuis draw an intriguing link between the nineteenth century convictions of Wilfrid Laurier—individual liberty and responsibility, minimal taxes and rules, maintenance of an open, competitive edge vis-à-vis the US—and the policy prescriptions needed to ensure a brighter twenty-first century for Canada. Their thoroughly documented analysis of the Redemptive Decade that ushered in Free Trade, the GST and deficit control, demonstrates how Canada has acted in its own best interest. Moreover, they show that if we establish a real advantage vis-à-vis the US on tax and other policies it will increase both our attraction with emerging powers and our leverage with the US. The question the authors pose is whether we have the wherewithal to finish the job."

—**DEREK BURNEY**, former Canadian Ambassador to the US, 1989–1993

"As the US and other nations struggle to defuse some potentially disastrous fiscal time bombs, *The Canadian Century* makes a compelling argument that the world should be looking to Canada for lessons on how to get reform right."

—**ROBERT KELLY**, Chairman and CEO, BNY Mellon

"Crowley, Clemens and Veldhuis tell a compelling tale of Canada's economic policy history over the past one hundred years from the perspective of Sir Wilfrid Laurier's vision. Many Canadians will be familiar with Laurier's boast that 'the twentieth century would be filled by Canada.' There will be less familiarity with his policy prescriptions and hence perhaps skepticism that the authors' approach can work. But it works exceedingly well. First because Laurier's ideas, once highly controversial, now seem so sound. Who now doesn't believe in individual freedom and responsibility; competitive taxes with fiscal balance and; self-confident engagement with the United States? Second, because the authors strike exactly the right balance with enough detail to keep the most ardent policy wonk captivated while writing in a breezy style that will engage non-economists. And as with a good novel the authors leave us in suspense.

The policy successes of the Redemptive Decade, highlighted by the federal and provincial governments slaying their deficits, have put Laurier's vision of Canadian world prominence back into our grasp. But some serious challenges, including the return to deficits and Canada's ailing productivity performance, make that grasp a bit shaky. I urge people to read this compelling tale and then like me, anxiously wait for a sequel to see how the story ends."

—**DON DRUMMOND**, Senior Vice President and Chief Economist, TD Bank Financial Group

"Sir Wilfrid Laurier proclaimed it would be 'Canada's century.' He put in place policies of open immigration, free trade and investment and a self-confidence attitude to our southern neighbour, that set in motion a half century of progress. Crowley, Clemens and Veldhuis, the authors of *The Canadian Century*, an engaging and informative romp through our last hundred years, convincingly demonstrate that prosperity does grow from liberty's soil.

The book is also an endorsement of the too often maligned Canadian federalism. Our founding fathers got it right. The provinces have come into their own as incubators of change, innovation and experimentation with application to the national level.

Entrepreneurship, hard work and self-reliance are deeply ingrained in our psyche. During the Redemptive Decade of the nineties these virtues were resurrected. In tandem with concerted actions by the different levels of government, we put right the debt and despair created by a couple of dark decades when we wobbled toward what the *Wall Street Journal* described as 'third-world status.' Limited government, light taxes and fiscal discipline, argue the authors, are the ingredients that bring gold in the Olympiad of nations."

—**COLIN ROBERTSON**, first Head of the Advocacy Secretariat at Canada's Washington Embassy

"This timely and provocative book will remind Canadians that the smart fiscal and trade policies pursued by governments of all stripes in the past two decades have made Canada a star at the beginning of this century. But history should not repeat itself. What we have achieved recently is what Wilfrid Laurier understood to be the right path forward for the last century. Instead, wars and economic depression led to inefficient government spending, high taxes and deficits, and protectionism. Canada should avoid this poisonous policy recipe in the coming years to fulfil Laurier's dream of a truly great nation of the North, which we should rightly be."
—**JACK MINTZ**, Palmer Chair in Public Policy, University of Calgary

"This wonderful book is an urgent wake-up call for Canada's current leaders—of all political stripes—and raises crucial economic issues that should be top-of-mind in coming federal elections. Crowley, Clemens and Veldhuis remind us of Sir Wilfred Laurier's ambitious vision for Canada in the twentieth century, founded on freedom, small but sensible government, and confident engagement with the world. After thirty years of expanding questionable social programs with borrowed money, they argue that Canada's Redemptive Decade of the 1990s saw us return solidly back toward Laurier's vision. But the danger now lies in the back-sliding that has occurred in the past decade, with rapidly growing government spending and a return to complacency about public debt. Now is the time to reaffirm the power of Laurier's vision, to make some courageous policy decisions, and to thereby ensure that the twenty-first century belongs to Canada in the way Sir Wilfrid intended a hundred years ago. Will Canada's political leaders pay attention."
—**CHRISTOPHER RAGAN**, Clifford Clark Visiting Economist, Finance Canada, Department of Economics, McGill University

"A generous helping of economic history, served up in a very appetizing way! Hopefully our public policy decision-makers will pay heed to this book and realize that those who do not learn from history are doomed to repeat it."
—**CATHERINE SWIFT**, Chairwomen, President and CEO, Canadian Federation of Independent Business

"Canada's remarkable journey from economic laggard to one of the developed world's best performing economies is the subject of this well-timed book. It is a story of sweeping Canadian policy reforms touching on fiscal management, taxation, pensions and social assistance—reforms that helped to position the country to manage its way through the recent global economic downturn. The authors have done a great service by summarizing the highlights and distilling the lessons of what they refer to as Canada's Redemptive Decade. They show how the achievements of that decade vindicate the vision of Canadian leadership associated with the prime ministership of Sir Wilfrid Laurier."
—**JOCK FINLAYSON**, Excecutive Vice-President, Business Council of British Columbia

THE CANADIAN
moving

CENTURY
out of america's shadow

BRIAN LEE CROWLEY | JASON CLEMENS | NIELS VELDHUIS

KEY PORTER BOOKS

Library and Archives Canada Cataloguing in Publication

Crowley, Brian Lee
The Canadian century: moving out of America's shadow / Brian Lee Crowley, Jason Clemens, Niels Veldhuis.

ISBN 978-1-55470-297-8

1. Canada—Politics and government—21st century. 2. United States—Politics and government—21st century. 3. Canada—Economic conditions—21st century. 4. United States—Economic conditions—21st century. 5. Canada—Economic policy—1971–1991. 6. Canada—Economic policy—1991–. I. Clemens, Jason II. Veldhuis, Niels, 1977– III. Title.

FC640.C769 2010 971.07 C2009-906878-8

ONTARIO ARTS COUNCIL
CONSEIL DES ARTS DE L'ONTARIO

The publisher gratefully acknowledges the support of the Canada Council for the Arts and the Ontario Arts Council for its publishing program. We acknowledge the support of the Government of Ontario through the Ontario Media Development Corporation's Ontario Book Initiative.

We acknowledge the financial support of the Government of Canada through the Book Publishing Industry Development Program (BPIDP) for our publishing activities.

Key Porter Books Limited
Six Adelaide Street East, Tenth Floor
Toronto, Ontario
Canada M5C 1H6

www.keyporter.com

Text design and electronic formatting: Marijke Friesen

Printed and bound in Canada

10 11 12 13 6 5 4 3 2 1

The Macdonald-Laurier Institute for Public Policy

exists to make poor-quality public policy in Ottawa unacceptable to Canadians and their political and opinion leaders by proposing thoughtful alternatives through non-partisan and independent research and commentary.

MLI's activities include:

Initiating and conducting research identifying current and emerging economic and public policy issues facing Canadians, including, but not limited to, research into defence and security, foreign policy, immigration, economic and fiscal policy, Canada–US relations, regulatory, regional development, social policy and aboriginal affairs;

Investigating and analysing the full range of options for public and private sector responses to the issues identified and to act as a catalyst for informed debate on those options;

Communicating the conclusions of its research to a national audience in a clear, non-partisan way;

Sponsoring or organizing conferences, meetings, seminars, lectures, training programs and publications using all media of communication (including without restriction, the electronic media), for the purposes of achieving these objects;

Providing research services on public policy issues, or other facilities, for institutions, corporations, agencies and individuals, including departments and agencies of Canadian governments at the federal, provincial, regional and municipal levels, on such terms as may be mutually agreed, provided that the research is in furtherance of these objects.

table of contents

preface

This book would not exist without two organizations. Appropriately, one is American and the other Canadian.

The first is Liberty Fund, Inc., of Indianapolis, Indiana. Liberty Fund is a foundation dedicated to ensuring that the intellectual case for human freedom is examined and understood around the world. The three authors of this book had the enormous good fortune to be participants in a Liberty Fund colloquium on *Liberty and Public Choice* that took place in Ottawa, Ontario, in March 2009.

A number of discussions around that colloquium table stimulated us to think more deeply about how Canada had changed over the course of the 1990s. Moreover, Canadian Chris Edwards of the Cato Institute in Washington, DC, was equally a participant at the Ottawa event and his knowledge of the American fiscal situation drew us into further discussions of how the paths being followed by Canada and the US, respectively, were diverging in Canada's favour. We realized that neither Canadians nor Americans had any inkling of how remarkably their relative positions had changed in recent years.

One immediate result of this fortuitous meeting of minds was the co-authoring of an op-ed by two of the present authors (Clemens and Veldhuis) along with Edwards. The piece, which appeared in the *Washington Post*, compared various aspects of Canadian and American economic performance over the last two decades. The disbelief of readers on both sides of the border when presented with the facts underlined for us the perennial quality of popular prejudices; they endure long after the reality that gave rise to them has been reshaped by events.

The writing of the op-ed forced the authors to examine in greater detail what actually happened in the two countries over the 1990s with specific emphasis on Canada's energetic and visionary reforms, contrasted with America's manifest difficulties in wrestling its fiscal and entitlement problems to the ground. The combination of the conference and the writing of the op-ed convinced the authors that these very different cross-border circumstances created an historic opportunity for Canada and motivated us to speak out to ensure that, if Canada fails to capitalize on this opportunity, it will not be out of ignorance. We are indebted to Liberty Fund for having brought us together, and to the other participants who helped us to understand how little Canadians and Americans really understood one another.

The other organization to which this book owes its existence is the new Macdonald-Laurier Institute for Public Policy in Ottawa. MLI ("Emily" to its friends) is a brand new institute aiming to fill a glaring gap in Canada's democratic infrastructure: the absence of a proper broadly based think tank in the national capital, talking to the national political personnel, the national media, and the national electorate about policy issues that matter to the Canadian nation. MLI is equally dedicated to the proposition that the founders and early architects of Canada endowed us with something of inestimable worth: the institutions and values on which a country might be built in what was formerly British North America.

As the three authors carried on the conversation begun at the Liberty Fund event, we began to place that discussion in the context of what we knew about those origins of our country, origins that might be distant in time but that left an indelible stamp on our institutions and our character as a people. As we teased out the changes that had produced such good results for Canada over the past two decades, we were quickly drawn to see how closely those changes mirrored the plan for Canada of one of our early prime ministers, Sir Wilfrid Laurier.

Thus was born MLI's Canadian Century project. You hold in your hand the first product of that project, but we hope it will be only one of many as the numerous fine minds associated with MLI begin to expand on the basic themes we have established in this book. Over the coming months and years the new institute will explore in more detail how smart policy in Canada can help to speed our country's return to Laurier's plan and the Canadian century he believed lay within our grasp. We want to thank MLI, its board of directors and supporters for the assistance and support they gave us as we struggled to tell the story of how and why Canada can, in the twenty-first century, move out of America's shadow and claim its rightful place in the sun.

Many people are due thanks for the direct role they played in turning this narrative from a mere gleam in our eye to the book you see before you. In particular we would like to thank the following people, all of whom read and commented on the draft at various stages or otherwise contributed to the content: Chris Edwards, Tad DeHaven, Nadeem Esmail, John R. Graham, Milagros Palacios, Vicki Murray, François Vaillancourt, Don Drummond, Don Johnston, Frank McKenna, David Perry, Jock Finlayson, Colin Robertson, Sean Speer, and Bob Knox. Canada's former ambassador to the US, Allan Gotlieb, honoured us with a foreword.

Financial support was received from numerous sources, including the Donner Canadian Foundation, the Aurea Foundation, a foundation that wishes to remain anonymous, and David Laidley.

At our publisher, Key Porter, we received the excellent editorial, technical, and marketing support that are its hallmark. In particular we would like to acknowledge the help of vice-president Tom Best, executive editor Jonathan Schmidt, designer Marijke Friesen, marketing manager Daniel Rondeau and publicist Kelly Ward.

We want to thank our families, and particularly our wives, Shelley Crowley, Kim Crosman, and Danielle Veldhuis, for the support and understanding they gave to us as we laboured under a very tight deadline to complete this book.

Finally, we would like to dedicate this book to Sir Wilfrid Laurier and his bold vision of a Canadian century, as well as to the many Canadians and their leaders who had the courage to put us back on his path to national greatness. May our generation and future ones be equal to the challenge they set out for us.

foreword

ALLAN GOTLIEB, former ambassador of Canada to the United States

Brian Crowley, Jason Clemens, and Niels Veldhuis have done a great service for Canada in writing this book. It isn't just that they have reminded Canadians of the remarkable vision and record of one of our greatest prime ministers, Sir Wilfrid Laurier, and shown how his plan for Canada is as relevant and vital to us today as it was in his day. It isn't just that they tell more comprehensively and more clearly than anyone before them the story of a reforming generation of Canadian politicians. Nor is it just that they paint as detailed and sobering a picture as anyone on either side of the border ever has of the tax, debt and spending trap which is daily ensnaring our American friends and allies.

What they have done is to go beyond each of these individual stories, weaving them together into a single comprehensive look at the opportunities that await Canada in the twenty-first century. In so doing they reveal something of the genius of Canada. We are neither a boastful nor a prideful people, but we think that we ought to do the right thing, even if it takes us a little while to figure out what that might be. And when we get the bit between our teeth, we see things through.

On the telling of Crowley, Clemens, and Veldhuis, this portrait of the Canadian character was on full display in what they have called the Redemptive Decade, a fertile period of reform that stretched roughly from Prime Minister Brian Mulroney's visionary initiative for a free trade agreement in 1988, to finance minister Paul Martin's tabling in the House of Commons of the first balanced budget in a generation. In between, politicians of all stripes wrestled with a host of policy challenges that had been left to fester for far too long.

They reformed entitlement programs such as the Canada Pension Plan and provincial welfare. They balanced budgets. They struggled to bring down debt and taxes. They focused governments on the things they do best; not smaller government for its own sake, but smarter government that was a more effective and less wasteful instrument to promote the well-being of Canadians. They ushered in an era of free trade with the

Americans, while reforming the structure of taxes through changes like the Goods and Services Tax (GST). In retrospect, as the authors lay it out for us, this group of reformers was an unlikely one. It included Saskatchewan New Democrats, Alberta and Ontario Tories, and BC and New Brunswick Liberals, as well as the Liberal government of Jean Chrétien, egged on by the Reform Party of Preston Manning, and the Progressive Conservative government of Brian Mulroney.

Region, party, and ideology took a back seat as they struggled to save Canada from self-imposed decline. And they did so remarkably successfully, creating one of the great fiscal and economic turnarounds the western world has seen in decades. Not a bad story for a country teetering on the brink, as the *Wall Street Journal* warned in 1995, of honorary membership in the Third World. Since Canadians put their shoulders to the wheel back then we have enjoyed a long period of growth greater than all our friends in the other G7 countries and Canada became a destination for world leaders seeking guidance and advice on how to achieve for their own countries what Canadians did for themselves.

What none of us realized at the time, but the authors of this timely and thoughtful book eloquently show, is that we were not the originators of the comprehensive reform program we were unwittingly putting in place. That honour belongs to Sir Wilfrid Laurier, the first French-Canadian prime minister and a man who saw perhaps better than anyone before or since, the boundless opportunity of Canada and knew just what was necessary to move the opportunity from promise to reality.

Liberty was Laurier's watchword. A Canada in which people are free—free in thought, word, conscience and action, free under the law, free from arbitrary and overweening government—this was a Canada that would attract the best and brightest from the world over. On that foundation of freedom, Laurier advised that we needed to build responsible public finances, limited but strong, and active government that promoted individual responsibility and shunned dependency, and a foreign policy that defended Canada's interests before anything else.

Taxes, Laurier thought, were a particularly vital part of his plan. He too was a tax reformer, taking on the special interests to reform the tariff, the source of most of his government's revenue. Ever the Canadian nationalist, Laurier also gave us a benchmark for our tax levels that he believed would invigorate Canadian entrepreneurship and innovation: we had to offer our people a tax burden that was not just competitive with the United States, but decidedly lower.

Speaking of the Americans, Laurier thought we could not leave the management of our relations with our neighbours to chance. Like Sir John A. Macdonald before him, he sought to tame America's economic power over Canada through reciprocity, or free trade. Unlike Sir John, he was actually able to strike a deal, although it was to go down to defeat in the general election of 1911, a defeat whose consequences reverberated across many generations of our political life.

Now that the authors of *The Canadian Century* have reminded us of Laurier's plan, it is easy to see why the actions we took in the Redemptive Decade brought Sir Wilfrid's prescriptions to mind. We thought we were just wrestling with the problems of the day, but now we can see that both the problems, and the right way to solve them, are bred into Canada's deepest history and character.

All of these reforms and the benefits they conferred on Canada, this return to Canada's roots in Laurier's plan, might have been enough to give Canada a shot at making the twenty-first century Canada's century. But the authors show that in fact our neighbour and long-time friendly competitor, the United States, is also contributing. Its contribution, sadly, is to stumble economically, leaving the field open for Canada to shine. Truth be told, American public finances are in a mess and that mess is deepening. If we want to see what would have become of Canada had we not lived through the difficult changes of our Redemptive Decade, we need look no further than Washington, DC, where unreformed entitlements and undisciplined borrowing are hobbling America's power to be a world leader and to outshine Canada on the economic front.

You don't need to agree with every one of the authors' prescriptions to be infected by their optimism about Canada's prospects. They are surely right to say that Canada cannot rest on its laurels from the Redemptive Decade. It would be easy to slip back into persistent government deficits, to allow stimulus spending to endure long after its justification has disappeared, and to fail to achieve for Canada the competitive tax advantage Laurier recommended. On the other hand, perhaps they are too optimistic about the appetite on both sides of the border for the kind of institutional deepening of our bilateral relationship that they recommend, and about Canada's prospects if we are so closely tied to an America with major economic problems.

Still, it is refreshing and encouraging to see these important policy thinkers in our country pointing out that Canada doesn't need to take a back seat to anybody, and that our fate lies within our own hands if we have the courage, the energy, and the enthusiasm to grasp it. It is not often that Canadians talk about moving out of America's shadow—for far too long we have simply assumed that being in that shadow was the natural order of things. Crowley, Clemens, and Veldhuis remind us that Sir Wilfrid Laurier thought that all things were possible for us, and today they show, with an impressive array of facts to support their argument, that Laurier's plan for Canada can still carry us through to that Canadian century we have all been eagerly awaiting for over a hundred years.

Toronto, January 2010

The good Saxon word, freedom; freedom in every sense of the term, freedom of speech, freedom of action, freedom in religious and civil life and last but not least, freedom in commercial life.

Sir Wilfrid Laurier, 1896

We are a free and happy people, and we are so owing to the liberal institutions by which we are governed, institutions which we owe to the exertions of our forefathers and the wisdom of the mother country.

Sir Wilfrid Laurier, 1877

Let us remember what Sir Wilfrid said and why he said it. "As the nineteenth century was that of the United States, so I think the twentieth century shall be filled by Canada," he told the Ottawa Canadian Club in 1904. Later that year he repeated himself, telling another audience: "I think we can claim that it is Canada that shall fill the twentieth century . . . For the next seventy-five years, nay the next hundred years, Canada shall be the star towards which all men who love progress and freedom shall come."

Robert Bothwell and J.L. Granatstein

part I

How to Have Your Very Own Century

LAURIER'S PLAN FOR CANADA chapter one

When in 1904 Sir Wilfrid Laurier[1] proclaimed that "the twentieth century would be filled by Canada," this was no mere boastfulness. We were one of the richest countries in the world; we enjoyed boundless natural resources, an energetic population, a privileged place in the great commercial empire established and defended by the imperial metropole, Britain, and reasonable access to American markets.

We had built a national railway across the vastness of the West, and immigrants were arriving on our shores in larger numbers, relative to our population, than anywhere else in the world. In the first twenty years of the twentieth century, our population grew by an unprecedented two-thirds.[2] Canada was a magnet to the world. Our future seemed assured.

Laurier had a plan to make sure that this unprecedented flowering would be no seasonal bloom, briefly drawing every passerby's glance before withering away. He was putting in place a plan to fill, not a decade or two, but a full century with Canada's rise to prominent adulthood on the world stage. It was a plan that found its roots deep in Canada's origins, in the ideas of its founders, and in the hard work and dogged determination of those who had already been building the country since the founding of the first colonies.

But just as Wayne Gretzky was rightly called hockey's Great One because he saw each play unfolding in his mind and knew what each player would do before he did it, Laurier was the one who saw and understood what had to happen for Canada to become a great nation. The whole plan was sketched out in his mind, and for almost sixteen years he patiently coached all the players in Canada, and slowly, methodically, he shaped our institutions, our landscape, and our relations with Britain and America to the end of making Canada the most prosperous, dynamic, and attractive country on earth.

Like all great leaders, it was less that he invented anything new than that he learned the secrets of how to call forth from each and every person the very best they had to offer, so that what emerged under his wise and thoughtful ministrations was simply the potential that he saw still slumbering within our awakening nation.

And that great awakening, that rise to full consciousness of Canada under his stewardship, remains a tale of heroic exploits still recounted in hushed and admiring tones by those who have not forgotten just how distinguished that period of our history was. For we were not merely *talking* about overtaking America as the world's awakening economic giant and the light unto the benighted masses of foreign lands; we were hard at work *creating* that future every day.

This was in marked contrast to the doldrums into which Canada, like much of the world, had sunk in the thirty years following Confederation. The new country, so full of promise, seemed in those early years to have lost something of its effervescence, even though no one can deny the great achievements of the era—the admission of three new provinces, the purchase of Rupert's Land, the completion of the Canadian Pacific Railway (CPR), and the country's survival of the upheaval and division of the Riel Rebellion. Still, having achieved the Herculean feat of piecing together the country, the government and the people then seemed progressively to lose economic energy, while indulging in fits of patronage, scandal, timidity, and self-destructive protectionism.[3]

Then, in 1896, came Laurier.

By 1910, half a million immigrants had entered Canada on Laurier's watch, many of them bound for the West, where the expansionist settlement policies of aggressive Minister of the Interior Clifford Sifton and his successors had made our "last best west" a magnet for the world's dispossessed. In that first decade of the new century, our population grew by over a third, from 5.4 million to 7.2 million. And nearly two-fifths of that growth came from immigration. As noted Canadian historians Robert Bothwell, Ian Drummond, and John English remarked, both of these figures are "extraordinarily high; nothing like them had been seen before or since."[4] Not only did immigrants come in vast numbers, but outmigration to the more prosperous United States—the bane of the country's early years—slowed to a trickle.[5]

The rush of newcomers was so great, and the attraction of the West so irresistible, that Laurier was obliged in 1905 to cut two new provinces out of the federally administered western territories. One of the new provinces, Saskatchewan, was seen to be such a land of opportunity that it quickly became the country's third-largest province by population and remained so for a number of years.[6]

The West's growth was more than mere dry statistics. Rather, it was the sum of choices by hundreds of thousands of people, each of their lives woven into the tapestry of Canada's emerging future. Both sets of maternal great-grandparents of Brian Crowley, one of this book's co-authors, were part of the great movement of people unleashed by the prosperity of the Laurier years. In 1891 Richard Lane and his wife, Mary Irving, were living in the rural Ontario of their birth; Crowley's grandfather, Russell Lane, and his twin brother, Richard, were born to them in Huron County that year. By 1901 the family was in Toronto, part of the exodus from rural regions to the prosperous cities. But soon on the move again, by 1906 they had left Ontario, headed for the promised land of Saskatchewan, where Crowley's mother was eventually born in North Battleford. Their initial destination was Saskatoon, a city that had barely existed a decade before.

Crowley's other maternal great-grandparents, Henry and Edith Bierschied, came from the United States in search of the free homestead land that had been largely exhausted south of the border but was still relatively easily available in the Dominion.[7] When they crossed the border from North Dakota at North Portal, Saskatchewan, in August 1911, they brought with them seven-year-old Grace, Crowley's grandmother. Henry was of German immigrant stock, and it was not unusual for the many ethnic immigrants who ended up in the Canadian West—the Poles, the Russians, the Germans, the Ukrainians, the Galicians, the Swedes, and others—to have tried their luck in the US first. In fact, this theme of the competition between Canada and the US for the best immigrants is one to which we shall return.

The Lanes and the Bierschieds were but two of the tiny trickles that together added up to a mighty torrent of humanity sweeping into the West, changing the politics, the economics, and the population of Canada forever. As one of Laurier's biographers, Joseph Schull, points out, the wheat yield in the three Prairie provinces rose during Laurier's time from eighteen million bushels to nearly one hundred and eighteen million.[8] This was the time when the West began to flex its muscles and the whole country saw the promise of the West as a powerful theme in the growing symphony of Canadian prosperity and optimism.

But there was more. The country's natural resources, its minerals, its timber, its agricultural products were flowing in ever-increasing streams to the markets of the world. As much as the West, the North was proving to be a treasure trove of natural wealth and a magnet for newcomers. Provinces such as Manitoba, Ontario, and Quebec were pressing to expand their borders northward to capture the spreading prosperity.[9] Manufacturing was booming and finding not just domestic markets behind modest protectionist barriers, but was part of a great Canadian effusion into foreign markets. Foreign trade tripled during this golden decade.[10]

William Cornelius Van Horne, the head of the CPR, saw his railway in terms that seem strikingly modern as we talk today about Pacific and Atlantic gateways to trade: Van Horne said that the CPR had one terminus in Euston station in London, metropolis of the greatest empire the world had ever seen, while the others were in Hong Kong and Sydney. And Laurier himself was "a convinced and ardent enthusiast for the 'All-Red Route' [red being the colour then reserved by mapmakers for the pieces of the far-flung British Empire, including Canada] which would link the British Isles with Australia and New Zealand by means of fast steamships and direct rail connections across Canada."[11]

Yet the CPR was not enough. The growth of Canada's production of every kind, and our energetic push into the world's markets, soon exhausted the ability of our single transcontinental tie to transport the fruits of our blooming, buzzing energy. Given the optimism of the day, it is perhaps no surprise that we ended up with more railways than we knew what to do with, although that may be as much due to our failure to stick with Laurier's plan as to any flaw in that plan itself.

Canada's boom cannot, however, be ascribed solely to exports. The new country was hungry for investment—it was not enough to plunk people in the wilderness and expect them to produce the New Jerusalem. They needed tools, homes, and institutions, things like railways, factories, mills, ships, equipment, roads, bridges, houses, schools, courts, customs houses, and churches. The new country was sucking in capital, chiefly from Britain and the United States, at a dizzying pace; the new investments themselves drove the boom even more than the exports that they made possible. "The value of new and repair construction increased by almost 400 per cent, while the value of exports went up just over 100 per cent. The size of the railway system and the quantity of residential housing increased much more rapidly than the volume of exports."[12] And contrary to the much-caressed prejudices of the big-government apologists and historical revisionists of our own time, historians are clear that this investment boom was led by the private sector, not government investment, although the government certainly played its part.[13]

And while we were predominantly a rural people, our cities—home to much of our manufacturing—boomed with the countryside: Montreal, Toronto, and Ottawa more than doubled in population, while Vancouver and Winnipeg far outstripped them in their rate of growth, quintupling in the same period. Hitherto empty plains saw cities suddenly mushroom in their midst, as Calgary, Edmonton, Regina, and Saskatoon became centres of the new prosperity.[14] The rate at which new companies were formed and chartered by the Dominion government grew over twelve times during the first decade of what Laurier felt in his bones was the Canadian century.[15]

A Man, a Plan, a People—Canada!

What was Laurier's plan, his vision for a Canada that would be the best the New World had to offer the Old, a plan that had already unleashed the greatest growth in our level of prosperity ever seen and that he expected would fuel our development for decades to come? That policy had four distinct elements.

1. Prosperity grows from liberty's soil

First, he thought it vital to preserve and protect the institutions brought to Canada by our forebears, the "British liberty" composed of the rule of law, free speech, freedom of conscience and religion, respect of minority rights, habeas corpus, parliamentary self-government, minimal state interference, low taxes, and respect of property and of contract.[16] That liberty and those institutions were, Laurier believed, the catalyst that released the energy and dynamism of those who lived under them, whatever their ethnic origin or religious convictions. When people were free to follow their own star, to determine what was important to them, to build their own relationships with family, friends, and colleagues, they built well and energetically—they had confidence in the future, they took risks, and they reaped the reward.

Laurier was convinced that the best people in the world would jostle one another at Canada's door, not just because they would enjoy a higher standard of living but, much more importantly, because in Canada they would be free: "I think we can claim that it is Canada that shall fill the twentieth century . . . For the next seventy-five years, nay the next hundred years, Canada shall be the star towards which all men who love progress and freedom shall come."[17]

A society like this, where people were responsible for themselves, made their own plans, and accepted that their fate was in their own hands, was one that could be open to immigrants on a vast scale. Newcomers could not be a burden to the government or the population, because if they succeeded, they became net contributors, and if they failed, they were no affair of the state.

Canadians today, used to thinking of themselves as more caring and sharing, and just altogether "nicer" than, say, our American neighbours, may be shocked to learn that this failure to use the state as a way to support the poor was not an oversight, and even less was it a matter of waiting impatiently until the country was rich enough to pay the bill. The very idea of the state acting so as to relieve people of responsibility for their own choices and actions was anathema to the entire political class.

> No one was interested in the devices which a later generation would call the "welfare state" . . . Neither Canadian governments nor the fashionable "reformers" were much interested in sickness insurance, old-age pensions, disability insurance, or unemployment insurance (not to speak of day-care centres!). Imperial and undemocratic Germany had provided sickness insurance and old-age pensions since the 1880s. Britain introduced such pensions, and a form of health insurance, in 1911, and New Zealand had already done likewise. These examples were not followed.[18]

Laurier's objection to such schemes, like that of his Liberal colleagues, was one of principle: when people were expected to take responsibility for themselves and their family, they made better provision for their needs and directed their productive efforts where they would do the country and themselves the greatest good. When this natural necessity to strive was diluted by an easy access to the public purse, the ever-present danger was of the enervation of the individual and the stagnation of the progress of society. "If you remove the incentives of ambition and emulation from public enterprises"—by which he meant the economic undertakings of individuals and businesses, not state enterprise—Laurier said on the subject in 1907, "you suppress progress, you condemn the community to stagnation and immobility."[19]

That individuals and families might occasionally need help to overcome the vicissitudes of life went without saying, but the appropriate institutions to deal with these hardships were ones that the community generated quite successfully itself, and no one in government saw any need to try to supplant the efforts that communities and families made together to protect themselves from the shoals and reefs of the human condition, such as illness and unemployment.[20]

2. Limited government, light taxes, and fiscal discipline

The second element of Laurier's plan was based on the view that once freedom, the rule of law, and key infrastructure had been created, the best thing that government could do was to then get out of the way, to keep taxes and rules to a minimum. Indeed, Laurier believed that the cost of government, and especially the tax burden, needed always to be kept below the level in the United States, so as to create a powerful competitive advantage for Canada. Small but efficient government, not big government, was, to Laurier's way of thinking, Canada's secret weapon in the competitive struggle with America.

Even beyond the absence of the welfare state, it may surprise many Canadians today the extent to which this belief in lean minimalist government in economic terms was also an article of faith for most of the first century of the Dominion's existence. Indeed, one of our leading historians of Canadian tax policy, David Perry, of the non-partisan Canadian Tax Foundation, points out that this consensus was assumed by its drafters to be part and parcel of the plan that inspired the British North America Act, later rebaptized the Constitution Act, 1867. In that document's scheme, both the major responsibilities and the major sources of revenue were granted to the central government in Ottawa, but the plan was not to create an expansive and activist government. Rather, it was to ensure that *no* government got too big for its britches by keeping them all, federal and provincial, on a meagre fiscal diet.

> The prevailing assumption in 1867 was that government should be unobtrusive and cheap. Its job was to prepare an environment in which private enterprise could thrive, and then stand to one side. So, although the federal government was to be stronger than the provinces, it was not to be very strong, or very expensive, in its own right.[21]

Today Canada's prime minister is excoriated in the press for suggesting that there are no good taxes;[22] the country's founders saw this view as unexceptionable. Sir Richard Cartwright, finance minister of the young Dominion in 1878, thundered during his budget speech to Parliament that

> All taxation ... is a loss *per se* ... it is the sacred duty of the government to take only from the people what is necessary to the proper discharge of the public service; and that taxation in any other mode, is simply in one shape or another, legalized robbery.[23]

Politicians stayed as far as they could from directly providing services or competing with private enterprise. They did not think it their job to provide what businessmen with proper incentives could do more cheaply and efficiently, while the voters wanted no truck nor trade with government masquerading as business, or even any expansion of the role already played by the state. As one set of historians of the time wrote, the public, "regarded 'national services' like the Public Works Department, Post Office, and Intercolonial Railway, all of them believed to be sinkholes of patronage, as painful necessities that ought not to be duplicated."[24]

Laurier believed that we lived in a world in which people and societies compete for the most desirable things—whether they be immigrants, industry, or capital—and that Canada could not win that competition by trying to throw up walls against it. Instead, the winner of the competition would be the country that proved most open and hospitable to these footloose forces. A vital part of his plan, therefore, was to find a way to create a distinctive set of Canadian advantages that would help the young Dominion win the competitive struggle with others, including the United States. Again, this preoccupation of Laurier's has an arrestingly modern feel to it.

As already noticed, in the early years of Confederation, Canada was the destination for a goodly amount of immigration, but our country too often proved to be only a way station for many of the newcomers, who slipped south of the border in search of better opportunities.[25] And in this vast, empty country, people were wealth; it took strong hands and stout hearts to bring European civilization to the new Dominion's empty spaces.

Governments, however, could not affect many of the factors that favoured one part of North America over another. If America enjoyed a more attractive climate, for example, or longer-established industry and infrastructure, there was little the government of Canada could do about it. Taxation, on the other hand, was something they controlled absolutely. In the battle to win a disproportionate share of people and industry for the Dominion, taxation was to prove a recurring and powerful theme.

> Competition for these mobile human resources, not to mention the capital with which these immigrants (be they farmers or businessmen) arrived, was fierce. Consequently, all Dominion governments were determined to keep their taxes low.[26]

No one displayed this determination more doggedly than Laurier.

Beyond rewarding energy and what we would today call entrepreneurialism and innovation, Laurier was deeply concerned that taxation that was too high, relative to the next-door neighbour's, would create a vicious circle in which loss of people and investment led to loss of revenue, which led in its turn to higher taxes and so forth.

> References were made [during the Laurier era] to the relative tax burdens between the two countries as an important political constraint. The economic loss of people and their resources to the U.S. would reduce the revenue bases available for taxation, necessitating higher tax rates or reduced government spending. Thus the potential economic cost of this horizontal tax competition [i.e., competition on tax rates between the two governments] would be reflected directly into higher political costs for the government.[27]

Not only, then, did Laurier's plan envisage taming, to the extent possible, American protectionism,[28] opening US markets to Canadian exports, it also envisaged attracting capital, enterprise, and above all people from under the American eagle's nose. This he planned to do by making it clear that people who came to Canada from south of the border or beyond the seas would find in the Dominion a society of free men and women where everyone was expected to work hard, and where, if they did so, they would keep more of the fruits of their labours than anywhere else, including the United States of America.

Laurier didn't merely willingly grasp the baton that was handed to him by his predecessors and the founders of the Dominion; he took it to be his duty and obligation to keep the burden that government imposed on taxpayers light and unobtrusive.

In this regard, he was himself a major tax reformer, for he believed that it was not enough to keep taxes low; it was also essential to impose the right kind of taxes and to the right degree.

Taxes were, of course, a rather different affair at the beginning of the twentieth century than at the beginning of the twenty-first. To understand Laurier's plan on taxes, one must realize that the major source of tax dollars for the Dominion government was not the income tax, a tax that was only to emerge with the exigencies of war in 1917,[29] nor the sales tax—it was the tariff on imports.

A tariff is a tax imposed on the value of imported goods. What we forget today, when governments have the administrative and technological know-how to impose and collect far more sophisticated and efficient taxes, is that tariffs can have their virtues in simple colonial societies. You can concentrate the machinery of taxation at the points of entry into the country, making the costs of policing relatively light. The revenue authorities need little in the way of coercive or surveillance powers over the domestic population, because the tariff is paid directly by those importing goods from abroad, and that tax is then passed on indirectly to consumers by being included in the final price.

Used to thinking of tariffs exclusively as a weapon in the protectionist's arsenal today, we forget the extent to which they were a simple and efficient way to generate cash for government a century ago. Indeed, they were the chief source of revenue.[30] Customs duties constituted at least 60 per cent of federal revenues from 1866 to 1917, a fact that finds a faint echo even today in Ottawa: control over tariffs falls, not under the jurisdiction of the Department of Foreign Affairs or International Trade or even Industry but that of Finance.

So as someone who believed that the tax burden should be kept light and simple, and who believed ardently as well in the principles of free trade, Laurier had his work cut out for him in tariff reform. He was dealing with the most important source of revenue the government enjoyed.

The competing principles that might guide thinking about the tariff were, on the one hand, that government should interfere as little as possible in the choices people made, including the choice to buy imported goods over domestic ones, and, on the other hand, the wish to keep the cost of raising revenue as low as possible. The solution, Laurier thought, was major tax reform: the steady move away from a "protectionist tariff" and toward a purer "revenue tariff."

The distinction today may seem a fine one, but then it was an important shift in policy. In the years prior to Laurier's rise to office, the protectionist role of tariffs had risen steadily to the fore. A protectionist tariff confers major benefits on domestic producers competing with imports. Naturally, the domestic lobbies, particularly for manufacturers, push the government to make its tariffs fall most heavily on their foreign competitors, rather than making the tariff a relatively neutral one, falling more or less equally on all kinds of imports. Not only did the tariff, as it grew up under the National Policy, pit manufacturer against importer, but it pitted, for example, the free-trading West against Central Canada's manufacturers, exacerbating regional tensions in the young country.[31]

A tariff is, by its nature, not economically neutral in its effects; it falls by definition on products coming from the outside, conferring an advantage on domestic production. That being said, however, the tariff itself could certainly be arranged in different ways. It could be used to favour domestic industries by placing its burden most heavily on industries in competition with domestic producers. Alternatively, its burden could be made to fall more or less equally across all imported goods, getting the government out of the business of using tax policy to favour some groups and industries over others.

Laurier's view, and it is one that has been shared by many of the historians who have come after, is that under the Tories, who had ruled with only a brief interruption since 1867, the tariff had become infected with politics, its revenue-raising role playing second fiddle to that of selective protection for favoured industries.[32] Originally, Laurier and the Liberals, guided by Edward Blake, their former leader, had been pure free traders, but after suffering electoral defeat on the issue, and given the Americans' manifest lack of interest in reciprocity negotiations, the Liberals trimmed at their 1893 policy conference, preferring tariff reform to outright abolition, at least in the short run.

This was done over the objections of Laurier, who proclaimed himself not only completely committed to free trade with the US but ready to adopt a customs union[33] with a single set of common tariffs and a pooling of the revenue that resulted—a policy of deeper integration with the United States than that which exists today.[34] But while Laurier would have preferred full steam ahead on free trade, he accepted that it was not going to happen any time soon, and once in power set about reforming the tariff. As John Dafoe wrote of Laurier's new policy, "A deft, shrewd modification of the tariff helped to loosen the stream of commerce which after years of constriction began again to flow freely."[35]

It was not the free trade, plain and simple, that a campaigning Laurier in earlier years had promised the West, and a revenue tariff, dress it up as you will, is still a tariff—but an important start had been made in getting the politics out of the tariff.

Even beyond that dilution of politics in the tariff, in another echo of modern practices of reciprocity in trade liberalization, Laurier's government introduced for the first time a tariff that would recognize and reward the efforts of countries that opened their markets to Canadian goods. In the words of Laurier's minister of finance, William Stevens Fielding, there would now be "one tariff for countries which are willing to trade with us and a different one for countries which are not."[36]

The other aspect of Laurier's plan to keep government small and costs under control was government borrowing. Laurier and Fielding were not anti-debt zealots. In most years, they borrowed a little. On the other hand, what constituted an acceptable level of borrowing for Laurier and Fielding was strictly limited by the interplay of three important factors.

First, given the extent to which the government was investing, as we have seen, in the development of a great deal of what we would call today infrastructure, and given the limited size of the borrowing in any year—

usually well below 1 per cent of gross domestic product (or GDP)—borrowing was clearly being used solely to finance genuine investment.[37] Laurier was not borrowing to pay for current expenditures, such as civil service salaries or public services. He limited debt to its proper use: to finance assets with a long productive life, spreading the cost of their construction over a long period so that all of the people who benefited from them over time would contribute to their cost.[38] As Fielding explained, "In a new country like Canada with a great many public works requiring to be assisted with many demands on the treasury, it would not be surprising that each year we would not only be obliged to spend our ordinary revenue but to incur some debt in order to carry on our great public works."[39]

Second, borrowing, which allowed the government to spread the cost of major investments over time, made an important contribution to Laurier's objective of keeping Canadian tax rates below those in the US. Laurier was balancing the demands of a growing nation against the need to keep the cost of government low.[40] Private finance built a lot of infrastructure, keeping the costs off the taxpayer's back, while what public borrowing there was was designed to further ease the burden on the taxpayer by spreading over many years the cost of constructing bridges, railways, wharves, and courthouses.[41]

Finally, Laurier and Fielding kept an eagle eye on international financial markets to ensure that Canada never borrowed beyond what lenders thought the young Dominion could support. They clearly feared that excessive debt would trigger higher interest rates, which would be followed by higher taxes and the loss of competitive advantage vis-à-vis the US. Laurier's legacy to us on this front was that reasonable levels of debt for the right purpose while living within the country's means contributed to Canada's well-being. But it was easy to get the balance wrong, and borrowing needed to be carried out carefully and in a disciplined way.[42]

3. Self-confident engagement with the Americans

The third part of Laurier's plan for the Canadian century was that Canada could not shrink before the challenge posed by American dynamism and proximity, but instead Canada must meet them head-on, turning them as best we could to our own account, especially as the British imperial power faded slowly from the scene. Laurier was a Canadian nationalist and a realist. He understood that Britain took but scant interest in Canada and that we were not strong enough to impose our will on America. Laurier believed, therefore, that we had to play cleverly and well the few cards that we had been dealt.

American arrogance and brashness; manifest destiny; hostility to the former colonial power, Britain, and its continued presence in North America; and the unsettled nature of the boundaries between much of Canada and the US helped to give rise to many conflicts between the two countries. Britain, which kept control over all questions of Canadian foreign policy—which they saw as merely a part of imperial policy—often sacrificed Canadian interests to further larger imperial objectives that required friendly relations with Washington.

Laurier lived through a classic example of Canada being sacrificed on the altar of British–US power politics in the resolution of the dispute over the border with Alaska in 1903. The three parties—Britain, the US, and Canada—had agreed to the creation of a joint commission to recommend how to resolve this long-festering issue. The issue had a special significance to Canada in that the Yukon gold rush was under way; Canada desperately wanted an outlet to the Pacific from the Yukon on Canadian soil so that Canadians would be the chief beneficiary of the wealth being created by the development of the Yukon's gold deposits.[43] American interests were equally determined that Canada should gain no such outlet and that Alaska should capture much of the economic benefit of the gold rush.

The commission was composed of six people: three Americans, two Canadians, and a Briton. Laurier was horrified when he realized that the British member of the Canadian delegation had marching orders to give in to the US to preserve transatlantic relations. Lord Alverston, the British judge in question, gave his name to a newly coined verb, to Alverstonize, that for years was just as prominent in Canadian political vocabulary as Captain Boycott's name became in Ireland's. And it was just as uncomplimentary a reference.[44]

The lesson that Laurier learned from disasters such as these was that Canada could not look to any power, whether Britain or the US, to protect the interests of Canada. We would always be sacrificed whenever it was convenient. Canada had to look to its own interests, while claiming from Britain increasing jurisdiction over its foreign relations. Beyond that, however, it had to seek to bind the more powerful nations to agreed and enforceable rules of behaviour that limit their ability to win their point through sheer brute force.

Moreover, Laurier understood that regardless of what Canada owed to Britain for its endowment of institutions and a culture of liberty, the rising power, and the one on Canada's doorstep, was America.

The fact that Britain was now a free trade nation, plus the extra cost of transatlantic shipping for Canadian exporters, plus the failure of British politician Joseph Chamberlain's scheme to create a free trade zone behind high tariff walls within the Empire, meant that Britain's role as the major trading partner for Canada was fated to fade with time.

America was on its way up in the world, and within North America was the obvious trade and commercial partner to step into the void being created by Britain's long goodbye.

During most of Laurier's long period in office, however, America was in no mood to bind its power through the kind of long-term commitments Canada needed if it was to reduce its vulnerability to American unilateralism. For Canada to invest in the US–Canada trading relationship required some certainty about Canadian access to American markets and some rules about how the US would treat exports from Canada.

This was a period of Republican dominance, and the Republican Party was the party of the Northern industrial interests that favoured high tariffs and considered Canada a direct commercial threat on their doorstep. Americans were in an ebullient mood, mirroring no doubt that of their president, Teddy Roosevelt. Roosevelt had been a hero of the Spanish-American War, which in 1898 led to a large expansion of US overseas possessions and power. He took over and completed the construction of the Panama Canal. He won the Nobel Peace Prize for brokering a peace settlement between the Russians and the Japanese. In 1901, he famously summed up the principles that he thought should guide American foreign policy thus: "Speak softly and carry a big stick, and you will go far."[45]

When Roosevelt had been the vice-presidential candidate on the William McKinley ticket, both he and McKinley—who was later assassinated, making Roosevelt president—stumped for prosperity at home behind high tariff barriers. These were truly unprepossessing partners for a Canadian government seeking freer entry to American markets and a taming of US power to damage Canada, by binding the US through enforceable trade agreements.

On the other hand, excessive and heedless use of power by American governments has traditionally exacted its own costs on that country. While powerful, America always somehow comes to realize that even it is not omnipotent and that even superpowers need friends and allies. William Taft, who succeeded Roosevelt as Republican candidate and president in 1908, was a Northerner and a protectionist; yet he and Congress proved to be on the lookout for ways to improve relations with the rest of the world. After having had his advances constantly rebuffed for a decade, Laurier suddenly found Canada's interest solicited in what we would call today an American charm offensive. Laurier lost no time in grasping the opportunity to put in place such a vital piece of his plan, binding the American colossus and subjecting its power to the rule of law, at least in its trade relations with Canada. But the chance slipped through his fingers—and ours. And thereby hangs a tale.

4. Free trade

Free trade deserves its own separate treatment as a central part of Laurier's plan. While the object of his efforts to negotiate free trade was the United States, free trade on a broad scale was, in his view, an end in itself. The fourth piece of Laurier's plan was therefore to move the country by degrees toward the regime of full free trade he so admired in Britain. Laurier believed that free and open trade was the cornerstone of economic prosperity and entrepreneurship and that government's role included working to throw open foreign markets to Canadian products while not obstructing the entry of products from abroad.

There was, of course, the tariff. We've already seen how Laurier dealt with the Canadian tariff. America,[46] emerging as the only rival to Britain as our chief trading partner—in 1896, these two markets purchased more than 90 per cent of Canadian exports—was a relatively high-protection economy. Only Britain, workshop of the world, levied no tariffs at all and posed no barriers to Britons buying and selling as they pleased.

For Laurier and his cabinet colleagues, British free trade was the ideal but politically unattainable in the face of the powerful manufacturing interests that had grown up behind the tariff curtain of Sir John A. Macdonald's National Policy.[47] In 1911, Laurier stoutly defended in the House of Commons his government's commitment to finding new markets for the country's burgeoning production: "Our policy has been, is and will be . . . to seek markets wherever markets are to be found."[48]

However much his eyes may have been fixed on markets wherever they were to be found, those same eyes could see clearly that the market that really mattered for the future was the United States. So the next major step in freeing Canadians' access to foreign markets was securing more favourable terms for the entry of Canadian products into the US market. That effort was crowned with success in 1911 when, after protracted negotiations, his finance minister, Fielding, returned triumphantly from Washington with a new reciprocity agreement with the Americans, one that seemed to set extremely favourable terms for Canada. The Liberals were ecstatic and the Tories despondent, convinced that the old fox Laurier, with his "sunny ways," had dished them yet again.[49]

To the surprise of almost everyone at the time, the outcome of the 1911 election was the rejection of reciprocity by the voters, for a complex tangle of reasons that need not detain us too long. In English Canada, an aggressive British imperialist movement called for the Empire to be made a kind of free trade zone complete with tariffs to keep out goods from elsewhere, including the US. In French Canada, by contrast, Henri Bourassa, and the nationalist movement into which he had breathed such life, abandoned the Liberals for being insufficiently ardent defenders of an independent Canadian policy in the face of growing imperialist sentiment. Even though the reciprocity agreement with the US continued protection for Canadian manufacturers, Central Canadian industry feared the thin edge of a tariff-busting wedge.[50] And of course the Americans, with the tin ear so typical of their sensitivity to Canadian concerns, gave Laurier's opponents lots of ammunition. Champ Clark, the speaker-designate of the House of Representatives, announced in Congress that "'I hope to see the day when the American flag will float over every square foot of the British North American possessions clear to the North Pole.'"[51] Reciprocity went down to defeat.

In our time, the anti-American protectionist crowd has so come to dominate the discussion of Canada–US relations in many universities and much of the media that many Canadians seem somehow to feel that Laurier's abortive attempt to establish free—or at least freer—trade with the US was an aberration in our history, one happily seen off by a vigilant Canadian electorate when given the chance in the federal election of 1911.[52]

One searches in vain for any justification for this view in the historical record.[53] Instead, it was the rejection of improved trade relations with the US that was the anomaly.

In fact, it would not be too much to say that Canada's development, indeed its very existence as a nation, owes a very great deal to the evolution of trade relations with both Britain and the United States, as well as the associated development of the tariff. Laurier knew this all too well, having lived through the difficulties created for the Dominion and its predecessors by the machinations of its two chief trading partners.

Britain had not always been a free-trading nation. When the Corn Laws were abrogated in 1846, and Britain put protectionism behind it, the consequences for the United Province of Canada (the union of Upper and Lower Canada created in 1841) were severe. It was Canadian grain, among others, that had sheltered behind the preferential tariff of the mother country. When the Corn Laws went, so too did protected access to our most important market. By the following year, the situation was dire in Canada and the decision was made, with imperial blessing, to seek reciprocity with the US as an alternative to the lost markets of Britain.[54]

While Canada was an ardent suitor, the Americans were a very discouraging object of our affections. They saw little benefit for themselves in such an arrangement, and Northern industrial interests were particularly leery. Moreover, the slave states, in this politically charged run-up to the Civil War, feared that reciprocity might lead to annexation and the reinforcement of anti-slavery forces in the Union. After all, slavery had been abolished peacefully by judicial fiat in Great Britain in 1772, and then throughout the Empire by simple act of Parliament in 1807, but America continued with what Southerners euphemistically called the "peculiar institution" until the issue was settled at the cost of many thousands of lives almost sixty years later.[55] The promise of access to Canadian waters for politically powerful New England fishing interests, however, ultimately tipped the balance within Congress, and a reciprocity agreement was signed in 1854. America, always the reluctant partner, gave in to protectionist pressures a mere twelve years later, abrogating the hapless and unloved agreement in 1866. Faced with no privileged access to either US or British markets, the third option for British North America was Confederation. Impelled chiefly by this economic logic, the federal union of three British colonies occurred the following year.[56]

The expanded markets made possible by Confederation, however, remained small beer in global terms. Reciprocity with our southern neighbour remained the holy grail of Canadian politics; Sir John A. Macdonald pursued it energetically in the face of massive American indifference, until even Old Tomorrow had to resign himself to the evidence. To fill the vacuum, he came up with the National Policy, which even he regarded as a poor second best. The National Policy—high tariffs to protect domestic producers against American competition, plus the completion of transcontinental ties, and especially the railway—became his signature policy in 1878. But in an early precursor of R.B. Bennett's boast that he would use high tariffs to "blast our way into the markets of the world or perish in the attempt,"[57] Macdonald was clear that his policy ought not to be taken as an *alternative* to reciprocity with the US, but rather as a *strategy for obtaining it*:

> The welfare of Canada requires the adoption of a National Policy, which, by a judicious readjustment of the tariff, will benefit and foster the agricultural, the mining, the manufacturing and other interests of the Dominion; that such a policy . . . will prevent Canada from being made a sacrifice market . . . and moving (as it ought to do) in the direction of reciprocity of tariffs with our neighbours, so far as the varied interests of Canada may demand, will greatly tend to procure for this country, eventually a reciprocity of trade . . . *It is only by closing our doors, and by cutting them out of our market, that they will open theirs to us . . . it is only by closing the door that we can get anything.*[58]

It was this policy that Laurier and his government inherited in 1896, that he moderated through tariff reform in the early days, and that he sought to subsume under a new reciprocity pact at the end of his reign. Surprisingly, the agreement Laurier negotiated would have left much of the protective tariff for Canadian manufactures in place but would have given free access for Canadian resources to US markets. A striking amount of the old National Policy would have remained intact. But the moment was not right. Laurier's political skills were not equal to the task after the wear and tear of fifteen years in power, and this key part of Laurier's vision became encrusted with a mythology of divisiveness and defeatism that would only be shaken off by slow degrees over the following century.

A COUNTRY AND A CENTURY DERAILED chapter two

What happened? How was such a promising start to what was to be Canada's century steered so quickly into the ditch?

In fact, the prosperity largely continued under Laurier's successor, Prime Minister Sir Robert Borden,[1] who, with the exception of reciprocity with the Americans, largely pursued Laurier's economic policies. The rapid growth in population, for example, continued right up until 1921, at which time 8.8 million people lived in the Dominion.[2] Under the later leadership of Laurier's handpicked successor as leader of the Liberal Party, William Lyon Mackenzie King, Canada continued to enjoy good levels of prosperity through much of the twenties, even if the frenetic effervescence of the Laurier years had gone.

But big changes were afoot. There was the human slaughter and benighted leadership on a vast scale of the First World War. In its wake were left broken trading relationships, barriers to the movement of people, the economic dislocation of Germany, the breakup of the Austro-Hungarian Empire, and the exhaustion of Britain, whose dynamism had so contributed to Canada's own. The Russian Revolution had let the genie of radical politics out of the bottle throughout the West, and it took the fall of the Berlin Wall more than seventy years later to put it back. This was part of a series of events that cumulatively, with the slowly gathering force of a locomotive, drove not just Canada but the entire industrialized world off course.

The big changes coming were perhaps masked at first by the return of prosperity in the decade following the end of the war.[3] Then in 1929 came the Crash, and the thirties that followed brought a worldwide depression and a protectionist surge that undid much of the remarkably free global movement of goods, services, capital, and people that had characterized the prewar years. Unemployed Canadians marched on Ottawa and queued for soup kitchens. The huge triangle of land in Alberta and Saskatchewan that the explorer and surveyor John Palliser had warned in 1863 was unsuitable for agricultural settlement had in fact been heavily settled during the Laurier years. Palliser had his revenge later when it turned out that "Palliser's Triangle" was a major contributor to the dustbowl of the 1930s that helped drag down Canada's economy.[4]

The Second World War, among other things, broke up this unhappy state of affairs in Canada as much as elsewhere, and the returning troops rushed into new jobs in a Canada determined to do better. Economically we entered an era of pronounced prosperity, as we reverted to a large extent to Laurier's policies and enjoyed the energy thereby set free. Britain was finished as an imperial power and as a major market for Canada. America confronted no serious competitor as our main market, our main supplier of capital, and the main alternative destination for the skilled immigrants fleeing Europe's postwar daze.[5] While we still lacked an institutional framework and strong rules to bind America's ability to run roughshod over Canada's interests, we had a powerful shared history as allies in the recent war and were partners in the construction of the postwar order.

America sat astride the world and found in Canada a respected neighbour who shared its world view. That had to be enough for the moment, in large part because the trauma of Laurier's defeat over free trade still lingered in the minds of the mandarins of Ottawa and the operatives of the dominant Liberal Party. Yet even in the face of this potent political bogeyman, it was only Mackenzie King's personal objections that prevented a new reciprocity agreement being consummated in the immediate postwar era. In 1948 a deal was struck and ready for signature in both capitals; in Ottawa the Liberal caucus and the senior mandarins were on board. At the last minute, Mackenzie King's still vivid memories of his political mentor's political humiliation over the issue won out over economic logic.[6]

The people who ran the country were keenly aware that our success depended on remaining competitive with America on every front, and indeed we kept our tax load and our newly emergent welfare state under tight rein to ensure that neither the cost of government nor the allure of an easy dependence would distract us from building a country equal to the promise of the continent we shared. In the fifties and sixties we intentionally positioned ourselves, as Laurier had recommended, as a low-tax alternative to the US.[7] Research comparing public spending over the three decades stretching from 1932 to 1963 show that over this period Canada remained close to the Laurier prescription. We were less inclined than the Americans to enrich social welfare but more inclined to invest in productivity-enhancing transport and communications. We spent less of our rising incomes on government; they spent more. And anticipating the critics, it is perhaps worth pointing out that the higher American defence spending does not account for the gap in favour of higher US spending: the gap between Canadian and US defence spending is considerably narrower than the one on social welfare.

> From 1932 to 1963 expenditure on health, education, and transportation rose slightly more quickly in Canada than in the United States, and expenditure on defence and social welfare and total expenditure more quickly in the United States than in Canada.[8]

Louis St. Laurent, the prime minister who most embodied the era of postwar progress and freedom, entertained no doubt that Canada's great good fortune was rooted in its inheritance of a tradition of freedom and individual responsibility—Laurier and St. Laurent were as one in their belief that our individual freedom was the cornerstone of all else and that the biggest danger to that freedom was an overweening state.

The St. Laurent government's policy could hardly have been closer in spirit and in detail to Laurier's vision. Canada's public finances were carefully managed to ensure regular budget surpluses to help pay down war debt. Modest expansions were made to social welfare programs, but these were kept under tight control and designed to ensure that they would not become an alternative to work for Canadians. The resistance to fashionable expansion of the size of government came not only from St. Laurent's government, but from the provinces as well. As a result of this measured frugality, Canada enjoyed the tax advantage that was so close to the heart of Laurier's plan, which was proving itself again in the mid-twentieth century as it had in Laurier's day.[9]

As late as the 1957 federal election campaign, St. Laurent was still firmly committed to Laurier's vision for Canada—and for the Liberal Party—when he said:

> [A]ny idea of non-essential interference by the government is repugnant to the Liberal Party. We believe that the private citizen must be left to his own initiative whenever possible and that if some help is required for the individual, that which is afforded by the national government must encourage rather than replace the help which the community or the province with its municipalities can give.[10]

We were not overtaking America, but the two nations of North America were together showing the rest of the world their heels.

The twenty years of growth and dynamism we enjoyed in the immediate post-war years amply demonstrated that Laurier's vision was not a mere product of its times but that it was a vision that stood the test of change and retained its power to inspire.

Again, however, Canadians got knocked off course—and this time the blame fell more on us than on world circumstances over which we enjoyed so very little influence.

Beginning in the mid-sixties, the confluence of many forces began to work a change in the minds of Canadians. A wave of nationalist anti-Americanism washed over Canada, fuelled in part by distaste for the Vietnam War and America's brash assertiveness on the international stage and in part by domestic alarm over a perceived American domination of the economy.[11] The counterculture movement that emerged in the US found echoes around the world, including in Canada, and Marxism, feminism, and various other isms began a long march through the academic institutions. Keynesianism, a naïve faith in the ability of government officials to "manage" the economy, became almost universal among Western governments, especially since memories were still reasonably fresh of the success of central planning controls during the Second World War.[12] In the seventies, a Republican president brought in price and wage controls, the ultimate expression of confidence in government's superiority over markets.[13]

Increasingly, government was being looked to to solve perennial social problems, such as when Washington moved in the 1960s against both racial discrimination, through the Civil Rights Act, and poverty, through the War on Poverty and the Great Society. All of these factors and more—

wider access to education, the emergence of effective contraception, the growth of cities and suburbs—affected Canada as much as they did other Western societies. Over and above that, we had special factors in Canada that exacerbated these trends. For example, we had the largest baby boom in the Western world, undermining our faith in the economy to provide work for all who wanted it, just as we saw the rise of a new breed of aggressive separatist nationalism in Quebec, which unleashed a torrent of spending designed to bind Quebeckers to the federal state.[14]

Laurier's belief in the rugged individualism of Canadians, and the freedom, within the rule of law, that made that individualism the source of great prosperity and social progress, seemed overtaken by events. The new zeitgeist called for an expansive state, great new social programs, and vast extension of state employment and state enterprise. Against all this Laurier had warned, and those warnings increasingly fell on deaf ears.

Government took an ever-increasing place in the economy and the lives of Canadians. Government was growing everywhere in the industrialized world, of course, but in few places like it did in Canada.[15] Armies of workers were drawn into public sector work in the federal, provincial, and municipal governments while the tax burden rose, public finances deteriorated, and the national debt took off. The expansion of welfare state programs drew tens of thousands into dependence as the value of benefits rose handsomely in real terms.

By the mid-nineties, over 12 per cent of the population of the country's largest and wealthiest province, Ontario, was on provincial social assistance. In next-door Quebec, one-fifth of the population was on some kind of public benefit, such as welfare or unemployment insurance.[16] Public employment rose in Ottawa, and those increases were mirrored in the provinces.[17]

The share of the national economy directed by government rose from about 28 per cent in 1960 to a peak of 53 per cent in 1992.[18] As we document more fully in later chapters recounting Canada's fiscal challenges, we didn't have a single balanced national budget between 1974 and 1998.[19] Taxes, and especially deficits, rose inexorably.

By contrast, America was a paragon of economic virtue, even though it too indulged in some expansion of the state. Over the same period, 1960 to 1996, the share of the national economy devoted to government also grew, and from the same starting point. But where they upped their spending by six percentage points, to 34 per cent of GDP, we nearly doubled ours.[20] Their national debt grew, but it went from being a little higher than ours to somewhat less—despite Vietnam, the Great Society, and the same percentage of national income spent on tax-financed health care as in Canada.[21]

Protectionism became something of a vogue as we threw up barriers to foreign investment and foreign cultural products like music, television, and magazines.[22] Unemployment became a national preoccupation, and after having kept even with US unemployment rates for decades, we began a long-term divergence of our rates that saw a larger share of Canadians than Americans consistently out of work.[23]

We slammed the door on immigration in many of the years of these lost decades, sometimes admitting as few as 71,000 people (1961)—a far cry from the 282,164 admitted at the postwar peak in 1957.[24] Taxes became uncompetitive compared to the US,[25] and we obsessed about brain drains to the south. Our standard of living in 1960—almost identical to the Americans'—slowed its growth, creating a gap that, by 1992, had reached about 22 per cent as a result of poor productivity growth, high taxes, and high deficits that crowded out private sector investment.[26]

The foreign investment controls introduced during this period merit a little further attention for the absolute reversal of policy they signal. The 1972 Foreign Investment Review Act, the product of a minority Parliament where Pierre Trudeau's Liberals were dependent on a virulently economically nationalist NDP for their survival, was a radical departure for Canada. As political scientist John Fayerweather noted in 1974:

> There have been virtually no general restrictions or even government administrative processes to impede new investors. Until the mid-fifties, the general tenor of Canadian attitudes was to encourage maximum inflows of foreign capital.[27]

Indeed we saw how the Laurier years had been ones of massive flows of capital into Canada. These flows were dwarfed by the St. Laurent years. The fifties saw the largest inflow of American capital in Canadian history up to that date.[28] For noted Canadian historian Michael Bliss, this phenomenon is easily explained: "American investors poured money into what was perceived as a friendly neighbouring nation, culturally indistinguishable from the U.S., rich in raw materials waiting to be processed to enrich the continental economy."[29] Clearly, the postwar relationship between the Canadian government and American investors was reciprocal—government was eager to attract huge levels of investment, and investors were equally as eager to invest in Canada.

This was regarded as a virtuous circle in the early postwar years, just as it had been regarded by Laurier and all the political leaders in between: "Until the mid-1950s, there was virtual unanimity in Canada that foreign direct investment created a net benefit for Canada."[30] In the seventies a modish economic nationalism made us skittish about foreign capital and investment, even though there was little evidence that we were any more reliant on that capital than we had been previously, and even less evidence that our traditional openness to foreign investment had been anything but beneficial, on balance, for Canada.

The actual degree to which foreign investment was obstructed is the subject of some controversy. Not many deals were actually blocked. On the other hand, the review process was long and cumbersome, and the simple fact of its existence created the kind of potentially costly uncertainty that business shies away from. Economist Harry Johnson passionately argued the line that Laurier, a proud Canadian nationalist, would have taken when he said in 1977 that "Canadian nationalism as it has developed in recent years has been diverting Canada into a narrow and garbage-cluttered cul-de-sac."[31]

In other words, we abandoned almost every tenet of Laurier's plan, and we paid a heavy price.

Still reeling from reciprocity's defeat in 1911, the political class shied away from any suggestion of broaching a broad-based trade agreement with the United States, but we were still mindful of the dangers to the Canadian economy posed by the possibility of American unilateralism, such as Richard Nixon's aggressive action against foreign trade. His 1971 New Economic Policy put paid to the notion that Canada could escape being the target of unilateral US trade action because of some ill-defined "special relationship," thanks to which we nice Canadians could always resort to special pleading to be excused from a protectionist spanking really intended for nasty foreigners across the seas. Nixon had Canada squarely in his sights. Canada had enjoyed a long-term trade surplus with the US, and Nixon most emphatically decided to include us in his surprise protectionist program. An across-the-board 10 per cent tariff was slapped on Canadian imports. Ottawa was shocked. Washington didn't care.[32]

With a comprehensive agreement off the table, Canada was thrown back on three strategies. One, which predated the shock administered by Nixonomics, was to negotiate more modest sectoral agreements with the US, such as the Auto Pact signed by Lester Pearson and Lyndon Johnson in 1965, which essentially created managed trade between our two countries in auto production and assembly.[33]

In 1959, following the cancellation of the Canadian Avro Arrow fighter plane project, we worked out a Defence Production Sharing Agreement. This seemed a sensible alternative to the Arrow's go-it-alone approach when we couldn't supply a market on the scale needed to produce complete defence systems at a competitive price; specialization for Canadian producers within a common continental defence equipment industry seemed a more efficient option, giving Canada a better bang for its buck. Gaining access to the US market by essentially being treated as domestic US suppliers paid off handsomely. In its first year alone, the agreement generated about $200 million in new revenues for Canadian suppliers of defence-related equipment.[34]

A third such agreement dealt with agricultural machinery.[35] But such agreements were few and far between, and being limited in scope didn't offer the kind of room for favourable trade-offs that a more comprehensive agreement would have done.

Under our second strategy, we were enthusiastic supporters of multilateral trade negotiations, looking to the General Agreement on Trade and Tariffs (GATT) and its successors to help discipline the US tendency to go it alone by dangling the prospect of improved access to world markets and not just Canadian ones. Like the sectoral trade agreements, these international agreements were useful, and throughout the period international trade grew consistently faster than domestic economies.

The third Canadian strategy was to seek to diversify trade away from the United States and toward other markets. This policy was an abject failure. Many Canadian governments came to office in the postwar years bubbling with enthusiasm for the unexploited or underexploited foreign markets that would reduce our reliance on American customers and vulnerability to American politicians. China, and to some extent India, plays that role in Canada today.

After the shock of Nixon's New Economic Policy, however, the pursuit of such diversified markets became a matter of high policy known grandiloquently as the Third Option, the other two options being the dysfunctional status quo or an unpalatably closer embrace of the US, a set of choices designed to make the Third Option appear highly attractive.[36] Talks were opened on special trading relationships with the European Community and Japan, for example, and Prime Minister Trudeau cultivated leaders of emerging economies around the world. These efforts foundered on the same shoals as all their predecessors: governments don't actually make trade decisions; companies do. And Canadian exporters were closely bound up with American markets. One acute observer of the time summed up the results with devastating accuracy: "Every Canadian government after 1945 hoped to diversify trade and every one left office with an increase in the proportion of trade with the Americans."[37]

Channelling Laurier's spirit, historian Michael Bliss dismissed all these efforts in the sixties and seventies as naïve attempts to deny Canada's real economic circumstances:

> The Galbraithian world of controlled markets, planning systems, and perpetual profits was a fantasy. Canadian governments' confidence in their ability to anticipate the future and shape economic events was pathetically absurd.[38]

One reason that Bliss's verdict on these lost decades may seem harsh, but is in fact quite justified, is that the policy of these years was based on an increasingly outmoded view. The truth of the matter was that it was becoming more and more misplaced to think of the Canadian and US economies as separate national economies. We had many highly integrated industries, such as autos, defence, and agricultural machinery, operating on both sides of the border as if the continent were a single economic entity. Autos and other manufacturing industries, however, weren't the only industries that were increasingly integrated across the international border. Our natural resources fed US production, for example, which was powered by our electricity, our oil, and our natural gas. To an ever-growing extent, we did not make products exclusively within our national borders and then trade those finished products with each other. Different pieces of complex production processes took place on both sides of the border; we traded less and less in the classical sense, and instead more and more we made things together. "Shifting" Canadian exports to other nations implied that Canadian exports were constituted of finished products we could sell to whomever we wanted, a naïve and dangerously outdated understanding of the unique degree of continental integration we were already achieving.[39]

Dawn of the Redemptive Decade

Slowly, groggily, Canada began to question the wisdom of the new course it had charted for itself, but once roused, Canadians began to demand change, and change they got. In fact, there is a decade during which Canada clearly changed course, beginning with the free trade election in 1988 and ending with Paul Martin's tabling of the 1997–98 budget, the first balanced budget in Ottawa in a generation. We call this the Redemptive Decade. Canadians and their leaders took bold steps to resolve problems that had been festering within the body politic for years. Actions that just a few short years before were conventionally viewed as "unthinkable" became not only thinkable but doable. And the country began to redeem itself, to return to Laurier's path of discipline and virtue after a long and uncharacteristic detour through self-indulgence.

Later chapters will lay out the blood, sweat, toil, and tears we expended to reduce our welfare dependence and put our public finances and tax burden on a sounder footing—or at least give them a strong push in that direction. But these were the last elements of our partial restoration of Laurier's plan for Canada. Others came earlier.

For example, we finally realized the limits of incremental trade deals with the United States in specific sectors, such as autos, especially as we began to see how signally we had failed to shift our trade to other nations. We could not beat the Americans—in large part because "beating them" implied being on a different economic team, which increasingly we were not—so we had to join them.

No politician was willing to call down upon his or her head the kind of repudiation that Laurier had endured on the issue, so progress was cautious and measured. We employed that handy standby called upon by all Canadian governments that hope to provoke change without taking responsibility for it—Pierre Trudeau appointed former federal finance minister Donald Macdonald to head a royal commission on Canada's economic prospects. After years of research and hearings, the Macdonald Commission delivered itself of a report, the content of which is now largely forgotten—except for the seemingly revolutionary recommendation to launch free trade talks with the Americans. The sentence from the Macdonald Commission's report that summed up that document's virtual repudiation of twenty years of poor policy was: "the message is that there is less and less place to hide [in the global marketplace]."[40]

While he would not deliver his report until the government that had commissioned it was long gone from office, Donald Macdonald let the cat out of the bag in an interview with William Johnson of the *Globe and Mail*: free trade with the US was going to be on the table.[41] His fellow Liberal, and the prime minister who appointed him, Pierre Trudeau, did not share Macdonald's enthusiasm. Even Trudeau understood that the old hiding places were offering less and less shelter, however, and had plans for expanding sectoral free trade agreements with the US—reciprocity in bite-sized pieces.[42]

Trudeau soon passed from the scene, and the Liberal government was defeated by the resurgent Conservatives under Brian Mulroney, who showed no interest during his 1983 Tory leadership campaign in opening free trade talks with the Americans. In his remarks on the subject he conflated two contradictory ideas: namely, that Canada is vulnerable to US unilateralism when it is in the Americans' interest and that the proper response to this threat is to refuse to negotiate an agreement with them that might limit the threat:

> Now there's a real honey—free trade with the Americans! Free trade with the Americans is like sleeping with an elephant. It's terrific until the elephant twitches, and if the elephant rolls over, you're a dead man. I'll tell you when he's going to roll over—he's going to roll over in times of economic depression and they're going to crank up the plants in Georgia and North Carolina and Ohio and they're going to be shutting them down here. That's why free trade was decided on in the election of 1911. It affects Canadian sovereignty, and we'll have none of it, not during the leadership campaigns, nor at any other times.[43]

But the Macdonald Commission recommendation became the idea that would not die, and the protectionist proclivities of the US Congress toward Japan, among other successful trading nations, breathed new life into the Nixonomics nightmare.

A debilitating recession gripped the economies of Canada and the US by late 1981. In both countries, unemployment levels rose steadily and economic output declined substantially. In addition, the Tokyo Round of multilateral trade discussions, which began in the mid-1970s, was concluded in 1979, to very mixed reviews. Although it helped bring down customs duties, for example, a number of seemingly intractable problems were left unresolved.[44]

In this context of economic and legal uncertainty, protectionist forces in the United States advanced an increasingly salient message that beguiled a far wider audience. Indeed, a steady increase in the US trade deficit provoked widespread despondency with multilateralism in general and the world trading system in particular. Early on, therefore, the Reagan administration—under strong pressure from a Congress determined to halt what was perceived as the unfair trading practices of America's major trading partners—was politically obliged to introduce a series of aggressive measures designed to curb imports despite Reagan's own free-trading instincts. While the US trade actions largely targeted Japan, the threat of sweeping import duties and quotas produced significant alarm in Canada. For the first time in decades, both business and government were forced to reassess the value to Canada of secure and enhanced access to the US market.[45]

As the country's economic prospects continued to darken relative to those of our southern neighbour, and the need to expose complacent Canadian business to the bracing shock of some continental competition became undeniable, Mulroney and the business establishment came to embrace free trade. An agreement was reasonably quickly struck with the sympathetic administration of Ronald Reagan and endorsed by a Congress by then in a rather different mood than in its most aggressive Japan-bashing days. Now they were imbued with the optimism of the president and buoyed by what seemed to be a resurgence of American power. It also helped that Canada, in the eyes of American policymakers, was not Japan but instead a friendly and trusted neighbour who seemed much less threatening.

Free trade was not to be an easy sell at home, however. Just as in 1911, and in earlier elections where free trade had been a central issue, feelings ran high. The parties might have reversed their respective positions—the Tories in favour of free trade, the Liberals opposed—but otherwise the script had been used before.

In June 1988, John Turner "took almost everyone by surprise" when he announced that he had instructed his senators not to allow the passage of the facilitating legislation until the Canadian people had been given a chance to vote on the issue.[46] The government could not postpone matters to 1989 if free trade was to be implemented on schedule in January. Therefore, on September 30, Prime Minister Mulroney called on the governor general and proposed an election for November 21.

Mulroney's election call precipitated one of the most emotionally charged campaigns in Canada's history.

In the months leading up to the election, the NDP's vociferous opposition to the agreement had contributed to that party's growing support in the polls. As the campaign commenced, Turner was determined to recapture potential voters who opposed free trade, and therefore, "It was the Liberals who gave it a higher profile once the campaign began."[47] By turning free trade into "the fight of [his] life," Turner plunged into the campaign with more zeal and passion than he had shown during his previous four years in opposition.[48] In one dramatic confrontation, he accused Mulroney of repudiating Canada's independence: "I happen to believe that you have sold us out." Ignoring Mulroney's reprimand and repeated interruptions, Turner, as historian Stephen Azzi eloquently points out, "found the words to tap into English Canada's perennial fear of falling into Uncle Sam's grasping hand":

> We built a country East and West and North. We built it on an infrastructure that deliberately resisted the continental pressure of the United States. For 120 years we've done it. With one signature of a pen, you've reversed that, thrown us into the north–south influence of the United States and will reduce us, I am sure, to a colony of the United States, because when the economic levers go, the political independence is sure to follow.[49]

The Mulroney Tories—and not John Turner's Liberals—won the election, however, and were able to use their parliamentary majority to pass the enabling legislation. Free trade was now a reality.

The agreement was not perfect, and in particular has proven frustratingly weak in its ability to put limits on America's unilateralist instincts. Still, it has proven a boon to the Canadian economy, and the higher degree of certainty that it introduced in Canadian business decision-making vis-à-vis US markets is reflected in subsequent significant increases in cross-border trade.[50]

Three-quarters of a century after his bitter defeat over this very issue, the building block that had always eluded Laurier in his plan for Canada was finally put in place.

In tandem with the drive for free trade, the Mulroney Tories pursued another Laurier tenet: tax reform, both for efficiency's sake and to regain lost competitiveness with the United States.

Laurier, we recall, wanted to avoid taxes and tariffs being higher in Canada than in the US, while also reforming the tariff to be less damaging in its effects on the Canadian economy.

While the structure of taxes evolved significantly over the intervening decades, the principles that Laurier sought to preserve and promote could not have been more apposite to the situation confronting Canada.

By the mid-eighties, federal revenues came chiefly from three sources: the manufacturers' sales tax, the personal income tax, and the corporate income tax.[51] Each was in severe need of reform.[52]

On the income tax front, Ottawa had allowed both corporate and personal tax loads to become uncompetitive compared with rates in the United States, and because of President Reagan's proposed tax reforms, that lack of competitiveness risked becoming acute if Ottawa did not act.

Regarding personal income taxes, Ottawa saw that the Reagan tax reforms were going to cut taxes by at least 30 per cent across the board.[53] Such a policy was in line with the advice many economists and the Department of Finance had been giving for years[54]—and that Laurier would instinctively have understood was right. Income taxes, especially ones that are highly progressive—i.e., where the tax rate on your income rises steeply as your income grows—fall most heavily on three highly valuable factors: effort, entrepreneurship, and productivity. As you work harder, and earn more as a consequence, your tax burden doesn't rise in lockstep with your income. It increases faster than your income. If the country's top rates are too high, then the reward for working harder and longer falls below what is needed to sustain that extra effort. As any economist will tell you, if you tax something, you'll get less of it. And in Laurier's plan, what Canada needed was more effort, more hard work, more risk-taking, more people striving to build the country, not less.

The finance minister at the time, Michael Wilson, didn't need much convincing that if the top rate on personal income had fallen to 28 per cent in the United States, Canada could not long attract and keep its most talented workers with top rates of over 50 per cent.[55] Accordingly, the 1987 federal budget outlined comprehensive personal tax reform, reducing the number of brackets to three from ten and lowering the marginal rates significantly.

Wilson's legislation to put these changes into effect, Bill C-139, broadened the tax base for personal income while reducing the tax rates. In the place of the traditional tax exemptions, the new regime relied on tax credits while getting rid of a number of personal income tax deductions.[56]

The situation was similar in the corporate income tax field. Economists were increasingly coming to the view that heavy taxation of corporate profits was undesirable because, among other things, it suppressed investment, left less money available for wages, reduced income for pension plans workers would rely on for their retirement, and caused multinational companies to try to report as much of their income in low-tax countries as possible. The 1986 US Tax Reform Act put US corporate taxes on the same reform track as personal income taxes. Canada was compelled to follow suit, and for exactly the reasons that Laurier believed were decisive: we live in a competitive world, especially vis-à-vis the US, and we could never allow our tax rates to rise above theirs without paying a painful price. In fact, given the other disadvantages Canada faced, having lower rates than the US was almost compulsory.

In putting his tax reform package forward, Michael Wilson sounded a Laurier-like note:

> Statutory corporate tax rates in Canada are above those in the United States and other countries, and without early implementation of

> significant reductions in Canada the gap would widen. If the gap between Canada and U.S. rates were not narrowed, considerable income-earning activities would shift to the United States. The gap would also encourage firms with operations in both countries to arrange their operations so as to allocate more of their taxable income outside Canada. The result of such shifts would be less economic activity in Canada and a significant erosion of our corporate tax revenues. The proposed reduction in Canadian statutory tax rates is designed to avoid these results.[57]

Of course, these reforms were only a down payment on what would come later, because while they reduced the gap between the tax burden borne by American and Canadian workers and companies, they did not eliminate it, and still less did they restore Laurier's ideal: a gap in favour of Canadian workers and companies. Still, just as Laurier had to be content in the early days with tariff reform rather than the free trade in which he so fervently believed, the movement was in the right direction, even if the way station fell far short of the cherished final destination.

Perhaps even more important than this early down payment on income tax reform was the wholesale reform of federal sales tax that Michael Wilson engineered.

The chief sales tax at the federal level was the manufacturers' sales tax (MST). A more foolish and damaging tax it would be hard to conceive. The MST was a tax that applied only to manufacturing, and even within that narrow field, taxed some activities but not others. Companies could organize themselves and their activities in such a way as to blunt or even escape much of the tax—practically a textbook definition of a poorly designed tax. Because the tax could be largely avoided with a little effort and imagination, Ottawa found its revenues from this source to be declining over the years.[58]

Yet leaving aside the misleadingly named MST, sales taxes per se have increasingly won approval from economists and policy thinkers because, if you are going to levy taxes, a well-designed tax on consumption is one of the least damaging. Unlike income taxes, which discourage work and effort and success, consumption taxes do not distort incentives to do these highly desirable things. And where saving is taxed—by the income tax and capital gains tax, which capture a part of the returns to savers—but consumption is not (i.e. when there is no sales tax), the absence of the sales tax also creates incentives for people to spend rather than save. Finally, a broadly based tax with few or no exemptions, and set at a low rate, means that the revenue is more reliable than under an MST-type tax, cause companies cannot escape the tax by artificial reorganization of their activities.

The highly courageous decision was therefore made by the Mulroney Tories to eliminate the MST and to replace it with the goods and services tax (GST). Unlike the MST, the GST was to be a "flow-through tax": when businesses bought raw materials or machinery or advertising or telecommunications services, the tax they paid on those "inputs" was credited against the GST they collected from the consumers of their goods or services. The hidden 13.5 per cent MST, applied to a narrow range of goods, was abolished and replaced with a much more transparent and easy-to-administer tax, applied to a wide range of goods and services but at the much lower rate of 7 per cent. The balance between saving and consuming was at least partially restored.

All of these good things were purchased, however, at a significant political cost. Because the new GST was so transparent and obvious, people had something quite concrete on which to focus their dislike of taxation, whereas the MST had been hidden and therefore called forth little popular agitation for its abolition. And it did not help that the introduction of the GST coincided with both a significant recession and a rise in the value of the Canadian dollar. A well-designed visible tax, even if it was replacing a badly designed invisible one, could only become a lightning rod for general economic discontent, and cross-border shopping with valuable Canadian dollars became an effective kind of tax protest.

The GST became a major money spinner for the federal government, although it was quickly forgotten that it replaced the revenue from the MST. The reception the tax received might well have been more positive had the government been able to follow through on their original plan to make it the centrepiece of a larger tax reform package that reduced income taxes and shifted the tax burden onto consumption, a highly desirable rebalancing of the tax load.[59] Unfortunately, the economic circumstances of the time, including the government's own inability to keep its spending under control, forced Ottawa to put off the planned reductions in personal income taxes until much later.

The GST was so politically unpopular that there is little doubt that, like Laurier's reciprocity proposal, it helped sink the party that brought it in. But the victorious Liberals of Jean Chrétien, once in office, quickly dumped their platform commitment to axe the tax, choosing instead to set in motion the other half of the sales tax reform that was necessary.

Paul Martin, Chrétien's finance minister, was given the job of finding some credible way of claiming that the Liberals had an "alternative" to the GST. The alternative he came up with was one that had been part of the original plan that the department of finance had put together for the GST but had fallen by the wayside in the face of the new tax's disastrous public reception: "harmonization," or the rolling of provincial sales taxes (PST) and the GST into a single tax, the harmonized sales tax (HST).[60] In fact this was not an alternative to the GST at all; rather, it was an attempt to bring up to date the extremely archaic and damaging provincial sales taxes, putting them on a modernized footing like the GST's.

Provincial sales taxes, like the old MST, were a tax that fell hard and damagingly on business. Every time a business bought something it needed for its production process, whether machinery or fuel or even restaurant meals for its workers, it paid a tax that had to be passed on to consumers in the final price, unless it got a specific exemption or credit. That put them at a disadvantage with competitors like Europeans, whose value-added tax (VAT) was a flow-through tax like the GST, or Americans, who generally faced much lower sales tax rates. PSTs were also levied on a unique mix of goods in each province and on a different mix than the federal GST. Each province had to pay for its own collection and verification machinery, although most of the cost of administering the tax fell on business, and businesses had to keep track of two different tax bases, tax rates, and audit and inspection requirements. It was all an expensive and counterproductive nightmare.

Martin was able to convince three provinces—Nova Scotia, New Brunswick, and Newfoundland—to agree to abolish their PST and simply tack the provincial consumption tax onto the federal GST, resulting in those three provinces in a combined HST rate of 15 per cent, composed of a 7 per cent federal tax and an 8 per cent provincial tax. Businesses in those provinces now had a flow-through tax that improved their competitiveness; Ottawa paid for all the administration and enforcement cost, removing that cost from provincial budgets; and Ottawa also gave the three provinces about $1 billion to help with the difficult politics of transition from the old regime to the new.[61]

Reflexively autonomist Quebec naturally decided not to harmonize with the federal tax but to do its own reform on similar lines, and to demand a higher payment from Ottawa to compensate the province for its administrative and transition costs. Four provinces were now essentially harmonized—five if you count Alberta, which is harmonized by the simple expedient of having no PST to harmonize.

Subsequent research shows that the promise of the HST has been amply realized: the lower costs that business faces are in fact passed on to consumers, and businesses invest more in productivity-enhancing equipment.[62] But the politics of provinces throwing in their lot with an unpopular federal tax have been so toxic that it is only now, twenty years after the original GST reform, that the logjam is really breaking and Ontario and British Columbia have agreed to sign on, leaving Saskatchewan, Manitoba, and PEI all clearly mulling how to make the move politically palatable to their own voters.

In summary, by the early 1990s, we were halfway through the Redemptive Decade and several key elements of Laurier's plan—the plan that would trigger the Canadian century—were in place. Reciprocity in trade with the Americans had finally been achieved within the context of a world where tariffs and other barriers to trade were falling. The free trade that Laurier believed in so passionately was increasingly carrying the day. Canada was engaging America directly and courageously, as Laurier had in his time, and seeking to put some restriction on Washington's poorly mastered urges to punish people who are good at selling to Americans, something Canadians are very, very good at.

Putting the tax structure on a sound footing was well under way, but while some modest progress was made on tax rates, the total tax load and tax structure remained uncompetitive with the tax regime in the US. That in turn was driven by the fact that the Canadian state remained bloated compared to the limited government that Laurier thought would unleash the creativity and entrepreneurialism of Canadians. Politicians were unwilling to impose on Canadian taxpayers and voters the kind of taxes necessary to pay the full cost of the services governments were providing, so to the heavy tax load had to be added the burgeoning debt. And against Laurier's firm advice, Canada had opened the taps on social welfare spending, drawing large numbers of people into dependence on the state and unable to contribute their energy and intelligence to the Canadian economy. America was also headed in a similar direction, but its progress was much slower than Canada's. The inevitable arithmetic was that Canada, relatively speaking, was losing ground all the time vis-à-vis the United States, whereas Laurier's advice to us had been always to keep ahead of the behemoth if we wanted to prosper. Free trade and tax reform were welcome reversions to the Laurier advice, but on most other fronts, Sir Wilfrid was still spinning at high speed in his grave.

The next chapters explain how we completed the Redemptive Decade, brought peace to Laurier's ghost, and reversed course so remarkably that the Canadian century Laurier believed was rightfully ours is visible on the horizon—and only a hundred years later than Sir Wilfrid predicted.

part II

Only in Canada, You Say? We Show the World How to Reform

FROM BASKET CASE TO WORLD BEATER: CANADA SHOWS THE WAY chapter three

Canada possesses an historic opportunity to forge a lasting economic advantage in North America, and indeed within the broader group of industrialized countries, that could make the twenty-first century the Canadian century. The basis of this opportunity lies in significant reforms that were undertaken federally and in many provinces throughout the Redemptive Decade of the late 1980s and early 1990s.

In particular, over the course of the second half of that remarkable decade of change, Canada did a fiscal U-turn, from nearly hitting a debt wall in the early 1990s to leading the G7 in economic growth for a decade, from 1997 to 2007.[1] While Canada has unfortunately regressed in a number of areas of fiscal policy over the past few years, the reforms of the Redemptive Decade continue to provide enormous benefits. What is needed now is a return to the successful policies of that remarkable decade, and then to extend them to meet our present circumstances.

Before we tell the story of the second half of the Redemptive Decade, however—the story of how we completed the reform package that began with free trade and the GST, of how we got back on track with Laurier's plan for Canada—it perhaps makes sense to start with the conclusion. In other words, the critics of the federal and provincial fiscal reforms that we are about to describe predicted dire, in some cases near-apocalyptic economic and social consequences for those reforms. In fact, the reforms of the 1990s ended up being a major—perhaps *the* major—contributor to the country's robust economic performance of the past decade.[2] By robust economic performance, we mean bread and butter prosperity for average Canadians in the form of lower unemployment, higher rates of investment and job creation, increasing economic opportunity, and rising incomes. The fiscal reforms at all levels, and Canada's decade of supercharged economic performance that followed, are the vindication of the plan Laurier bequeathed to us.

As governments reduced and constrained spending in the 1990s, a greater share of the resources in the economy began being controlled by individuals, families, and businesses rather than governments. In other words, individual Canadians were increasingly making the decisions about how best to use and allocate resources instead of governments. It's not surprising that Canada began to prosper, since individuals with skin in the game—vested interest—are far more likely to make productive decisions than remote bureaucrats and politicians with little or no vested interest in the outcomes of such decisions.[3]

As deficits were eliminated and debt (relative to the size of the economy) declined, interest rates came down and private investment increased. Tax reductions that followed improved the incentives for work, savings, investment, and entrepreneurship. As a result, Canada exceeded the US and most other G7 countries on a host of economic indicators.

Indeed, Canada received international recognition from *The Economist* magazine in 2003 when the newspaper labelled Canada "rather cool" and characterized the country on its cover as a moose with sunglasses. *The Economist* noted that Canada had made a U-turn on fiscal policy and was witnessing the economic benefits:

> Deficits have been left far behind and the public debt slashed. Since the late 1990s, Canada's economy has outperformed the rest of the rich world. It no longer depends only on lumber, mining, oil and cars. Like any economy, Canada's is vulnerable to shocks . . . But Canada has begun to close the gap between its living standards and those in the United States.[4]

Economic Growth

Perhaps most indicative of Canada's economic success after the fiscal reforms of the 1990s is our stellar economic growth.[5] Many of the critics, relying on a Keynesian view of the world, predicted that Canada's effort to put its fiscal house in order would provoke a collapse of GDP growth and social unrest. The reality was exactly the opposite.[6]

From 1997 to 2007, Canada fared well on economic growth relative to other industrialized countries. Specifically, average economic growth among the thirty-member group of industrialized countries known as the Organisation for Economic Co-operation and Development (OECD) was 2.7 per cent, compared to 3.3 per cent in Canada.[7] While seemingly small, these differences have a material impact on the growth of economic activity when compounded over the course of several years—much like interest in a bank account.

Canada also truly stood out among the smaller subset of the G7 countries—France, Germany, Italy, Japan, the United Kingdom, and the United States, in addition to Canada—by achieving the highest average rate of economic growth.[8]

In terms of GDP per person, the most commonly used measure of average income, Canada again excelled. From 1997 to 2007, inflation-adjusted per person GDP grew 2.3 per cent in Canada, higher than any G7 country including the United States, which registered per person GDP growth of 2 per cent.

Jobs, Jobs, Jobs

Another important measure of economic performance is the ability to generate jobs. High job creation rates lead to increases in the demand for labour—workers—and ultimately drive up wages.

From 1997 to 2007, Canada outperformed most other OECD member countries in terms of average employment growth. Specifically, Canada ranked sixth out of thirty OECD countries, with an average total employment growth of 2.1 per cent, nearly doubling the OECD average of 1.1 per cent. Moreover, total employment growth between 1997 and 2007 exceeded employment growth in the United States, which was at 1 per cent, and that of every other G7 country.

Investment—Building for Future Prosperity

Between 1997 and 2007, Canada outperformed most OECD countries in attracting business investment. Business investment is critical for Canadian living standards, as increases in the amount of capital (i.e., machines, equipment, technology) each worker has at his or her disposal ultimately makes him or her more productive. When workers become more productive, they can produce more and/or higher-valued goods and services in a given amount of time. And workers who produce more for each hour they work are able to demand higher wages. Indeed, the key single factor explaining wage growth over time is productivity. Make people more productive, and they will earn more.

Canada experienced an average increase of 5.4 per cent in investment from 1997 to 2007 compared to an average of 3.2 per cent among the thirty members of the OECD. Moreover, Canada's growth in such investment was greater than in any other G7 country, including the United States, from 1997 to 2007.

All Boats Rose on the Reform Tide

Perhaps of most concern to critics of the changes in government policies during the Redemptive Decade was the potential implications for the less well off. Indeed, many critics predicted a dramatic increase in poverty and hardship for lower-income Canadians as a result of the spending cuts and fiscal reforms more generally. Fortunately, Canada's growing economy, in large part due to reforms at both the federal and provincial levels, benefited rather than hurt those with the lowest incomes.

In 1997, 15.3 per cent of all Canadians were considered "low-income."[9] Families are considered low-income if they devote a larger portion of their income to food, shelter, and clothing than does the average Canadian family.[10] By 2007, the proportion had decreased to 9.2 per cent, a reduction of nearly a third.[11]

Poverty rates, which are distinct from low-income measures,[12] also fell substantially between the mid-1990s and the mid-2000s. Specifically, 6.8 per cent of all Canadians were in poverty in the mid-1990s compared to 4.9 per cent in the mid-2000s.[13]

Restoring fiscal prudence in Canada through reduced spending, the elimination of deficits, and reductions in taxes not only reduced the debt burden Canadians were passing on to future generations, but also contributed greatly to Canada's economic performance. On a host of indicators, from economic performance, job creation, and business investment, Canada outperformed most industrialized counties from 1997 to 2007. Importantly, the robust economy Canada experienced also provided benefits to the less well off.

So now we know the destination we arrived at, the one Laurier had confidently predicted we would reach. Here is the story of how we got there, a story that has won Canada admiration and plaudits from around the world.

Spitting Distance from the Debt Wall

In the mid-1990s Canada was in a full-scale fiscal crisis. The federal government had run substantial budget deficits consistently for twenty years; Ottawa's indebtedness was reaching crisis levels; and a third of all federal government revenue was being used to simply pay interest on the debt. The status quo had become unsustainable. Without significant fiscal reform, Canada was at risk of hitting the "debt wall"—when investors stop financing government debt.[14]

Specifically, in 1993 the federal budget deficit was $38 billion.[15] This was the amount that the federal government had to borrow in 1993. Its budget that year provided for total spending of $167 billion. In other words, Ottawa had to borrow nearly 25 per cent of the money needed to pay for its spending.

This unprecedented and unsupportable level of borrowing was not isolated. Over the preceding ten years, the federal budget deficit had averaged nearly $30 billion a year. As a result, by 1993 the federal government's debt—the cumulative amount it had borrowed—had ballooned to $557 billion, nearly 80 per cent of the economy (GDP).[16] On a per person basis, each Canadian owed $19,440 in federal government debt alone in 1993.

As Canadians understand from their own household finances, one of the main problems with significant debt levels is that borrowed money isn't free. You must pay interest on your debts. In 1993, interest payments on the federal government's outstanding debt amounted to $39 billion. With a yearly deficit of $38 billion and interest payments of $39 billion, essentially all the money borrowed in 1993—and then some—was used to pay interest on past borrowings.

Also of concern was the fact that Canadians were left with little in terms of long-term benefits to offset these costs. Most of the spending that was financed by deficits was spent on services and transfers consumed in a single year rather than on long-lived assets such as roads and bridges.[17] We were borrowing too much, for the wrong reasons, and spending it on the wrong things.

The federal government was caught in an unsustainable cycle: higher interest costs were leading to higher deficits, which required more borrowing, which further increased interest costs as investors demanded higher returns to compensate them for the increased riskiness of lending to the Canadian government.

Indicative of the seriousness of the federal fiscal situation and the dramatic action needed was the influential warning from John Fund, a member of the *Wall Street Journal*'s editorial team, in an article published in the *Journal* on January 12, 1995. Mr. Fund wrote:

> Turn around and check out Canada, which has now become an honorary member of the Third World in the unmanageability of its debt problem. If dramatic action isn't taken in next month's federal budget, it's not inconceivable that Canada could hit the debt wall . . . it has lost its triple-A credit rating and can't assume that lenders will be willing to refinance its growing debt.[18]

The article set off a wave of concern around the world regarding Canada's debt problem. The federal government had produced a fiscal time bomb that threatened to wreak havoc on the Canadian economy and our standard of living. It had become clear that things needed to change.

A Fiscal Time Bomb in the Making

How did Canada's federal government find itself speeding toward an ever-nearing debt wall?

The central cause of the fiscal crisis was Ottawa's inability to control spending and its unwillingness to raise taxes commensurate with that spending. From 1965 to 1993, federal government spending per Canadian increased from $2,593, adjusted for inflation, to $6,810—an increase of 163 per cent.[19]

While spending per person provides an informative measure of the level of government spending, it does not take into account Canadians' ability to pay for government programs. The ability to pay for government programs is closely related to the level of economy activity in

Canada—gross domestic product (GDP), the total value of all goods and services produced. It is entirely possible for government spending per person to increase over time while spending as a share of the total economy either remains the same or even declines. It all depends on how fast the economy is growing relative to government spending. It is therefore important to examine the federal government's spending by comparing it to the size of overall economy (GDP). This measure indicates both the extent to which the government takes resources from the companies and workers that create wealth in the economy and to what extent it makes the decisions about how Canada's wealth will be spent and invested.

Government spending can be and most certainly is a positive force in the economy. Governments provide vital services that increase freedoms and lead to a well-functioning economy, with the provision of services like defence, an effective legal system, adequate infrastructure, and the protection of persons and property. As governments grows, however, they can increasingly become involved in areas that do not lead to improvements in—or, worse, have dragged down—economic performance. Examples of such programs include business subsidies and regional diversification programs. As these less helpful forms of spending take up more of a government's budget, the overall level of economic growth and living standards tend to suffer.[20]

In addition, increased spending, as a percentage of GDP, must ultimately be financed by higher taxes. Since taxes can affect, sometimes very significantly, the benefits of working, saving, investing, and entrepreneurship, they have a negative impact on the growth rate of the overall economy, especially once they exceed certain levels.[21]

From 1961 to 1993, Canada pursued an almost uninterrupted path toward larger government. Federal spending increased from a low of 14.8 per cent of the economy (GDP) in 1965 to 23 per cent by 1993.[22] While federal spending increased significantly, politicians failed to raise taxes to keep pace. As a result, a substantial gap opened between revenues and expenditures from the mid-1970s onwards. While spending increased significantly, revenues remained between 15 and 18 per cent of GDP in most years.

Deficits and Debt: Can't Have One without the Other

Increases in government spending that were not matched by increases in revenues (or the government's income) resulted in large federal deficits from 1975 onward. Specifically, federal deficits averaged 4.4 per cent of GDP from 1975 to 1993. In other words, the federal government was spending 4.4 per cent of the economy on benefits and programs each year but transferring the cost of these programs on to future generations. The interest payments on the debt, and ultimately the debt itself, would have to be paid back in the future through higher taxes, lower spending, or some combination of the two. Future generations of Canadians were increasingly being burdened by the government's fiscal actions.

The increases in the deficit had other harmful economic consequences. When governments borrow, they ultimately compete with other borrowers in the private market (i.e., individuals and businesses) for the pool of available savings. As governments compete with individuals and businesses for money—credit—a greater demand for credit is created, and in turn the cost of borrowing increases through higher interest rates. That is simple supply and demand at work. To finance their deficits, governments are forced to offer a more attractive return to investors, adjusting for risk, than is offered by private borrowers. This is not to say that governments actually pay higher rates than private sector borrowers but rather that they had to pay a higher rate than they would have if their finances had been more solid. In other words, governments have to pay higher interest rates to compensate investors for the perceived higher risks of Canadian government debt. Investors channel their savings into government bonds and end up "crowding out," or displacing, private borrowers. This has severe consequences for Canadians' productivity, wages, and living standards, as the amount of capital available in an economy is one of the main drivers of productivity.[23]

As a result of persistent annual deficits, the level of Canada's government debt increased significantly. In 1975 the value of gross federal debt was $213 billion, adjusted for inflation and presented in 2002 dollars, or $9,200 per Canadian.[24] Over the next twenty years, the federal debt increased threefold, to $651 billion in 1993, or $22,700 per person.

More critically, the federal debt as a percent of the economy (GDP) reached almost 80 per cent in 1993. To understand the seriousness of this level of debt, consider the analogy of an average Canadian family. This family would have taken out loans equivalent to 80 per cent of their annual income to cover their yearly spending. In other words, this borrowing was not done to purchase a home or car, assets that produce benefits to the family over time.

Big Debt Means Big Interest Payments

Paying down the debt was the last thing on the mind of Ottawa budget makers in the early 1990s. The problem of massive interest payments, on the other hand, occupied their every waking moment. Interest costs cannot be avoided, so, as they grow, governments find that these costs eat away at the money available for ordinary spending like programs and services, civil servants' salaries, pensions, EI benefits, and so forth. That is, the larger the interest costs, the less money available from current tax revenues for current spending on government programs and transfers.

As the federal debt increased, the interest costs associated with the debt became an ever-increasing burden on Canadian taxpayers. In 1974, one-tenth of federal government revenue was used to pay interest costs on the debt. By 1993, interest payments on the federal debt were consuming a third of every dollar in revenue collected by Ottawa. Think about our hypothetical family again. Close to one-third of their income would have been used simply to pay the interest on their accumulated debt. No family can survive, let alone prosper, with this type of financial burden.

As debt and interest costs increased significantly, Canadians were increasingly wondering what benefits they were getting to offset these costs. What annual borrowing wasn't being used to pay for interest payments on previous borrowing—debt—was being spent on many federal programs and transfers that provided little in terms of longer-term benefits. For instance, in the ten years preceding 1993, the federal government's investment in new capital (i.e., infrastructure) and the maintenance of existing assets averaged only 2.5 per cent of total spending.[25] In other words, federal spending was primarily dedicated to programs, services, and income transfers that were enjoyed exclusively in a particular year and did not provide benefits over time. If the majority or even a meaningful amount of the spending were dedicated to long-term assets—projects that are enjoyed over time and thus deliver benefits over time—such as bridges, highways, and other infrastructure, then the cost of interest would have been at least partially offset by these benefits.

Higher interest costs also increase the risk associated with the underlying debt. When governments are faced with higher interest costs, government bonds become riskier in the eyes of lenders, who have to worry about the possibility of default or of governments using inflation to reduce the real value of the debt. Investors then require higher interest rates to compensate for the higher risk. This can become a destructive cycle in which higher interest rates lead to higher interest costs, higher deficits, and more borrowing, which further increase interest cost, risk, and interest rates—a cycle that becomes almost inescapable.

Canada experienced this destructive cycle as its debt and interest costs increased. As both the federal debt and interest costs increased, Canadian government debt became much riskier to hold. Lenders required higher interest rates to compensate them for this additional risk.[26]

Federal fiscal policies from the mid-1960s to the mid-1990s left Canadians in a serious situation. Not only did the federal government become much larger, it was also leaving a fiscal time bomb of increased debt and rising interest costs to future generations of Canadians. Among the worrying trends were the increase in federal spending from 15 per cent of the economy (GDP) in 1965 to 23 per cent in 1993; the shift to consistently large deficits from 1975 to 1993; the increase in federal debt from 35 per cent of GDP in 1976 to nearly 80 per cent in 1993; and interest payments that ended up consuming over 30 cents out of every dollar in revenue collected by the federal government.[27] The federal government's fiscal policy was simply unsustainable.

The 1995 Budget—Ottawa Changes Course

In October 1993 the Liberal Party of Canada, led by Jean Chrétien, won a convincing victory in the federal election.[28] The new government inherited a dismal fiscal situation with a deficit of 5.3 per cent of GDP in 1993. Federal debt had ballooned to nearly 80 per cent of GDP, and interest costs consumed 31 per cent of federal revenues.

While the Liberals pledged to address the deficit in their campaign by promising to reduce it to 3 per cent of GDP by 1996–97, their first budget was timid and largely accepting of the status quo.[29] Indeed, the 1994 budget proposed an increase in program spending, an increase in government revenues, and a rather small decrease in the deficit.[30] To shift spending to where it would do the most good and reduce waste, the 1994 budget did include a pledge to "review" every government agency and program over the course of 1994 with an eye toward ensuring appropriate "size, scope, composition, and cost."[31]

The Liberals' first year in office, 1994, proved to be a difficult one for the government's fiscal plan. Throughout the year, interest rates increased, in part as a response to the lacklustre 1994 federal budget.[32] With the federal debt at $596 billion and interest costs already consuming 30 per cent of revenue, the increase in interest rates threatened to significantly increase interest payments on the federal debt and therefore increase the federal deficit.[33]

Pressure mounted on the Liberals throughout 1994 to enact more aggressive fiscal reforms. For instance, the media turned against the rather timid 1994 budget almost immediately.[34] The media reaction was also representative of a broader shift in public opinion. By 1994 several provinces, including Alberta and Saskatchewan, had already enacted fiscal reforms and were moving toward balanced budgets. These provinces provided real-life Canadian examples of fiscal reform initiatives.

The composition of Parliament after the 1993 election also increasingly put pressure on the governing Liberal Party. The collapse of the Progressive Conservative Party in the election removed most members of Parliament tied to previous fiscal policies. The primary beneficiary of the PC's collapse in English-speaking Canada was the Western-based Reform Party.[35] The Reform Party spoke out strongly for an end to fiscal deficits through spending reductions. Even though the other beneficiary of the Tories' collapse, the Bloc Québécois, was the nominal official opposition, the Reform Party provided intellectual leadership for the rest of the country. For the first time in many years, the government in Ottawa faced sharp criticism from fiscal conservatives on the opposition benches.

The collapse of the Mexican peso in December 1994 illustrated the problem of massive government debt. Shortly after the collapse, the *Wall Street Journal* highlighted Canada's debt problem and suggested the country was nearing bankruptcy.[36] The *Journal* article itself caused a sharp devaluation of the Canadian dollar and an increase in interest rates. Indeed, then associate deputy minister of finance and later governor of the Bank of Canada David Dodge called the *Journal* article a "seminal event."[37] Finally, international organizations such as the International Monetary Fund and the Organisation for Economic Co-operation and Development were calling for faster reductions in Canada's deficit.[38]

The Liberals delivered their much-anticipated second budget on February 27, 1995. This document set in motion a fundamental change to the status quo and ultimately became a defining moment in Canada's fiscal history. In his budget speech, finance minister Martin boldly stated the new direction for the government and the government's almost sole focus: getting the debt and deficit under control. In outlining the government's fundamental challenge, Martin noted that:

> The debt and deficit are not inventions of ideology. They are facts of arithmetic. The quicksand of compound interest is *real.* The last thing Canadians *need* is another lecture on the dangers of the deficit. The *only* thing Canadians *want* is clear action.[39]

More broadly, Martin articulated a new direction for the federal government: "We are acting on a new vision of the role of government . . . smaller government . . . smarter government."[40] In other words, seen in the context of the first two chapters of this book, finance minister Paul Martin did not announce a radical new departure for Canadian finances or for the Liberal Party of Canada. Rather, the tone and much of the specifics of the budget speech heralded a return to the fiscal principles espoused and advocated by Sir Wilfrid Laurier, Louis St. Laurent, and others, although this connection was never made by the Liberal Party or the media.

The budget plan included a host of concrete actions:

- A substantial reduction in the size of the federal government—spending and employees—to reduce the deficit
- Reform of government programs with an increased focus on efficiency
- Reform and a reduction of the employment insurance (EI) program[41]
- Substantial reductions in business subsidies
- Restructured and reduced provincial transfers

Ottawa Gets Serious about Controlling Spending

Perhaps the most significant change in the 1995 federal budget was the substantial decrease in government spending. Specifically, the federal government proposed a $4.3-billion decrease in program spending in 1995–96 and a $6.1-billion dollar reduction in 1996–97.[42] Over those two years, the federal government aimed to reduce program spending by $10.4 billion, or 8.8 per cent. These cuts were pivotal; up to that point every government that had tried to deal with the deficit had simply tried to slow the growth in spending. No government had actually proposed, let alone enacted, spending cuts.

More importantly, the size of the federal government as a share of the economy (GDP) was projected to decrease from 16.2 per cent in 1994–95 to 13.1 per cent in 1996–97. With revenues relatively stable, the proposed spending cuts would offset the expected increases in interest payments on the debt and still achieve the government's pledge of a deficit of no more than 3 per cent of GDP by 1996–97.

As part of the cuts, the budget significantly reduced the size of the public service, i.e., governmental employment. All told, the budget proposed eliminating 45,000 employees—a 14 per cent decline in federal government employment once fully implemented.[43]

Getting Government Right—Program Review

The proposed reductions in program spending in the 1995 budget were largely the result of the program review—a comprehensive examination of federal departmental spending announced in the previous budget and carried out throughout 1994.[44] Ministers in every government department put their departments under the microscope. In particular they applied six tests to everything their departments did:

1. Serving the public interest
2. Necessity of government involvement
3. Appropriate federal role
4. Scope for public sector/private sector partnerships
5. Scope for increased efficiency
6. Affordability

The program review led to a significant structural change in the federal government's involvement in the Canadian economy. Major reforms included:

- Dramatic changes in the federal government's involvement in large parts of Canada's transportation system[45]
- A complete change to the federal government's approach to agricul-

ture, including a move away from an emphasis on income support to income stabilization[46]

- A massive reduction in the federal government's involvement in the business sector, including a proposed 60 per cent cut in subsidies to businesses[47]
- A change in the way in which departments delivered services to Canadians, including an increased focus on efficiency[48]

All told, the federal government proposed $9.8 billion, or 18.9 per cent, in reductions in departmental spending from 1994–95 to 1997–98. All areas of direct federal spending save two—justice and legal programs, and social programs—were reduced by over 10 per cent.[49] The largest planned reductions were in transportation, where spending was to decline by over 50 per cent, and industrial, regional and scientific support programs, which were set to decline by nearly 40 per cent.

Restructured and Reduced Provincial Transfers

A major piece of federal spending was money given to the provinces in support of provincial programs. The 1995 budget also proposed a wide-ranging reworking and reduction in these transfers. Specifically, the budget proposed a move away from federal transfers based on federal–provincial cost-sharing programs to a block-grant approach in which the amount transferred by the federal government to the provinces did not depend on provincial spending.

Prior to the 1995 budget, the federal government provided two major transfers to the provinces for certain programs: established program financing (EPF) and the Canada Assistance Plan (CAP).[50] The EPF was a "block" transfer for health and post-secondary education, and the amount transferred did not depend on how much the province actually spent on the related programs.[51] The Canada Assistance Plan (CAP) was a cost-sharing program in which the federal government paid up to half of the amount that provincial governments spent on social services and social assistance.[52]

One of the major problems with the cost-sharing approach to social services was that the provinces could finance an extra dollar of spending on social programs with just 50 cents of their own money. The federal government provided the rest. This arrangement meant that the federal government did not control this portion of their own spending. The provinces decided on the amount of social services and social assistance spending, and simply sent the federal government a bill for half the cost.

What the federal government *did* do was to exercise some control over certain standards for social services by attaching conditions to their transfers to the provinces. But these federal conditions ended up preventing provinces from experimenting with better ways of providing for social welfare.[53]

The 1995 budget proposed the replacement of the Canada Assistance Plan and established program financing with the Canada Social Transfer,[54] a new block transfer, starting in 1996–97. As a result, the damaging impacts of cost-sharing under the Canada Assistance Plan would be eliminated. The move to a large block grant represented a significant step forward in allowing for flexibility and greater provincial control of social service provision.[55]

Much to the dismay of the provinces, the 1995 budget also included a major reduction in the total amount transferred to the provinces over the following two years. The EPF and CAP cash transfers combined were to fall from $17.3 billion in 1994–95—the current fiscal year—to $16.4 billion in 1995–96. In 1996–97, when the Canada Social Transfer would replace the EPF and CAP transfers, the total amount was set to fall to $12.9 billion. Over the course of the two-year budget plan, transfers to the provinces overall were set to decline from $25.8 billion in 1994–95 to $22.2 billion in 1996–97, a decline of 14 per cent. In percentage terms, the cut to provincial transfers was significantly deeper than reductions in the federal government's own programs.

What About Taxes?

Finance minister Paul Martin claimed in his 1995 budget speech that the government "must focus on cutting spending—not raising taxes."[56] It didn't quite turn out that way. The budget did raise some economically damaging taxes. For example, taxes on investment increased, which made investing in capital equipment more expensive for Canadian businesses.[57]

Despite the tax increases, the budget framework presented by the Liberals was truly an historic event. The tax increases contained in the 1995 budget amounted to an additional $940 million in tax revenue in 1995–96 and $1.28 billion in 1996–97. However, compared to the proposed spending cuts, the revenue measures were quite small. Specifically, for both 1995–96 and 1996–97, spending reductions were more than four and a half times larger than revenue increases.[58]

After the Reforms: Let the Good Times Roll

The importance of the 1995 fiscal reforms can scarcely be exaggerated. The size of the federal government shrank significantly and balanced its budget within three years. Canada's federal government transformed itself from a fiscal basket case to the envy of the industrialized world.

While the 1995 federal budget proposed significant cuts to program spending over the following two years—$10.4 billion, or 8.8 per cent—the actual reductions in spending ended up being even larger.[59] Specifically, federal program spending (total spending minus interest payments) fell from $123.2 billion to $111.3 billion, a cut of nearly 10 per cent in two years. As a share of the economy, program spending decreased from 16 per cent of GDP to 13.3 per cent of GDP over those same two years.

All told, federal government spending (program spending plus interest payments) as a percentage of GDP fell from 21.7 per cent in 1994–95 to 17.9 per cent in 1997–98. While federal spending decreased, revenues grew. Specifically, revenues increased from 17 per cent of GDP in 1994–95 to 18.2 per cent in 1997–98 as a result of both tax increases and economic growth.[60]

Indeed, 1997–98 marked the first time in nearly twenty-five years that Ottawa had had a balanced budget. In fact, it was better than balanced. The significant cuts in federal government spending and the growth in revenues resulted in a budget surplus that year of $2.95 billion. The federal budget had gone from a substantial deficit, $36.6 billion, or 4.8 per cent of GDP, in 1994–95 to a $3-billion surplus in just three years.

After the government balanced its budget in 1997–98, it ran eleven consecutive budget surpluses, at times reaching nearly 2 per cent of GDP, which reduced the federal government's debt. With the federal government paying down debt and the economy expanding, the total public debt plummeted from 80.5 per cent of GDP in 1997–98 to 45 per cent a decade later.

With a declining debt, the gap between the money collected by the government—taxes—and the money actually spent on programs and transfers shrank. Lower interest costs meant that more money was available for government programs and transfers.

By 2008–09, the interest costs on the federal debt fell to under 13 per cent of federal spending, down from 30 per cent in 1996–97. Put differently, the federal government went from spending 30 cents of every dollar on interest payments on the federal debt to spending 13 cents by 2008–09.

As a result of dramatically lower interest payments, the federal government was able to reduce its overall spending as a percentage of GDP yet increase its program spending as a percentage of GDP at the same time. The promise of fiscal discipline was realized: more tax dollars were being spent on programs and transfers instead of being used to pay interest on the debt.

Taxing Right, Taxing Light

One of the keys to Canada's economic success in recent years is that many governments used the benefits of balanced budgets, lower interest costs, lower spending, consistent surpluses, and the resultant improvement in economic performance to make pro-growth tax cuts.[61] Tax relief was thus an indispensable supplement to the fiscal discipline of the second half of the Redemptive Decade. Working, saving, investing, and being entrepreneurial (i.e., taking risks) had all been discouraged by the rising taxes of the previous decades, helping to explain our mediocre growth. Cutting taxes correspondingly spurred Canada's economic performance. Indeed, a more competitive and less economically damaging tax system, made possible by spending control and debt reduction, contributed to Canada's leading the G7 countries in growth for a decade until 2007.[62]

Understanding these connections is critical; much of the backsliding in government finances that has occurred post-2000–01 is a result of government using the spoils of a robust economy simply to spend more rather than continue to focus on balancing their budgets, controlling spending growth, and promoting economic competitiveness and productivity.

Not All Tax Cuts Are Created Equal

Taxes make some good things possible. We cannot, however, ignore the fact that the process of raising those taxes causes economic damage. In this context, we must not lose sight of the fact that not all tax cuts affect the economy in the same manner. While all current forms of taxation are economically damaging—that is, they discourage desirable economic behaviour, be it consumption, investment, savings, or hard work—some taxes are certainly more damaging than others.[63]

Taxes change the reward, or benefits, people receive from undertaking certain activities. If we make certain activities, such as investing, more expensive by imposing taxes, we simultaneously make alternatives to investing less expensive. By intervening in this manner, governments cause less investment and more of the alternative, consumption, solely because of the way their taxes affect our behaviour. Our decisions, which are influenced by taxes, have an impact on the economy by increasing or decreasing the amount and intensity of activities like hard work, savings, investment, and entrepreneurship.

Taxes on capital (corporate income taxes, capital gains taxes, and corporate capital taxes) and on personal income impose much higher costs on the economy than some other taxes, such as consumption (sales) taxes.[64] The reason is that taxes on capital make it less attractive for businesses to invest in buildings, plants, factories, equipment, and other tools that make our economy productive. Similarly, personal income taxes, especially high and increasing tax rates, reduce the returns to and therefore incentive for individuals to increase their work effort, save, invest, and take business risks. Efforts at both the federal and provincial levels have reduced these damaging taxes—for now.

Federal Tax Relief

As we've seen, when Paul Martin first tackled Ottawa's deteriorating fiscal position in 1994 and 1995, reducing taxes was not in the cards. He needed every penny of revenue he could get his hands on, and indeed his early budgets contained tax increases, albeit small ones relative to spending reductions. In particular, capital gains taxes,[65] the corporate capital tax, and the corporate surtax, all quite damaging types of taxes, were increased.[66]

It was not until the federal government balanced its budget in 1997–98 that it began to turn its attention to cutting taxes. Nearly every budget from 1997 to 2009 contained important tax reductions.[67] In particular:

- The general corporate income tax was reduced from 28 per cent in 1997 to 19 per cent in 2009. It is set to further decline to 15 per cent by 2012.[68]
- The federal general corporate capital tax, yet another tax on capital, was completely eliminated in 2006.[69]
- Personal income tax rates were reduced significantly and the thresholds were indexed to inflation.[70]
- Capital gains taxes were lowered.[71]
- Tax-free savings accounts, with a contribution limit of $5,000 per year, were introduced to improve the incentive to save.[72]

Most of the reductions were squarely focused on decreasing capital-based taxes and personal income taxes, which improved the incentives for productive economic behaviour like hard work, savings, investment, and entrepreneurship. Reductions in economically damaging taxes contributed to Canada's economic success from 1997 to 2007.

The Lack of a Fiscal Anchor

There was, however, a worm gnawing away at the heart of the apple of Ottawa's fiscal success. While the government racked up ten years of budget surpluses and the country's finances grew rosier while the tax burden declined, the federal government quickly lost its way. For three years the federal government focused on eliminating the deficit, almost to the exclusion of everything else. What was little understood at the time was the extent to which the government and the voters were motivated by that simple but compelling goal: to balance the books. Once that feat was accomplished, the government lacked another clear goal, or fiscal anchor, for its policy, such as reducing the debt by a specific amount.

In fact, the absolute decline in the level of federal debt was relatively small from 2000–01 to 2007–08: $21.3 billion. By comparison, the cumulative budgeted surplus between these years exceeded $81.7 billion dollars. Put differently, the majority of surpluses after 2000–01 were spent rather than used to pay down debt, although some of that money was devoted to tax cuts.

In addition, program spending began increasing faster than the economy after 2000–01. Specifically, since 2000–01, program spending increased by an average of 6.7 per cent per year compared to the average rate of economic growth of 5.6 per cent. This means that government began again to control and decide on the uses to which an increasing portion of society's resources would be put. Increases in program spending also made it harder for Ottawa to cut taxes as much as it might have, although some taxes were cut.

2008 and Beyond: Falling off the Wagon?

Governments, both Liberal and Conservative, spent liberally once the country's dodgy finances had been put on a sounder footing. When times were good, they spent as if the country was in need of a jolt of government spending, when the truth was that the economy was enjoying a period of strong expansion. But what goes up must come down, and the long period of growth fell to earth with a bump in 2008.

In response to the collapse of financial markets and the ensuing recession, governments around the world increased spending in attempts to "stimulate" the economy. Canada was no different.

Initially, however, the Conservative government attempted to hold the line on balanced budgets by cutting spending. In its *Fall Economic and Fiscal Statement*, delivered in November 2008, the government emphasized the need to "protect our hard-won fiscal advantage."[73] The government also indicated that any further recession-driven deterioration in the government's finances would be temporary.

Circumstances changed significantly between November 2008 and early 2009. Specifically, the Liberal Party and New Democratic Party agreed to form a minority coalition government, with the Bloc Québécois agreeing to provide support though not formally to join the coalition. These parties threatened to bring down the government, in part because the *Fall Economic and Fiscal Statement* lacked "stimulus" spending.[74]

Largely in response to the threat of defeat at the hands of the "coalition," the 2009 federal budget significantly increased the size of the federal government and returned to deficit financing.

The 2009 budget proposed to increase program spending by a whopping $29.7 billion over two years. As a result, program spending as a percentage of GDP is to increase from 12.9 per cent in 2008–09 to 14.5 per cent by 2010–11. The budget also forecast deficits of $33.7 billion in 2009–10 and $29.8 billion in 2011–12. These measures would largely return Ottawa's spending to where it was before the reforms of the late 1990s.

The federal government has stated its intention that the stimulus package would be temporary: "Canadians regret the need to run a deficit in order to invest in our economy. Our government shares that regret . . . it will be temporary."[75]

But as successive federal governments found in the years prior to Paul Martin's fiscal reforms, it is easier to promise fiscal discipline and spending reductions than it is to deliver them. While much of the spending contained in the government stimulus package are one-time expenditures focused on new infrastructure and bailouts for specific industries,[76] other initiatives (e.g., increased spending on culture and arts, tourism, agriculture, funding for the new southern Ontario development agency, and increases in employment insurance benefits) will be much more difficult to scale back.

It isn't only on fiscal discipline that Ottawa has started to lose focus. It is also starting to lose sight of the justification for fixing the tax burden, ensuring that when Canadians pay taxes, they do so in a way that is the least damaging possible to work, growth, investment, and risk-taking in the economy. Tax reductions, and especially the right kind of tax reductions, have been a highly successful part of the pro-growth strategy of the past decade.

A major departure from this successful recipe of reducing economically harmful taxes in order to promote economic growth occurred under the leadership of the Conservative Party. In the 2006 election, the Conservatives ran on and won a mandate to reduce the GST, perhaps one of Canada's least costly and most efficient taxes but nonetheless one of its most vilified.[77] Between 2006 and 2007, the GST was reduced from 7 to 5 per cent. The reduction resulted in $12 billion less in tax revenues for the federal government and little improvement in economic incentives. Put differently, had those revenues been used to reduce taxes that damage economic incentives, such as corporate or personal income taxes, we would have expected to see greater work effort, more savings and investment, more entrepreneurship, and a generally stronger economy.

Whether or not, and how quickly, the federal government will return to the successful policies of the 1990s remains unclear. Despite the strong statement from the finance minister, estimated deficits for 2009–10 and beyond have increased significantly. Specifically, the government is now expecting a deficit of $55.9 billion in 2009–10, amounting to 3.7 per cent of GDP.[78] The government is planning to have deficits for at least the next six years. The GST rate reduction, plus a jungle of "boutique tax credits," for things like transit passes and schools sports activities, are all symptomatic of Ottawa forgetting the rationale for reducing taxes and reducing them the right way. There is substantial risk that current federal policy will undo the fiscal reforms of the Redemptive Decade. Indeed, a great deal of the progress has already been undone.

FISCAL REFORM: UNSUNG PROVINCIAL HEROES chapter four

Over the course of three decades, the mid-1960s to the mid-1990s, the federal government created a serious debt problem that left Canada heading toward bankruptcy. The direction of the provinces differed little from that of Ottawa. Provincial governments increased in size, ran budget deficits, and built up substantial deficits. Fortunately, like the federal government, a marked change in provincial policy occurred in the second half of our Redemptive Decade.

The change in provincial fiscal policy was led by three high-profile transformations that occurred in Saskatchewan under NDP premier Roy Romanow in 1991, Alberta under Progressive Conservative premier Ralph Klein in 1992, and Ontario under Progressive Conservative premier Mike Harris in 1995. In all three cases, the provincial governments pursued a policy of spending reductions and a shift from deficits to surpluses. Reforms in Saskatchewan and Alberta were particularly influential, as they set the stage for other provinces (i.e., Ontario) and the federal government to follow.

Nearing the Wall: Provinces Exacerbate the Problem

As was the case with the federal government, the central cause of the Canadian provincial governments' fiscal crisis was their collective inability to control spending.[1] From 1961 to 1993, provincial government spending increased nearly sixfold, from $1,300 per Canadian in 1961 to $7,400 in 1993.[2]

Provincial government spending as a share of the economy (GDP) also increased substantially in these decades.[3] In 1961 all provincial government spending combined represented less than 10 per cent of the

Canadian economy. Over the next thirty years, provincial spending increased steadily and dramatically, reaching 25 per cent of GDP by 1993.

Provinces Sink Into Debt

Equally worrying was the growing gap between provincial revenue and spending. From 1961 to 1980, provincial governments generally collected more in revenue than they spent. In 1980 this ceased to be the case and for nearly twenty years the provinces consistently spent more than they collected in revenue. Deepening debt was the only course open to them.

From 1961 to 1979, the budgets of all the provinces taken together were balanced or in surplus. After a recession-induced deficit in 1980, the provinces never returned to a balanced or surplus position in the following thirteen years. From 1980 to 1993, provincial governments collectively ran persistent deficits.[4] To make up the shortfall between revenue and expenditures, the provincial governments were forced to borrow heavily, and the provinces were thus big contributors to Canada's overall fiscal problem.[5] In 1970 gross provincial debt was approximately $3,175 per Canadian, adjusted for inflation and presented in 2002 dollars.[6] Over the next twenty-three years, provincial debt increased to $12,745 per Canadian in 2002 dollars. Put differently, by 1993 every Canadian owed roughly $12,745 in provincial debt in additional to $22,711 in federal government debt.

More telling is the size of the burden of debt compared to the overall economy. From 1970 to 1993, provincial government debt as a share of GDP more than doubled, from 15.2 per cent of GDP in 1970 to 43 per cent in 1993.[7]

Just as with Ottawa, as the provincial debt increased, the interest costs associated with the debt became an ever-increasing burden on the taxpayer.[8] By 1993, interest payments on provincial debt were consuming nearly 15 cents out of every dollar in revenue collected by the provincial governments, a percentage that had nearly tripled over the preceding two decades.

The provincial governments' deteriorating fiscal situation largely mirrored that of the federal government. Provincial governments expanded in size, ran nearly twenty consecutive years of budget deficits, and significantly increased their debt. The result was an unsustainable fiscal situation in which interest costs on the debt began consuming an ever-increasing portion of provincial government revenues.

Saskatchewan, Alberta, and Ontario Step Up

Just as spendthrift provincial policies exacerbated Ottawa's fiscal crisis, so the reversal in the country's fiscal fortunes in the late 1990s was hastened along by a few provinces that repented of their irresponsible behaviour. In particular, Saskatchewan, Alberta, and Ontario enacted substantial fiscal austerity programs and indeed provided an example for other Canadian governments. Few Canadians seem aware that Saskatchewan's and Alberta's reforms actually preceded those of Ottawa and helped change the climate of public opinion about spending reductions to balance government budgets.[9] Their stories also deserve to be told.

Saskatchewan: The NDP Leads the Way in Fiscal Reform

The fiscal reforms in Saskatchewan, while less significant than those implemented in Alberta and Ontario, were critical and essential for two reasons. First, Saskatchewan was the first Canadian government to seriously and genuinely tackle its deficit problem. Indeed, it was the first government actually to reduce nominal spending in an attempt to balance its books. Second, the fact that these fiscal reforms were enacted by a government led by the NDP, which historically had championed expansive government spending, was critical in establishing the non-partisan, non-ideological importance of balanced budgets. Indeed, the changes enacted by Saskatchewan's NDP government provided the ultimate stamp of credibility for federal finance minister Paul Martin a few years later when he sought public support for wrestling with the deficit: "Debt and deficits are not inventions of ideology. They are facts of arithmetic."[10]

During the decade that ended in 1992, Saskatchewan's fiscal situation deteriorated significantly. During this period, the government, led by Progressive Conservative premier Grant Devine, ran a budget deficit every single year without pause.[11] And not only did the government run deficits consistently over that decade, but the annual deficits averaged over 3 per cent of provincial GDP.

As a result, over that same decade, the province went from a reasonably strong financial position in which its financial assets were greater than its total liabilities to having net debt of 28 per cent of GDP. In other words, the citizens of Saskatchewan, through their provincial government, owed the equivalent of 28 per cent of the provincial economy in government debt. Interest payments on the growing debt also became a serious problem, consuming an ever-growing portion of government revenues. Specifically, interest costs increased from an almost negligible 1.6 per cent of revenues in 1982–83 to 12.4 per cent in 1991–92.

Dissatisfaction with the fiscal management of the Progressive Conservative government helped bring it down in the 1991 provincial election. New premier Roy Romanow's NDP government was committed to "restoring sound financial management" by "eliminating the budget deficit and returning to balanced budgets."[12] In this, the Saskatchewan NDP returned to a long tradition of fiscal discipline stretching right back to the province's first CCF/NDP premier, T.C. Douglas.

In May 1992 the Romanow government presented its first budget, which genuinely attempted to deal with the province's $843-million deficit, which amounted to over 4 per cent of the provincial economy (GDP). The situation faced by the province and the tough decisions that needed to be made were highlighted in finance minister Ed Tchorzewski's budget address:

> Today our Province stands at a critical crossroads. We must choose a path for the future . . . we must start to live within our means because it is the only way to rebuild Saskatchewan.[13]

The Romanow government's strategy for reducing the deficit centred on reviewing all government programs and services with an emphasis on starting "first with spending cuts." Minister Tchorzewski's candid comments in delivering the budget highlighted the dramatic change in direction: "We can no longer pay for all the services government provides. Programs that we simply cannot afford will be eliminated."[14]

And eliminate programs and public sector positions they did. The 1992 budget ultimately eliminated more than twenty programs, including the mortgage protection plan, the Saskatchewan pension plan, and the feed grain adjustment program. More than 500 government positions were eliminated. Overall, the measures resulted in a $73.1-million, or 1.8 per cent, reduction in program spending for the coming fiscal year. This was a rather stark departure from the average program spending increases of 5.6 per cent witnessed over the preceding four years.

The 1992 budget also proposed to reduce the budget deficit by nearly 40 per cent, from a forecast $845 million in 1991–92 to $517 million in 1992–93. To achieve that target, the government also raised taxes in addition to cutting spending. For example, personal income taxes increased by $60 million. Taxes on investment also increased, which made investing in capital equipment more expensive for businesses in Saskatchewan.[15] Several other taxes, including liquor, sales, gas, and tobacco taxes, were also increased. All told, the tax increases were estimated to bring in an additional $303 million to the government. Most of the $328-million decrease in the deficit in the first year was the result of tax increases rather than spending reductions.

The 1993 Saskatchewan Budget—Securing Our Future

By the time the next provincial budget was delivered, Saskatchewan was still saddled with a significant deficit. Clearly, more action was required. The 1993 Saskatchewan budget pledged to balance the books by 1996–97.[16] To back up that goal, the province laid out a detailed "Balanced Budget Plan" that relied on both spending reductions and revenue increases.

In terms of spending, the 1993 budget proposed a $141-million, or 3.3 per cent, cut in program spending for the coming year. The budget proposed zero growth in program spending for the year after that, and small increases in the two subsequent years.[17] Savings were expected in government administration such as office, communications, and staff development costs. In addition, the budget proposed the elimination of one-quarter of all government agencies, boards, and commissions. Finally, significant cuts were made to funding levels for hospitals, school boards, universities and colleges, and municipalities.[18]

The government proposed to slash the deficit in half over the course of the coming year, 1993–94, to $296 million from a forecasted $592 million in 1992–93. The $141 million in spending cuts in 1993–94, however, were not near enough to achieve the goal of halving the deficit. As was the case in the previous year's deficit reduction, the government relied heavily on tax increases. The province increased a number of taxes, including investment taxes, sales taxes, and fuel taxes.[19] All told, the tax increases were estimated to bring in an additional $176.1 million to the government in 1993–94. Going forward, the government was projecting that further tax increases would be unnecessary to achieve a small surplus of $20 million by 1996–97.

Saskatchewan Reaps the Benefits of Reform

While the Saskatchewan government laid out a plan to balance the budget within five years, it actually achieved its goal two years early. In just three years, the NDP government went from an $845-million budget deficit to a $128-million budget surplus. The NDP government had broken with its traditional predilection to champion increases in the size of government, instead reducing program spending by over $300 million, or 7.1 per cent, in its first two years in office.

What ultimately differentiates the reforms in Saskatchewan from the more aggressive reforms in Alberta and Ontario discussed below is that Saskatchewan relied on large tax increases and moderate spending reductions to achieve a balanced budget. Both the 1992 and 1993 budgets increased taxes of all kinds from personal income, corporate, tobacco, fuel, liquor, and sales taxes.[20] None the less, while the reforms in Saskatchewan were not as aggressive in terms of spending reductions as those pursued in Alberta, the transformation from a significant deficit to a budget surplus in just three years indicates that the willingness to deal with fiscal issues transcended partisan and ideological politics.

Alberta: Creating the Alberta Advantage

Like Saskatchewan's, Alberta's fiscal situation was spiralling out of control in the early 1990s. The collapse in oil prices in 1986 hit Alberta's economy and provincial finances particularly hard. Government revenues from resources, chiefly oil and gas, fell by over 60 per cent that year, while total revenue dropped by nearly 30 per cent and the deficit increased to over $4 billion, or 7 per cent of GDP.[21] Newly elected premier Don Getty famously noted that his government had "inherited an economy and budget based on $40 oil and the price of oil was $13."[22]

Unfortunately, Premier Getty's government assumed that oil prices and the economy would rebound quickly and budgeted accordingly.[23] Oil prices, however, remained low, government revenues stagnated, and the government largely continued to spend as if high oil prices would soon return. The result was a long, nine-year stretch of substantial budget deficits.[24]

The fiscal plan of Premier Getty's government was built on illusion and false hopes; the debt burden it left behind was horrendous. By 1992–93, the province's annual deficit was $3.3 billion, almost 4.5 per cent of GDP.

Alberta's provincial debt had increased to $20 billion, or nearly 30 per cent of GDP, a fourfold rise in roughly a dozen years. Government debt had reached over $8,000 per Albertan. As a result, interest costs had steadily increased from a negligible 1 per cent of government revenues in 1985–86 to a significant burden of 10 per cent of revenue by 1992–93.

Alberta was caught in a fiscal spiral of persistent and substantial annual deficits, ever-increasing government debt, and a growing interest burden. With evidence increasingly pointing to the fact that oil prices had adjusted downward for the longer term, it became evident that a new fiscal plan was needed.[25]

As a result of the increasing unhappiness with his performance, Alberta premier Don Getty stepped down as leader of the Progressive Conservatives in December 1992. The ensuing party leadership race was won by Ralph Klein. In the race for the party leadership, Klein campaigned on the need to restore fiscal responsibility, including decreasing the size of government, balancing the provincial budget, and paying down the provincial debt.

The first two budgets of Ralph Klein's tenure as premier of Alberta fundamentally changed the status quo in Alberta, and indeed Canada. The fiscal austerity programs delivered in 1993 and 1994 budgets were bold, innovative, and aggressive. The government of Alberta was determined to end the downward fiscal spiral that threatened Alberta's future.

The 1993 Alberta Budget—A Plan for Change

Premier Klein's first budget was delivered in May 1993 and became the platform upon which he would run and win the June 1994 election. Premier Klein clearly stated his intended direction in his 1993 *Message from the Premier*:

> Reducing government spending . . . changing the way we do business . . . getting out of the way of business and other organizations so they can get the job done . . . balancing the budget. Those are the key elements of the new course for Alberta.[26]

The 1993 Alberta budget presented the new course by significantly reducing program spending, decreasing government employment, and proposing a plan to balance the budget within four years.

Specifically, the budget introduced the Deficit Elimination Act, legislation that forced the government to balance the budget within four short years. The act included scheduled reductions in the deficit and required that any slippage from the targets be made up with tougher spending cuts the following year. To meet the four-year pledge, the budget also called for a reduction of 20 per cent in program spending.

In the first year of the fiscal reform package, the budget proposed a $700-million, 5.5 per cent cut in program spending and a 17 per cent reduction in the budget deficit. Government program spending would fall substantially: from 17 to 15 per cent of GDP in one year. Furthermore, the budget proposed to reduce government employment by 2,575 jobs, a reduction of 7.6 per cent.[27]

The spending reductions and layoffs were government-wide and touched nearly every government department. As was noted in the budget, "All areas of government are on the table . . . A balanced budget cannot be achieved unless savings are found in all program areas."[28] Of the seventeen departments, fourteen had their budget cut—some by over a quarter.

At the same time, Alberta enacted broad reform of its welfare system. The changes were focused on preventing people from entering welfare before other possible avenues of support, including employment, were exhausted. Other changes were put in place to reduce fraud.[29] In part as a result of the reforms, 172,000 people left the province's welfare rolls between 1993 and 1996, while social assistance spending fell by $250 million, or 20 per cent, over that period.[30]

The actions presented in the 1993 budget were bold and represented a dramatic departure from the status quo; even so, the government promised that more cuts were coming: "The expenditure cuts will have to go deeper . . . our work has just begun."[31]

Budget 1994—A Plan for Securing Alberta's Future

By the end of the 1993–94 fiscal year, the Alberta government had actually exceeded the targets laid out in the previous budget. Program spending was reduced by $830 million, or 6.4 per cent, a greater reduction than the planned 5.5 per cent. The deficit was reduced by nearly 30 per cent, and the public service was reduced by 2,847 positions.[32]

Despite these successes, much work remained to get Alberta's fiscal house in order. The provincial deficit by the end of 1993–94 was still $1.97

billion, almost 2.4 per cent of GDP. Alberta's provincial debt was now $27.8 billion, or $10,415 per Albertan. And interest costs had increased to 11.6 per cent of government revenue.

Throughout 1993, the government reviewed every department and prepared a detailed three-year fiscal road map for Alberta. The 1994 budget outlined the government's plan to achieve a balanced budget, with no tax increases, by 1996–97, as set out in the Deficit Elimination Act. As finance minister Jim Dinning noted in his budget speech, "We've chosen to get rid of [the] deficit once and for all, not slowly, not a little bit at a time, but decisively and completely."[33]

For the coming fiscal year, 1994–95, the budget proposed a significant $956-million, 7.9 per cent reduction in program spending. All told, a further 1,787 public sector jobs would be eliminated in 1994–95, a decrease of 5.7 per cent. Again, the spending reductions and layoffs were government-wide and affected nearly every government department.

Further, over the three-year plan, program spending would be reduced by nearly $2 billion, or 15 per cent. The substantial budget deficit of nearly $2 billion in 1993–94 was to be eliminated and indeed a surplus of $362 million was planned for 1996–97. All told, the government was planning for a 20 per cent reduction in the public service over four years.

While the government was making clear that its ambitious plan required it to reduce spending and cut public sector jobs, it was also laying out its vision of what it should be doing: investing in people, building a prosperous province, providing essential services for the health and well-being of Albertans, maintaining quality infrastructure, and providing law and order.[34] The government's efforts were to be focused squarely on these core functions while cutting back less essential programs, eliminating waste and duplication, and streamlining administration.

Every department was required to develop a three-year business plan with missions, strategies, performance measures, and benchmarks. In addition, there was a move away from government-provided services to making increased use of the private sector and charging user fees for government services so that people who use the services would pay.[35]

Alberta's Fiscal Reforms Pay Off

Examining Alberta's fiscal turnaround leaves no doubt about the importance of the 1993 and 1994 fiscal reforms. In the first four years of Premier

Klein's tenure, government program spending decreased from $16.1 billion in 1992–93 to $12.7 billion in 1996–97, a reduction of over 20 per cent.[36] Spending fell from 21.5 per cent of GDP to 12.9 per cent.

While revenues also fell, spending fell even faster, resulting in a budget surplus of 1.1 per cent of GDP in the second year of Premier Klein's reforms, a remarkable change from a deficit of nearly 4.5 per cent of GDP in 1992–93.

After the government balanced its budget in 1994–95, it ran consecutive budget surpluses for the next fourteen years. These surpluses were in part used to pay down the provincial debt. In fact, by 2004–05, Alberta had eliminated its provincial debt.[37]

Perhaps one of the most beneficial aspects of the reforms enacted by Premier Klein was the elimination of the gap between the money collected by the government—taxes—and the money actually spent on programs. Just as was the case in Ottawa, fiscal discipline and debt reduction lowered interest costs and made more money available for spending on government programs. Interest costs reached a peak of $1.7 billion, over 10 per cent of revenues, in 1994–95. After 1994–95, interest costs plummeted and are now negligible.

Alberta's fiscal austerity program in 1993 and 1994 fundamentally changed the status quo. The changed budgets were bold and implemented quickly. As a result, the downward fiscal spiral that was threatening Alberta's future was reversed within just two years. Indeed, Alberta's remarkable and substantial reforms reinforced the changes implemented in Saskatchewan and set the course for other reforming provinces, particularly Ontario, and the federal government to follow.

Ontario: Mike Harris's Common Sense Revolution

In the mid-1990s, Ontario's provincial government, like many others, was in a fiscal crisis. The 1991 recession saw government revenue fall by 5 per cent in a single year. The provincial deficit exploded from $3 billion to nearly $11 billion.[38]

The recession, however, was not the only culprit behind the exploding deficit. The Ontario government, led by NDP premier Bob Rae, had increased government program spending by $5.3 billion in 1991–92, a 12.7 per cent increase. The dramatic increase in program spending was preceded by a similar $4.8-billion (12.9 per cent) increase in 1990–91. In fact, in just two years the Ontario government had gone from a small surplus to an $11-billion deficit. While revenues only decreased by $472 million (1.1 per cent) from 1989–90 to 1991–92, total spending increased by $10.5 billion, up over 25 per cent in just two years.

Ontario's substantial deficits persisted over the next three years, never falling below $10 billion despite increased revenues. Over the course of the five years to 1994–95, the Ontario government accumulated $49 billion in debt. The provincial debt, which had stood at 14.3 per cent of GDP, more than doubled. By 1994–95, each Ontarian owed $8,100 in provincial government debt. The now-familiar pattern repeated itself: interest costs steadily increased, from 9.3 per cent of government revenue in 1989–90 to 17 per cent by 1994–95. Each Ontarian was contributing $716 a year simply to pay for interest on government debt. Ontario was caught in a spending-induced downward spiral of persistent and substantial deficits, increasing government debt, and growing interest costs. Like Saskatchewan's and Alberta's, Ontario's status quo was simply not sustainable.

As a result of the rapidly mounting fiscal crisis, Premier Rae's government had become unpopular. Capitalizing on this discontent, the Progressive Conservative leader, Mike Harris, seized the opportunity to present his so-called "Common Sense Revolution" platform in 1994. This plan was to cut spending to eliminate the deficit. In the June 1995 provincial election, Harris's party won and he became premier.

Harris came to office ready to act. In just under a month, his government released a fiscal overview and outlined its plan to deal with the budget deficit. The July 1995 Ontario statement was followed by a landmark budget in 1996 that presented a three-year austerity program to end the province's fiscal crisis.

Ontario Fiscal Overview, 1995

Premier Harris noted in the *1995 Fiscal and Economic Statement*, presented on July 21, 1995, "The fiscal situation is not good. In fact, it is critical . . . the status quo is unacceptable."[39] The document outlined the government's financial plan for the 1995–96 fiscal year and presented the government's medium-term plan for dealing with its spending and deficit. Finance minister Ernie Eves noted the urgency of reform: "We must get Ontario out from under the burden of rising interest costs . . . the size of our debt and the interest we pay on it mean we have to act quickly."[40]

Despite being four months into the current fiscal year of 1995–96, the *1995 Fiscal and Economic Statement* proposed an $850-million cut in program spending and $307 million in capital spending in 1995–96. Each minister was also assigned an additional target for further reducing spending in their ministry, with the goal of achieving another spending cut of $500 million in 1995–96. If all the reductions came to pass, the fiscal review would reduce spending by $1.9 billion in 1995–96.

As was the case in Alberta, welfare reform was singled out as a high priority in the *1995 Fiscal and Economic Statement.* In the preceding decade, Ontario had loosened eligibility requirements, raised welfare benefits, and reduced enforcement of welfare eligibility criteria.[41] As a result, the percentage of Ontario's population collecting welfare more than doubled and reached 12.8 per cent of the population in 1994. In its fiscal review, the new government immediately reduced welfare rates by 22 per cent, tightened eligibility requirements and reduced fraud, saving an estimated $1.46 billion over two years.[42]

Finally, the government proposed a goal of reducing program spending by $3 billion within two years, setting the stage for the 1996 budget, which outlined the government's full austerity program.

Ontario Budget, 1996

The first budget of the Harris government was delivered on May 6, 1996, and presented the government's plan to achieve a balanced budget while decreasing taxes within four years. Two central components of the budget were the balanced budget plan—which would have the budget balanced by 2000–01—and a reduction in taxes.[43]

To meet its balanced budget target, the 1996 Ontario budget pledged to reduce government administration costs by a third in one year, saving $300 million annually; improve efficiency and restructure operations to save $1.1 billion per year by 1997–98; cut subsidies to businesses by $230 million a year; reduce funding to agencies, boards, and commissions by $220 million per year; and cut government grants by $1.4 billion a year by 1997–98. For the coming fiscal year, the government proposed a big $2.4-billion, 5.3 per cent cut in program spending. Total spending, including program and capital, would decline by $2.7 billion.[44] Furthermore, over the Harris government's full three-year austerity plan program, spending would be reduced by $4.3 billion, or 9.5 per cent. The budget deficit would decrease by 36 per cent to $6.6 billion in 1997–98 from $10.3 billion in 1994–95.

Despite the attack on the deficit, the government also proposed a significant tax cut to improve the incentives for Ontarians to work, save, invest, and engage in entrepreneurial activities. Specifically, Ontario's personal income tax rate would be cut by 30 per cent over three years.[45] Personal income taxes would be reduced by $1.2 billion in 1996–97 and $4.8 billion per year when fully in place in 1999–2000.

Results of the Common Sense Fiscal Plan

Ontario's fiscal turnaround under Premier Harris highlights the importance of the 1995–96 fiscal reforms.

In his seven years at the helm of the province, Premier Harris reduced government spending from 18 per cent of GDP to 14.5 per cent. By 1999–2000, the reductions in government spending resulted in a budget surplus, the government having succeeded in achieving the goal set out by the balanced budget plan one year earlier than planned. For the first time in over a decade, Ontario's provincial government ran a small surplus. In five years, the Harris government turned a $10-billion deficit into a $300-million surplus.

Provincial Fiscal Policy, 1993–2008

When one looks at how the budgets of all the provinces and territories evolved over the course of the 1990s, it quickly becomes clear how fast their collective situation changed, even if a few of the provinces did most of the heavy lifting. The provincial governments, led by Saskatchewan, Alberta, and Ontario, contributed significantly to Canada's fiscal turnaround. Having looked at the performance of the leaders, it may now help us to understand the magnitude of the provinces' contribution if we look at their performance collectively over the period of reform.

Revenues, Spending, and the Deficit

From 1993 to 2000, the size of provincial and territorial governments decreased from 25 per cent of GDP to 20 per cent of GDP, a level that had not been seen since 1981, nearly twenty years prior. The downward trend, however, was short-lived, with provincial spending stabilizing at 20 per cent of GDP from 2000 to 2008. Provincial revenues also decreased, from 22.2 per cent of GDP in 1993 to 19.7 per cent in 2003, before increasing to 20.9 per cent in 2008.

After consistent deficits from 1980 to 1998, provincial governments ran surpluses in six of the ten years from 1999 to 2008. Indeed, the turnaround in the provincial deficits from nearly 3 per cent of GDP in 1993 to the small surplus posted in 1999 was quite remarkable.[46]

Declining Provincial Debt and Lower Interest Costs

Between 1980 and 1999, the provinces together ran up considerable debt. Once they determined to change course, however, they were able to eliminate deficits and reduce their debt fairly quickly. Specifically, provincial government debt consistently increased from nearly 21 per cent of GDP in 1980 to nearly 50 per cent in 1996. From 1996, provincial government debt as a percentage of GDP began to decrease, falling to approximately 40 per cent of GDP by 2007.

As a result of the ramping up of provincial debt, interest payments reached a high of 15 per cent of revenue in 1995. Thanks to reform, by 2008 interest payments as a percentage of revenue had fallen precipitously to 8.6 per cent.

Provincial Tax Relief

Many provincial governments, like Ottawa, have reduced capital and personal income taxes. Indeed, all provinces with the exception of Nova Scotia reduced both middle and upper personal income taxes rates between 1995 and 2008.[47] The most aggressive provinces—Ontario, Saskatchewan, Alberta, and British Columbia—reduced their top personal income tax rate by over 20 per cent from 1995 to 2008.

All provinces, save for Newfoundland and Nova Scotia, also decreased taxes on capital through substantial reductions in provincial corporate income tax rates from 1995 to 2008.[48] The western provinces of British Columbia, Alberta, and Saskatchewan enacted the most aggressive reductions, with corporate income tax rates decreasing by roughly 30 per cent.

Most provinces—Newfoundland and Labrador, New Brunswick, Nova Scotia, Ontario, and British Columbia—also have or are in the process of harmonizing their provincial sales taxes with the federal GST.[49] Prior to harmonization, the independent sales taxes in these provinces applied to many business costs ("inputs"), which significantly increased the cost of investing in capital. Since the GST is a true value-added tax, business inputs (i.e., machinery, equipment) will now be exempt from sales taxes in these jurisdictions.[50] Reducing taxes on new business investment improved the incentives for investment and leave firms with more money to reinvest.

From the early 1960s to mid-1990s, the provincial governments' deteriorating fiscal situation largely mirrored that of the federal government. Provincial governments expanded in size, ran nearly twenty consecutive years of budget deficits, increased debt. and as a result faced continuously increasing interest costs. Fortunately, like that of the federal government, the provincial fiscal situation changed markedly in the 1990s. Government spending as a percentage of GDP decreased and debt as a percentage of GDP began to fall, as did the portion of government resources required to pay interest. Like Ottawa, many provinces cut taxes, improving the incentives for work, savings, investment, and entrepreneurship. In other words, much credit is due to those provincial governments that contributed significantly to Canada's fiscal turnaround.

REFORMING CANADA'S ENTITLEMENTS—GLASS TWO-THIRDS FULL chapter five

The reforms of the 1990s were not limited to just government spending and taxes. Some profound changes were made to some of Canada's longest-standing government entitlement programs. The financial sustainability of these entitlement programs, which include public pensions, health care, and social assistance, are challenging governments around the world. The fundamental premises upon which the funding for many of these programs were based, namely increasing populations and high rates of economic and income growth, have proven faulty over time.[1]

Canada has a number of programs that guarantee Canadians specific benefits, also known as entitlements. These programs include retirement benefits (Canada Pension Plan—Quebec maintains its own stand-alone public pension[2]), income security (social assistance or welfare), and health care benefits. There is a mix of federal and provincial involvement in each of these programs, including financing, regulating, and providing services. Therefore, solutions to the problems facing these programs inevitably require action at both the federal and provincial levels.

The record of reform in these programs by Canadian governments over the last twenty years is mixed. In two cases, social welfare and the Canada Pension Plan (CPP), substantial reforms were enacted in the 1990s, reforms that have proven overwhelmingly positive. Worryingly, health care remains largely unreformed. As the third rail of Canadian politics, its problems are mounting fast. By better understanding the successes of welfare and Canada Pension Plan reform, we can better understand the clear path to successful reform of Canada's health care system.

Canada Pension Plan—Real Reforms with Real Success

In the 1990s, Canada reformed its public pension arrangements. Understanding those reforms to the Canada Pension Plan is critical for two reasons. One, it illustrates that Canadians and their governments can come together to work successfully for the good of the country in politically sensitive areas. And, two, it illustrates Canada's real advantages with respect to public pensions compared to other countries, whose public pensions are slowly—quickly in some cases—disintegrating. This is particularly important for our comparisons to our southern neighbour.

Canada's public retirement system is based on several separate programs. The best known and the focus of this section is the Canada Pension Plan.[3] However, there are other important components of the public system worth noting. The Old Age Security (OAS)[4] program provides a flat benefit of up to 15 per cent of the average wage regardless of an individual's work status.[5] In other words, this benefit is not tied to an individual's history of employment earnings. The OAS benefit is paid for by general federal revenues.[6]

In addition to the OAS, there is also the Guaranteed Income Supplement (GIS) program.[7] This program, like the OAS, is financed by general federal revenues and is not tied to individual earnings. It is a means-tested benefit given to seniors deemed to have low incomes. In other words, it's a minimum-income scheme for seniors.[8]

But the main pillar of the public retirement system is the Canada Pension Plan. It provides workers a retirement benefit of up to 25 per cent of pensionable earnings, which in 2009 was $46,300. Thus, the maximum monthly benefit offered by the Canada Pension Plan in 2009 was $908.75. The CPP is financed by a dedicated payroll tax of 9.9 per cent, applied on earnings above the exemption of $3,500 and up to $46,300.

In the early 1990s, there was an increasing realization and recognition that the CPP was not financially sustainable. That is, revenues from yearly CPP contributions and the assets that had been accumulated in years in which CPP revenues exceeded expenditures were insufficient to cover the benefits for the coming wave of retiring baby boomers.[9] In 1996, under the leadership of then finance minister Paul Martin, Prime Minister

Jean Chrétien, and a number of officials in the Department of Finance, the federal government engaged its provincial counterparts in an effort to reach agreement on a solution to the CPP's longer-term financial problems.[10]

In what should be viewed as an historic achievement, the federal government announced in early 1997 that an agreement on CPP reform had been forged with the provinces and that it would take effect in 1998. Four broad changes were agreed to and put into effect in 1998:[11]

1. The payroll tax that pays for the CPP was increased to 9.9 per cent. It stood at 5.6 per cent in 1996 but was scheduled to increase to 10.1 per cent in 2016 and was expected to reach 14.2 per cent by 2030. By bringing forward the increase in the contribution rate—payroll tax—larger surpluses could be recorded immediately. These fresh funds were used to invest in assets that would underpin the CPP's ability to honour its pension obligations. By bringing in an increase in the payroll tax earlier than planned, it is expected that no further increases beyond the current 9.9 per cent payroll tax rate will be needed.
2. Prior to the reforms, the accumulated surplus from CPP contributions were invested passively in low-interest provincial bonds. One of the major reforms enacted was to establish the CPP Investment Board (CPPIB),[12] which actively invests the surplus funds with an aim to maximize the risk-adjusted rate of return of CPP assets.
3. The value of earnings exempted from the payroll tax was frozen at $3,500. That is, no one has to pay CPP premiums on the first $3,500 of income. The aim of the exemption was to exclude individuals whose earnings were deemed minimal from having to pay CPP premiums.[13]
4. A series of small benefit changes were brought in, which in total were expected to reduce overall benefit spending by 9.1 per cent by 2030. Among the benefit changes agreed to were a more stringent set of rules for eligibility for the disability benefit; limits on the earnings-related survivor benefits; a reduction and freezing of the death benefit—lump-sum benefit—to $2,500; and a change in the calculation that determines an individual's benefit.

People might quibble with the specific reforms and certain risks they may present in the future. For example, the reforms ignored the possibility of allowing for individual provincial programs that could compete with one another and offer citizens more choice. Indeed, the reform process outright rejected the privatization option that a number of participants favoured. In addition, the reforms did not increase the age at which Canadians could claim partial and/or full benefits despite the large increases in life expectancy witnessed since the inception of the CPP.[14] There are also clearly risks for increased politicization of the CPP and the CPPIB.[15]

One cannot deny, however, that the reforms enacted have successfully stabilized the long-term viability of the CPP. Perhaps different reforms could have achieved similar results at a lower cost, but one must acknowledge the success of the reforms implemented. Indeed, these successes have consistently been noted in the regular actuarial reports published by the Office of the Superintendent of Financial Institutions.[16]

The most recent report, published in 2006, reiterated the favourable performance and financial footing of the CPP. Among a number of findings was that the 9.9 per cent contribution rate remains sufficient to cover expected benefit payments, assets continue to grow and to increase as a ratio against spending, and income and assets are more than sufficient to cover expected spending.[17] Put more succinctly, the 1998 reforms meant that the CPP is fully funded with little or no risk of having to increase contribution rates, decrease benefits, and/or incur debt to finance benefits in the future.

While the next report will not be published until 2010, financial reports from the CPPIB indicate that the stock market meltdown of 2008 hurt the CPP fund. Specifically, the $122.7-billion CPP fund fell by 23.8 per cent in 2008 to $106 billion.[18] The CPP fund strongly rebounded in the second quarter of 2009, however, increasing to $123.8 billion. The CPPIB also remains confident that the fund will fully recover and assist in carrying the Canada Pension Plan through the coming demographic shift as the baby boom generation retires.[19]

The reforms enacted in the late 1990s will enable the fund to withstand the pressures associated with the coming bulge of baby-boom retirees. Perhaps equally as important when seen in comparison to the situation south of our border, the reforms mean that younger workers are actually contributing to a program from which they can reasonably expect to enjoy benefits somewhat commensurate with its costs. The forging of this solution by governments of all stripes shows that politically sensitive problems can be solved.

Canadian Welfare Reform: Decentralization and Incentives Matter

Perhaps the best example of social program reform in Canada over the past twenty years was the changes made to our welfare system.

As we know, the federal and provincial governments in the late 1980s and early 1990s battled continuously with budget deficits and how to constrain spending. One of the reasons spending had increased in many provinces was the significant rise in the number—and percentage—of Canadians receiving welfare.[20] The combination of needing to restrain and reform spending, coupled with growing welfare dependency, set the stage for fairly dramatic reforms to the welfare system in the mid-1990s.[21]

The fundamental reform of welfare began in 1995, triggered by Paul Martin's dramatic changes to the financing of social programs in the 1995 federal budget.[22] Specifically, Martin initiated the switch from a system of cost-sharing grants to a block grant to the provinces to provide social assistance.[23] This meant that any new extension of programs or benefits would be paid for by the provinces exclusively. It clearly placed the financial responsibility for these programs on the shoulders of the provincial government. Crucially, the reforms also provided more flexibility and autonomy to the provinces with respect to the delivery and design of social programs, excluding health care.[24]

Provinces Tackle Welfare Reform

One common feature of reform among the provinces was a reduction in benefit levels, particularly for single employable people. While the narrative of reform's opponents regarding the benefits was often about balancing the books on the backs of the poor, the changes were actually rooted in an increasingly widespread acknowledgement that incentives mattered for low-income work decisions.[25] Specifically, people understood that when welfare benefits surpass comparable income available from low-paid work, strong incentives are created for people to use the welfare system rather than work.[26]

Another common reform was to integrate welfare and related services with employment programs provided by the province. For example, Saskatchewan,[27] Newfoundland, and the Northwest Territories all moved fairly quickly to integrate welfare delivery and government-provided employment services. In addition, a number of provinces, including Alberta, Ontario, British Columbia, and Quebec, undertook initiatives to improve the administration of welfare and related programs, including reducing fraudulent claims.

Unsurprisingly, given the altered incentives, many provinces also reformed their welfare systems to reduce dependency, improve value for money in the services and support they offered people, and control cost. But different provinces focused their attention on different things, tailoring reform to their local circumstances.

Alberta

Alberta was really the first province to pursue genuine and broad welfare reform in Canada. In 1993, even before the federal transfer reforms, Alberta overhauled the administration and ethos of its Ministry of Family and Social Services.[28] The cultural and administrative changes shifted the emphasis *away* from determining eligibility and mailing cheques and *toward* preventing people from entering the welfare system before other possible avenues of support, including employment, were exhausted. The underlying premise of the change was that once people entered the system, they had a much higher probability of using it again in the future. Thus, people were helped by making sure that every other possible alternative, such as finding or staying in work, was exhausted before they could enter the welfare bureaucracy. Additional measures were taken to reduce fraud, such as adding investigators and review officers.

The combination of focusing on alternatives to welfare and bringing benefit levels in line with low-paid employment opportunities resulted in marked improvement in outcomes for former welfare recipients. One study concluded that almost half of the 172,000 people who left the province's welfare rolls between 1993 and 1996 found full-time employment.[29] In other words, Alberta was able to reduce welfare dependency by adopting reforms that promoted work and employment, which in turn led to better results for its citizens while reducing provincial spending.

Ontario

Ontario's welfare system had profound problems.[30] Despite the fact that it was at the time Canada's wealthiest province, by 1994 Ontario had the highest rate of social assistance to population in the country at 12.8 per cent, its spending was increasing at an unsustainable rate, and its benefit levels were encouraging ever-higher rates of welfare use.[31]

As discussed above, Ontario elected a new government in 1995 that immediately brought in a number of changes, including reduced benefit rates, an increased focus on diversion to non-welfare alternatives, greater focus on employment, and administrative improvements such as reducing fraud and ensuring accuracy in determining eligibility.

Ontario's unique reform, though, didn't arrive until 1998.[32] Ontario Works was introduced in 1998, making Ontario the only province with a formal and fairly broad "workfare" program. The goal of the program was to determine and secure the shortest route to paid employment for welfare recipients. The focus on employment was mandatory for all employable adults collecting welfare benefits. The result of the reforms, as well as a much stronger economy, meant that Ontario's welfare rolls were reduced to a greater extent than observed nationally.[33]

British Columbia

British Columbia was one of the last provinces to enact reforms. In 2001 a newly elected Liberal government moved quickly to implement wholesale changes to the province's welfare system.[34] Most noticeable in their reform package was a rolling benefit time limit, which echoed one of the core US reforms. Specifically, each month a recipient received welfare benefits counted toward a twenty-four-month limit within any five-year period. The program was announced in 2001 and effective on April 1, 2002.[35] For employable individuals, reaching the limit would result in stiff reductions in benefits, to zero in some cases, while more difficult cases, like families with children, would suffer much smaller reductions in their benefits. Put differently, the program was aimed at forcing employable individuals and couples with no children to think about welfare as an insurance program rather than simply as a potential source of income.

The results were dramatic. To a much greater extent than expected, single employable individuals basically stopped using welfare as a source of income and moved much more quickly back into the labour force. The result was a plunge in welfare dependency rates, as well as a reduction in welfare-related spending.

Provincial welfare reform highlights the power of decentralized delivery of government services and the varied and innovative approaches different provinces took to improve their welfare and related programs. The results of these reforms were dramatic. By 2000, the number of welfare beneficiaries in Canada had declined to a little over 2 million, or 6.8 per cent of the population, from a peak of 3.1 million, or 10.7 per cent of the population.[36] In addition, welfare-related spending had been curtailed, helping governments balance their budgets. Most importantly, however, the programs being delivered seemed to be achieving better results by getting more employable individuals into the job market and dealing with some of the more pressing underlying problems that caused people to consider welfare as an alternative to work.

Health Care: Reform's Black Hole

The country's public health care system, on the other hand, has avoided any real, substantive reforms over the past two decades. While the federal government provided the provinces with substantially more flexibility and autonomy with respect to the delivery and design of social programs like welfare, the same cannot be said for health care. In fact, one of the primary reasons for the lack of reform and experimentation is that the federal government uses the threat of reduced transfers to ensure that the provinces abide by the federal government's vision of health care as set out in the Canada Health Act.[37]

As a result, the state of Canada's universal health care system remains a serious concern for Canadians. While provincial governments have increased health spending significantly, their efforts have produced little in the way of results.[38] The reality is that the problems with Canada's health care system will have to be dealt with more fundamentally over the coming decade as increasing pressures are placed on the system and related finances due to an aging population, continued advances in medical and related technologies, and no effective means to keep demand for publicly funded health services within reasonable bounds. Unless, of course, you consider making people queue for needed services to be an effective means.

Canada's Heath Care System: A Case of Life Support?

Canada's health care system is, on an age-adjusted basis, the developed world's third-most-expensive health care system after Iceland and the United States.[39] Looking at only those systems that maintain universal approaches to health insurance, Canada's health expenditures in 2005 were 22 per cent higher than in the average universal access nations, which includes countries such as Austria, Belgium, France, Germany, Japan, Luxembourg, and Switzerland.[40]

The future for increased health expenditures does not look bright. Just as in many other nations, health care expenditures in Canada are rising faster than growth in the economy as a whole and are straining government budgets as a result.[41]

Despite this internationally high level of spending, Canada has remarkably long waiting times for health care services. In 2009 the median waiting time for treatment across twelve major medical specialties was 16.1 weeks from GP referral to treatment by a specialist.[42]

Part of the explanation for long wait times lies in the shortage of medical professionals and a failure to invest in new medical technologies. Specifically, Canada's physician-to-population ratio is one of the lowest in the developed world.[43] Similarly, Canada has many fewer MRI machines and CT scanners per million population than the OECD average, while many pieces of medical and diagnostic equipment in Canada are outdated and in need of replacement.[44]

Attempts at Health Care Reform

The most challenging barrier to reform of health care in Canada is the federal government and the billions it transfers to the provinces for health care. These funds are available only to those provinces who abide by the rules, regulations, and federal interpretations of the Canada Health Act.[45] The act specifically prohibits a variety of beneficial policies being implemented in other developed nations that also maintain universal access health care systems but deliver better care at lower costs. The prohibitions require provinces not to allow cost sharing or extra billing for medically necessary care and have been used as a barrier to allowing the private funding of medically necessary care.

While the Canada Health Act has stifled innovative reforms at the provincial level, a number of small changes have been made in an effort to improve access to health care services and reduce the rate of growth in health expenditures. The reforms undertaken by the provinces since the early 1990s fall into three broad categories: (1) reforms intended to improve government management of the system, (2) reforms intended to change the incentives for providers delivering care, and (3) reforms aimed at controlling spending.[46]

For its part, the federal government has altered the method by which it shares the cost of health care with the provinces and introduced targeted funds for health care reform, medical and diagnostic equipment, and wait times.[47]

While it is difficult to examine the impact of each of the individual reforms listed above, efforts expended by governments in total have not taken the health care system off life support.

These reforms in total also seem to have had no effect on the unsustainable nature of public health spending. In 1993, provincial health expenditures constituted roughly 33 per cent of provincial program expenditures. By 2008, that proportion was estimated to have risen to approximately 39 per cent.[48] Further, the average annual rate of growth in per capita provincial health spending between 2003 and 2008 was above the average rate between 1988 and 2008.[49] This all suggests that expenditures are just as unsustainable now as they were in the past, or may have actually become even less sustainable than they were previously.

Conclusion

Highly successful reforms to the Canada Pension Plan were a vital addition to the fiscal—spending and tax—reforms enacted successfully by the federal government and a host of provincial governments in the 1990s. The CPP is now positioned to weather the storms of the retiring baby boomers and provide benefits to both old and young Canadians. Similarly, when Ottawa freed the provinces to experiment with welfare reform and gave them incentives to do so, reform was remarkably successful.

The great unreformed entitlement is Canada's public health care system. Federal and provincial governments have avoided any real, substantive reforms over the past two decades. The problems in the health care system will have to be dealt with more fundamentally over the coming decade as increasing pressures are placed on the system and related finances. With health care consuming an ever-growing portion of government spending, fundamental reform will be required if Canada is to build on the successful fiscal policies of the 1990s.

part III

America Loses the Script

WHERE'D YOU GET THAT SUIT? U.S. BUCKLES ON FISCAL STRAITJACKET chapter six

The significant reforms undertaken successfully in Canada, both federally and in many provinces, have laid the foundation for the current economic opportunity before our great country. However, this moment of opportunity is not solely based on good decisions and successes of the past in Canada as we draw back from the mistaken and damaging policies of the sixties, seventies, and eighties and revert to the plan that Sir Wilfrid Laurier established for us a century ago. Our opportunity is amplified by something that Sir Wilfrid never contemplated: that America would stumble and lose its way. In other words, the historic economic opportunity facing Canada is a result of good decisions by Canada in the past and is further amplified by poor decisions made and being made in the United States. American missteps offer Canada a chance to become more dominant as a destination for talented and diligent people, business investment, and entrepreneurship within North America.

Leaving aside the renewed engagement with the Americans, at their heart the Canadian reforms in the Redemptive Decade were largely about living within our means—balancing the spending and taxing of government to avoid deficits—and asking what we really needed from government. The combination of having our governments live within their means while fundamentally re-evaluating what we needed from them resulted in a smaller, smarter government in Ottawa and in many provincial capitals. These fiscal lessons have generally not yet been learned, let alone acted on, in the United States.

This chapter tells the story of how and why public finances in the United States got into a terrible mess and why that enhances the opportunity available to Canada to create a lasting economic advantage in North America. Let us be clear though, the entrepreneurial spirit that characterizes and drives the US economy will survive and indeed thrive despite the serious policy missteps of US governments. The opportunity for Canada exists in the fact that these missteps by US governments will constrain their ability to sustainably reduce taxes for the foreseeable future. Indeed, as we shall see, tax increases are almost inevitable south of the border. Such constraints mean that Canada has an opportunity to create a lasting tax advantage over the US while reforming our government programs to ensure greater value and effectiveness. Such competitive advantages translate into more investment and entrepreneurship, and therefore more employment and opportunities in Canada as our great nation becomes a beacon for investment in North America.

Assessing the US Federal Fiscal Situation: Retrospective and Prospective

Deficits as Far as the Eye Can See

There may be no single policy area where the performance gap between Canada and the United States is wider over the last two decades than with deficits. Recall that deficits are simply the borrowing of money by government in any given year when spending exceeds revenues. The debt of a country or a province is largely the accumulation of these deficits.[1]

The US federal government has demonstrated a near-absolute inability to solve its deficit problem, while Canada has been a leader among industrialized nations in balancing its financial affairs for more than a decade, or at least it was up to 2008. Because deficits necessarily mean an accumulation of debt and interest costs, this divergence between Canada and the US means that while Canada has enjoyed reducing debt and interest costs through surpluses, the US has struggled with the opposite: increasing debt and interest costs.

Deficits have been the overwhelming norm in the United States since 1980, surpluses the rare exception.[2] Over the years spanning 1980 to 2009, there were only four years[3] in which surpluses were recorded, 1998 to 2001.[4]

Looking back over these decades, Washington's finances can be divided into three periods.

The first period, 1981 to 1993, which encompasses the presidencies of Ronald Reagan and George Bush Sr., is characterized by deficits averaging a little over 4 per cent of the economy,[5] or GDP.[6] With rising public deficits and debt came rising anxiety—among politicians and voters alike—about the state of government finances.[7]

That anxiety was founded on a legitimate concern: Americans were increasingly becoming worried about the legacy of debt they were leaving their children. Instead of Americans paying enough in taxes each year to finance the public services they were receiving, their national government chose to borrow the equivalent of roughly 4 per cent of the economy (GDP), on average, each year to finance a portion of current spending.

But this is nothing more than a sleight of hand. A deficit is merely taxes deferred into the future, because at some point the bill—with interest—for these deficits comes due and it is the taxpayer who must pay. These deferred taxes are ultimately paid for by future generations in the form of higher taxes, lower spending, or a combination of the two.

The turnaround in government finances enjoyed during the administration of Democratic president Bill Clinton was made possible in large part by mounting public concern over the debt.[8] Beginning in 1993, the size of the annual deficits began to fall and eventually turned into surpluses starting in 1998. The surplus in 2000 reached 2.4 per cent of GDP, which is fairly sizable, particularly when viewed against the experience of the previous two decades of red ink.

The final period began in 2002 under Republican president George W. Bush, Jr., and looks set to be extended under his Democratic successor, President Barack Obama. Deficits reappeared in 2002 and remained through to today but, as we shall see, appear to be worsening. Although the size of the deficits under President George W. Bush were not as large as those incurred under his father and President Reagan, there were still some fairly sizable deficits: 3.5 per cent and 3.6 per cent, respectively, in 2003 and 2004. It would thus appear that the respite from deficit financing achieved during the Clinton administration can rightly be looked at as an aberration in US government finances over the last thirty years.

American Exceptionalism

The forecasts of the non-partisan Congressional Budget Office[9] (CBO) for the next ten years confirm that the United States plans to extend the fiscal policies and deficits of the Bush administration rather than return to the successful policies implemented during the Clinton administration.[10] According to the Congressional Budget Office's long-term analysis of US federal finances,[11] the national public debt—the accumulation of deficits—will increase by $7.14 trillion over the next ten years, reaching $14.3 trillion in 2019.[12] Interestingly, however, on the same day the CBO's analysis appeared, the Obama administration's Office of Management and Budget increased its ten-year estimate of debt accumulation—deficits—even further, to $9.1 trillion.[13] To get a sense of the magnitude of the deficits being faced in the United States, the non-partisan Tax Foundation estimated that, assuming current spending levels, US personal income tax rates would have to triple to raise enough revenue to bring the budget into balance in 2010.[14]

The CBO's long-term forecast of the federal budget indicates persistent deficits averaging roughly 4 per cent of the economy over the next ten years.[15] The average expected deficit as a share of the economy equals or exceeds the average deficits incurred during the 1980s, which rightly caused great concern across the political spectrum.[16] Indeed, there may actually be a gap, and perhaps a growing one, between the American public and the governing political class on the subject of responsible public finances. In polls taken as early as June 2009, Americans began to express deep concern over the size and persistence of the federal deficit.[17]

What is clear from Washington's past experience as well as its future plans is that it cannot seem to come to grips with its deficit problem in a significant and lasting way. The US federal government seems all too willing to continue to spend considerably more than it collects in taxes while slipping the remainder of the bill to future generations. Indeed, in many ways, US fiscal policy resembles the Canadian experience pre-1995.

Guardians of Public Finances Sound the Deficit Alarm

Congress is not sleepwalking unawares toward a fiscal wall, nor can President Obama plead ignorance. Peter Orszag, President Obama's director of the Office of Management and Budget,[18] offered quite dire warnings about the effects of increasing budget deficits[19] when he was the director of the non-partisan Congressional Budget Office. Specifically, in a May 2008 report, Dr. Orszag concluded that:

> Sustained and rising budget deficits would affect the economy by absorbing funds from the nation's pool of savings and reducing investment in the domestic capital stock and in foreign assets. As capital investment dwindled, the growth of workers' productivity and of real (inflation-adjusted) wages would gradually slow and begin to stagnate. As capital became scarce relative to labor, real interest rates would rise.[20]

Orszag listed a series of harmful economic effects emanating from rising and persistent deficits, effects that included lower private investment, lower wages, and higher real interest rates.

Despite these earlier—and warranted—conclusions, Orszag, as the president's lead person on budgets, now proposes large and increasing deficits.

Nor has the Congressional Budget Office changed its tune in its post-Orszag era. The CBO recently reiterated its concerns about the economic effects of persistent and increasing deficits in its analysis of the federal government's long-term budget outlook.[21] Specifically, they concluded that:

> Large budget deficits would reduce national saving, leading to more borrowing from abroad and less domestic investment, which in turn would depress income growth in the United States. Over time, the accumulation of debt would seriously harm the economy. Alternatively, if spending grew as projected and taxes were raised in tandem, tax rates would have to reach levels never seen in the United States. High tax rates would slow the growth of the economy, making the spending burden harder to bear.[22]

Plain English translation: the American government has been unable to tackle its deficit problem. While Americans won a brief reprieve from fiscal purgatory during the Clinton administration, 1993 to 2000, the situation worsened under his successor, President George W. Bush, from 2001 to 2008, and is now expected to worsen even further under President

Obama.[23] Continued deficits will inevitably put increasing pressure on US government finances by increasing debt and interest costs.

It's Just Arithmetic, Part I: Deficits Mean More Debt

Unsurprisingly, given the persistence of deficits, the US federal debt[24] has increased markedly since 1980.[25] As we know, there are a number of ways to think about the significance of such growing indebtedness. We have chosen to focus largely on how the size of US government debt compares to the overall size of the economy (GDP).[26] In simple terms, we're comparing a country's accumulated debt to its income, just as families compare their debt—such as mortgages, car loans, and credit card debt—against their annual income.

US federal debt was on a fairly stable upward path until 1993, increasing from 26.1 per cent of the economy (GDP) in 1980 to 49.4 per cent of GDP in 1993. Federal debt as a share of the economy then began to decline in 1994 through to 2001.[27] Debt as a share of the economy remained fairly stable between 2002 and 2008. In 2009, however, federal debt as a percentage of the economy spiked, increasing from roughly 38 per cent in 2008 to nearly 54 per cent.[28]

Given the iron rules of arithmetic and the size of the expected deficits over the next ten years, the national debt of the United States must necessarily increase. The CBO estimates that US national debt will reach nearly 68 per cent of GDP in 2019.[29] Let's place this in the context of a Canadian family: imagine that the value of a family's debt reached more than two-thirds of its annual income. Worse, unlike most families, who purchase assets with debt such as homes and cars that last a long time, very little of the accumulated national debt in the US is linked with long-lasting assets like roads and bridges that deliver benefits over the long term. Rather, most of the debt accumulated and expected to be accumulated will finance annual spending.

In late 2009 the Obama administration and many members of Congress were proposing large increases in both deficits and debt. Specifically, they were proposing an increase in the public debt to 82.4 per cent of the economy (GDP) by 2019.[30] Clearly, both deficits and debt are increasing, both in absolute terms and compared to the size of the US economy.[31] In other words, the US national public debt is increasing in dollar terms as annual deficits accumulate, but because the debt is also growing faster than the economy, it means the national debt is becoming larger and larger when compared to the US economy.

It's Just Arithmetic, Part II: More Debt Means More Interest Payments

As discussed in the Canadian chapters, there is a real, immediate effect from higher deficits and debt, namely higher interest costs. These increased costs mean less government revenues available for spending on actual programs. They also mean more pressure on the economy, because the economy bears the cost of the taxes but gets no benefit from that money—that was obtained in an earlier year, when the original spending occurred. And because higher levels of borrowing mean greater risk of default, the potential is always present for interest rates to rise even higher, multiplying these negative effects.

Obviously, the higher interest costs[32] go, the less money is left over in government's coffers to pay for public spending. This "slice off the top" of all government revenues is sometimes called the interest wedge.[33] In other words, the larger the interest wedge, the larger the gap between what taxpayers are paying in taxes—costs—and what they actually receive in programs, or benefits. Thinking about a family, the interest wedge is the amount of the family's income that must be used to pay the interest on their various forms of debt, such as mortgages, car loans, and credit card debt.

In addition, interest wedges can also raise alarm bells about the sustainability of current fiscal policies. Any government experiencing a consistent increase in interest costs as a share of its revenues will at some point face serious difficulties in paying all its bills. Why? Because when interest payments get too high compared to overall revenues, lenders get nervous that governments may default on their debts or resort to inflation to lower the cost of carrying the debt.

Looking back, there are essentially three distinct periods in recent US budget history as regards the impact of interest. These periods essentially mirror those three distinct debt periods already described. Interest costs as a percentage of revenues climbed steadily between 1980 and 1986, increasing from 10.2 per cent in 1980 to 17.7 per cent in 1986. They remained fairly stable as a percentage of revenues between 1987 and 1995, ranging from 16.1 per cent of revenues to 18.4 per cent. Interest costs as a share of revenues then started a marked decline beginning in 1995, reaching 8.5 per cent of revenues in 2004.[34] Between 2004 and 2009, interest costs as a share of revenues increased slightly. Again, please recall that these percentages represent the portion of resources that the US federal government must allocate simply to pay the interest on its debt.

Unfortunately for the American economy and taxpayer, the Congressional Budget Office and indeed most forecasters expect the US federal interest wedge—interest costs as a share of revenues—to rise over the next decade. This means less and less of the resources—taxes—collected by the US government will actually be spent on services. More and more of these resources will be spent simply servicing the existing debt—interest costs—from previous spending. More specifically, the Congressional Budget Office expects the US federal government to be spending an extraordinary one out of every six dollars of revenues collected in 2019 simply to pay the interest on the national debt.[35]

It is quite clear from the CBO analysis that deficits, debt, and the required interest costs incurred to finance them are expected to increase over the next ten years. These costs will restrict the flexibility and options available to the US federal government for the foreseeable future. More specifically, the larger deficits and the necessary rise in debt and interest costs mean that the reforms required for the US government to bring taxing and spending into balance will be more painful and potentially take more time because the magnitude of the problems are worsening rather than improving. This supertanker cannot turn on a dime.

This is an important insight with respect to the opportunity available to Canada. Our conclusion is not that the US economy is about to implode. Far from it, we believe the entrepreneurial capitalism[36] that exists at the heart of the US economy will persevere and return to a path of economic expansion. The latest CBO estimates, for example, indicate real growth in the US economy of 2.8 per cent in 2010, 3.8 per cent in 2011, robust economic growth of 4.5 per cent in 2012 and 2013, and then more moderate growth of 2.4 per cent in the out years of their estimate (2014 to 2019).[37] However, the combination of higher government spending, larger deficits and debt, and rising interest costs will constrain what the US federal government can do, particularly with respect to taxes. It is this constraint on the US federal government that heightens the opportunity in

Canada to create lasting economic advantages, which will be detailed later in the book.

Spending Increases

Understanding Washington's finances is indispensable to understanding the opportunity at hand for Canada. The US government suffers both from an inability to control spending and an aversion to match spending with current-year tax revenues (i.e., using deficits to finance current spending). The result of this fiscal sleight of hand is that at some point, future taxpayers will have to pay for the goods and services being financed now through deficits. America's future therefore holds less public spending, more taxes, or most likely both.

In real terms (i.e., eliminating the effects of inflation), the US federal budget has grown from $1.6 trillion in 1980 to an estimated $3 trillion in 2008.[38] Once the stimulus package[39] and omnibus spending bills are included,[40] federal spending skyrocketed by $1 trillion in a single year, 2009, alone. Put another way, federal spending in 2009 increased by nearly a third, to almost $4 trillion. In addition, some of the so-called temporary spending included in the stimulus bills looks like it will become part of the permanent, ongoing spending by the federal government.[41]

Again, let's think about all this share of the economy (GDP) being devoted to government spending. When viewing government spending as a share of the economy, two historical trends are evident. One, Washington's spending was declining as a share of the economy between 1983 and 2000. This is particularly important. The size and in many ways the scope of the federal government declined, albeit to varying degrees, under three consecutive presidents—Reagan, Bush Sr., and Clinton; two Republicans and one Democrat. In fact, the largest declines in federal government spending compared to the economy took place not under, say, the Republican Ronald Reagan but rather under the Democrat, Bill Clinton. On Clinton's watch, federal government spending as a share of the economy declined markedly, from 22.1 per cent in 1992 to 18.4 per cent in 2000. Again, recall that the key feature of declining government spending as a share of the economy is the increasing reliance on individuals, families, and businesses to make decisions about the use and allocation of society's resources, which they tend to do much better than government. In other words, under President Clinton, individual Americans were increasingly in control of and making decisions about the resources of the US economy compared to the national government.

The reforms enacted during the Clinton administration might well have been a more permanent turning point in American fiscal history had they been built upon and continued by the subsequent Bush administration. However, the second period, beginning in 2000, shows government spending as a share of the economy beginning to increase, in part illustrating a departure from the successful fiscal policies of the Clinton administration. By 2008, the last year of the Bush administration, federal government spending as a share of the economy reached 21 per cent of GDP[42] compared to an average of 19.9 per cent under the Clinton administration.[43]

This may be the best indicator of how large a difference exists between the fiscal policies implemented under the previous Democratic president, Clinton, and those implemented by President Bush and now being pursued by President Obama.[44] Virtually all of the spending discipline introduced in the Clinton years has now been cast aside. The Congressional Budget Office expects US federal spending as a share of GDP to average 23.4 per cent over the 2010 to 2019 period, which doesn't include the spike in stimulus spending in 2009.[45]

The specific numbers are, however, less important than the overall trend, which is clearly for the federal government to assume a larger role in the economy, at least as measured by the government's spending. In other words, rather than recognize and adopt the successful policy mix of the Clinton administration during the 1990s that saw deficits reduced and eventually turned into surpluses, the current administration and Congress are intent on continuing the spending policies of the Bush administration coupled with higher deficits, more debt, and eventually, inevitably, increasing taxes and cuts in spending.[46]

New Revenues Don't Help

Two fairly clear periods emerge when revenues are compared with spending. The first begins with the Reagan administration and ends on a high note with the Clinton administration. This extended period is generally characterized by rising revenues and falling government spending as a share of the economy. This combination of rising revenues and declining spending is most pronounced under the Clinton administration; it was this combination that produced the budget surpluses now seen as one of Clinton's greatest achievements. The rising revenues were largely a result of a robust economy rather than increasing tax rates. Indeed, after 1994, a number of important tax cuts were implemented by the Republican Congress and Democratic president.

The exact opposite trend begins in 2000: falling revenues combined with increased spending. The reduction in government revenues as a share of the economy is the result of both weakness in the economy post-2001 and a series of tax cuts enacted by the federal government. And it is generally this latter mix of policies, namely increasing spending without sufficient revenues, which the Obama administration is advocating for America over the next decade.[47]

State and Local Governments: With Friends Like These . . .

Like Canada and its provinces, the United States is composed of strong states that have taxing and spending authorities. Although the United States is more centralized than Canada, and its states are not in practice as powerful as our provinces, it is still important to understand how the decisions of the states contribute to the overall fiscal position of the United States.[48]

Maxing Out the State Credit Card

State and local debt has also increased over the past thirty years, although not as badly as Washington's. This is important to note, since almost every state's constitution prohibits it from running operating deficits, which should limit its ability to incur debt. None the less, state and local debt increased as a share of the economy from 11.6 per cent in 1980–81 to 16.7 per cent in 2005–06.[49]

The years between those two periods are generally characterized by a stable level of state and local debt as a share of the economy: 15.3 per cent in 1985–86 and 15.3 per cent in 2000–01.[50] Please recall, however, that the 1990s were generally a very prosperous period characterized by low unemployment and strong economic growth.[51]

Not surprisingly, as the debt of the state and local governments has increased, so too has the interest owed on that debt. In real terms (i.e., stripping out the effects of inflation), annual interest costs for the states and localities has increased from $48.6 billion in 1980–81 to $103.8 billion in 2005–06.[52]

Lots of Taxing and Spending to Go Around

Like the US federal government, the taxing and spending of the US states and municipalities has been increasing over the last three decades, although not to the same extent. Removing the effects of inflation, aggregate spending by the states and municipalities has increased from $860.7 billion in 1980 to an estimated $2 trillion in 2008.[53] Revenues have also increased in real terms (i.e., inflation-adjusted) from $883.7 billion to $1.9 trillion.

More important, however, is the growth of state and local government compared to the economy.[54] The tax take of states and local governments was just over 12 per cent of GDP in 1980. By 2008 this had risen to a little over 13.5 per cent of GDP.[55] More striking, however, is the increase in spending by these governments. Total state and local expenditures increased from a little under 12 per cent of GDP in 1980 to just over 14 per cent in 2008.[56] Although less pronounced than the increases at the federal level, both spending and revenues for state and local governments have been increasing over the last thirty years as a share of the economy. So, like Washington, states and municipalities have been increasing their take of the economy, which necessarily means more political decisions and fewer private decisions in the US. In other words, governments at all levels in the US have become more prominent at the expense of individuals, families, and businesses.

The state of US fiscal policy is more than a little worrisome.[57] Indeed, a number of government agencies, including the non-partisan Congressional Budget Office, have concluded that the current fiscal policies of the United States are "unsustainable" and threaten the long-term prosperity of the US economy.[58] In other words, there is increasing recognition that the current mix of spending, taxing, and borrowing simply cannot continue and that, at some point, change will become unavoidable.

The US federal government, along with the states, has increased spending over time, resulting in a larger government. They have not, however, financed this expansion of government with current taxes. Rather, both the federal government, and to a lesser extent the states, have decided to borrow to finance this largesse.[59] The growth in government debt has meant increasing interest costs compared to revenues, and those costs are expected to increase even further over the next decade. The pernicious fiscal policies of the federal government (i.e., more and more spending financed by borrowing) and to some extent similar policies among the states have created a difficult and unsustainable fiscal environment: spending cannot continue to increase—either taxes must increase or spending must be cut, or some combination of the two.

The state of US finances is critical in understanding the Canadian opportunity in that the mix of policies in place right now in the US is increasingly placing the country in a fiscal straitjacket with very limited options. We have no doubt that the US will turn the corner and begin rectifying these problems and that the entrepreneurial nature of the US economy will continue to provide economic growth and opportunity. In the interim, however, these destructive fiscal policies by government will weigh on the US economy by restricting governments' ability to enact meaningful reform and in particular tax relief. This opens the door for Canadian reforms that are proactive in establishing lasting economic advantages.

ARE AMERICANS ENTITLED TO THEIR ENTITLEMENTS? SOCIAL SECURITY AND MEDICARE chapter seven

As startling and worrying as the previous chapter may be, it is far from the entire story. Indeed, the state of US finances is much worse once future obligations such as the US Social Security program[1] and Medicare are included.[2] These programs are similar to Canada's public pension plan and health care system in that specific benefits are promised to citizens over time. Unlike Canada, however, the United States is aggressively increasing promised benefits across a number of different programs without bothering to match these cost increases with new income.[3] These rising but unfinanced obligations tighten what was already a very tight-fitting fiscal straitjacket that will afford the United States very little, if any, fiscal flexibility for the foreseeable future.[4]

Social Security

Before discussing the hole in the finances of Social Security, let's spend a moment looking at its benefits and comparing them to the Canada Pension Plan benefits available to Canadians.

Social Security does more than just provide retirement income. It also includes survivor benefits, disability benefits, and a supplemental income program.

The best-known Social Security benefit provides retirement income based on the employment earnings of individuals over their working lives. The current maximum payment provided for someone retiring in 2009 at age 66[5] with maximum earnings eligibility is $2,323 per month. As of 2009, these transfers are financed by a payroll tax of 12.4 per cent on taxable earnings up to $106,800.[6] By contrast, the maximum monthly benefit for the Canada Pension Plan for 2009 was $909.75[7] and the payroll tax that underwrites the CPP is set—sustainably—at 9.9 per cent. Social Security, like the CPP, also provides for benefits for survivors such as widows and children in certain circumstances, as well as a disability benefit.

Largely unknown, even to many Americans, is the Supplemental Security Income (SSI) program.[8] This program provides supplemental income financed by general taxes rather than the social security tax to low-income seniors and people with disabilities. This program is similar to Canada's Guaranteed Income Supplement (GIS).[9] Supplemental Security Income is meant to provide a means-tested minimum amount of income to cover basic necessities such as food, clothing, and shelter. As of 2009, the current maximum benefit is $674 for an individual and $1,011 for a couple.[10]

Each year the trustees of Social Security and Medicare issue reports detailing the current operation of the programs as well as prospects for the future.[11] According to the 2009 annual report of the Social Security trustees, the annual cost of Social Security will begin to exceed revenues collected from the payroll tax in 2016, a year earlier than estimated in the previous annual report. At that point, the notional assets[12] of the fund will begin to be drawn down and will be fully exhausted in 2037.[13]

To understand the enormity of this problem, the trustees highlight the fact that to solve the financial shortfall immediately would require a 16 per cent increase in the payroll tax, from 12.4 to 14.4 per cent, an immediate reduction in benefits of 13 per cent, or some combination of the two.[14] These estimates, however, are fairly optimistic in that, for example, they assume the increased revenues would be saved and invested.[15] What is indisputable is that the spending pressures emanating from Social Security on the federal government will increase in the future and further constrain US federal finances.[16]

Last year's dire warnings about the unfunded costs and future tax increases and/or benefit reductions required to keep Social Security solvent are consistent with previous annual reports. The implication of the findings is relatively clear: there are simply not enough expected revenues and accumulated assets to cover the expected costs of Social Security in the future without increasing taxes, decreasing benefits, and/or increasing borrowing. It seems evident that some combination of these rather unpopular alternatives will have to be implemented at some point to sustain the Social Security program.[17]

There is an additional consideration to ponder: political constraints. The leading edge of the vote-rich baby boomer generation is entering retirement; the rest of that generation is well into planning for their retirement and plans on drawing on Social Security when they do retire. In these circumstances, it is unclear how a political coalition could be constructed in favour of reforming Social Security if reform meant any cuts in benefits for those retired or about to retire. In addition, given the enormity of the obligations, any move to reform would likely require a longer phase-in or transition period than observed in other countries where public pension schemes have successfully been reformed.[18]

Medicare

In 2008 the US Government Accountability Office (GAO)[19] characterized the long-term deficit and fiscal outlook of the United States as unsustainable, largely because of rising health care costs and demographic changes.[20] The Congressional Budget Office recently analyzed the long-term budget outlook for the federal government and concluded that it was unsustainable, in large part due to rising costs emanating from Medicare[21] and Medicaid.[22] Indeed, there is a fairly broad consensus that the problems in Medicare far exceed the already daunting ones observed in Social Security.[23]

Before discussing the specific current status and future expectations of Medicare, it is important first to have a broad understanding of the program. It's also important to differentiate between Medicare and Medicaid.[24]

Medicaid is a state-delivered program aimed at providing low-income people with hospital and medical coverage. Medicare is the national health insurance program for people over the age of sixty-five. The program is partially financed by a payroll tax of 1.45 per cent for both employer and employee for a total of 2.9 per cent of eligible income, assessed alongside Social Security.

Medicare is divided into four distinct programs. Hospital insurance, commonly referred to as Part A, covers in-patient care and some related expenses. Medical insurance, or Part B, assists in paying for doctor services and related medical services that are not covered by hospital insurance. Medicare Advantage, Part C, is an option for Medicare beneficiaries to use private plans to provide for the benefits covered in parts A and B. Finally, the recently added prescription drug coverage, or Part D, covers prescription drugs and some related treatments.

The conclusions contained in the trustees' report for Medicare are even more dire than those for Social Security. Spending on hospital insurance, which is funded by the payroll tax, already exceeds revenues, and the notional trust fund is expected to be exhausted by 2017.[25] The report characterized the state of the hospital insurance fund as an "urgent concern,"[26] which is fairly strong language for this type of report. The extent of the problem is highlighted by the immediate solutions offered by the trustees' report: a 134 per cent increase in the payroll tax, from 2.9 per cent to 6.78 per cent; a 53 per cent reduction in spending; or some combination of the two.

The report also concluded that financial concerns for Part B of Medicare, the supplementary medical insurance portion, and for Part D, the prescription drug coverage program, were less urgent because the legislation for this program automatically provides financing for its costs. The report, however, ignores the effects of increasing costs in these programs on general government finances. Specifically, as the costs escalate for these two programs, taxes do not rise. Rather, existing tax revenues are automatically diverted to pay for these two programs. Since these diverted revenues are already being spent on other things, increasing pressure will be placed on the finances of the federal government. To sustain the remaining government programs, and indeed finance expanded programs and services as proposed by the Obama administration, additional resources (i.e., taxes) will have to be raised.

Orszag Tells It Like It Is

Dr. Peter Orszag, President Obama's director of the Office of Management and Budget, analyzed the cost pressures and tax implications of Social Security and Medicare when he was director of the Congressional Budget Office. In a May 2008 response to the congressional Committee on the Budget, then CBO director Orszag concluded that *primary spending* by the federal government (i.e., including Social Security and Medicare, national defence, and the various services provided by government but excluding interest on the national debt) would increase from 18 per cent of GDP in 2007 to 28 per cent in 2050 and 35 per cent by 2082.[27] These estimates were recently reaffirmed by the Congressional Budget Office in an analysis of the US federal government's longer-term fiscal outlook.[28]

More tellingly, Orszag's analysis included a set of likely implications for taxation in the United States as the result of the cost pressures of Social Security and Medicare. He concluded that:

> Individual income tax rates would have to be raised by about 90 per cent to finance the projected increase in spending between 2007 and 2050. The lowest tax rate on individual income would have to be increased from 10 percent to 19 percent; the tax rate on incomes in the current 25 percent bracket would have to be increased to 47 percent; and the highest statutory rate would have to be raised from 35 percent to 66 percent. The top corporate income tax rate would also have to increase from 35 percent to 66 percent.[29]

A Whole Lot of Obligations

The Peter G. Peterson Foundation[30] is dedicated primarily to raising awareness of the enormity of the financial obligations being loaded onto future generations of Americans and providing solutions to this problem. Their recent documentary, *I.O.U.S.A.*, was nominated for an Academy Award.

One of the Peterson Foundation's endeavours is to regularly calculate the total value of debt and program obligations owed by Americans. In 2008, the latest year for which an update was available, the total value of program obligations, which includes Social Security, Medicare, publicly held debt, and civil service retirement benefits, was $56.4 trillion.[31] This represented a debt of $184,000 per American in 2008. There is no doubt, given the budget and reports discussed above, that the 2009 update will show an increase in the total debt and obligations of Americans well in excess of $57 trillion. Yes, that is trillions, with a "t."

It is abundantly clear that the United States has prepared a rod for its own back; some combination of tax increases, benefit reductions, and/or additional debt financing is unavoidable now to manage the pressures of

Social Security and Medicare over the next decade and beyond. These pressures simply add to an already difficult and unsustainable financial position for the country.

The fiscal condition of the United States is troubling. It seems clear that under even the best economic conditions, the US will continue to run deficits for at least the next decade, increasing its national debt and the interest costs needed to service that debt. This fiscal reality, coupled with the dire state of Social Security and government health care programs, means that US public finances will be in a painful vise grip for the foreseeable future.

It will take enormous effort and unusual bipartisanship to tackle these problems and the solutions will be neither easy nor quick because the US has delayed reforms for so long that the problems are now much larger than they could have been. It will take time to correct these problems, but we're confident that the United States will solve them eventually. In addition, no one should underestimate the power and strength of the entrepreneurial capitalism that characterizes the US economy. In the interim, however, there is a real opportunity for Canada to create and extend an economic advantage based on a better business and investment environment than our friends to the south will enjoy. We need feel no discreditable *schadenfreude* to recognize that our own hard work has created an opportunity for us, and we should not hesitate to seize it.

NOT WHAT THE FOUNDERS HAD IN MIND: REPRESENTATION WITHOUT TAXATION chapter eight

The US government will clearly face some challenging fiscal decisions over the next two decades or so, including reforming government spending and major programs like Social Security, to place their financial house in order and achieve a sustainable set of fiscal policies. While we're confident that the resilience and ingenuity of the US system will triumph and thrive, these pressures will impose costs on the larger US economy. And we have by no means exhausted the economic challenges to which America must rise in the coming decades. Over that time, our southern neighbour will experience profound pressures that will inevitably leave it a different nation than the one that stands next to us now. Importantly, the US tax system currently poses a number of challenges to the country's economy that likely cannot be tackled until the larger problems of deficits, debt, and government spending are solved. These are important to at least acknowledge, since they again amplify the Canadian opportunity and provide some contours in terms of the reforms needed in Canada to capitalize on this historic opportunity.

Taxes: Not As Competitive As You Think

The US economy faces four principal economic challenges embedded within the country's tax system that are worthy of note.

The first, which is generally recognized, is that the US tax system is highly complicated and imposes enormous compliance costs on taxpayers and the US economy as a whole.[1] Put more simply, it is nearly impossible for average citizens and small businesses to navigate the labyrinth of the US tax system. This necessitates the use of tax accountants and lawyers to a greater extent than most countries.

Canada already possesses, to some extent, an advantage over the United States in this area,[2] although recent federal budgets have increased the complexity of our country's tax system,[3] thus reducing this advantage.[4] After all, outside of tax accountants and attorneys, very few people in an economy benefit from complicated, convoluted tax codes. It is increasingly acknowledged that such complications in the tax system impose enormous costs on society.[5]

The other three problems, which are generally not well known or understood, relate to (a) the total tax burden incurred by Americans; (b) the tax structure or mix used in America to collect needed revenues; and (c) the distribution of the tax burden. The surprising and counterintuitive result is that America is no longer the low-tax jurisdiction it once was. Compared to other countries, it relies on costly—less efficient—taxes, and it increasingly collects taxes from a shrinking group of taxpayers. These considerations are important to understand, since they place additional constraints on the United States in terms of the choices available to them in the future for reform and magnify the opportunity for Canadian reform.

Who's Smaller Now?

Many analysts have examined government revenues, or the more narrow measure of tax revenues, among industrialized countries and concluded that the United States imposes a smaller tax burden than most other nations.[6] The problem with this analysis is that it ignores deficits, which, as we know, simply push today's taxes off into the future. Once deficits are properly understood as a (deferred) tax, the US tax advantage is significantly reduced, if not eliminated.

Indeed, one of the most revealing comparisons between Canada and the United States is that of total revenues, including deferred taxes, or deficits, compared to the size of the economy. Such a measurement really focuses attention where it belongs: on spending, which is ultimately the driver of taxation.

The following graph illustrates all government spending in Canada and the United States as a share of the economy beginning in 1990. The decline in government spending in Canada since 1992 is nothing short of remarkable. As discussed in the Canadian chapters, government spending declined from a high of 53.3 per cent of the economy in 1993 to 39.1 per cent in 2007. It has since inched up to 43.6 per cent as a result of the recession and increased government spending in Canada.[7] However, the longer term trend in Canada is clearly towards less government compared to the economy.

The story in the United States is quite different. While Canada markedly reduced government spending compared to the larger economy, the US has been increasing since 2000. Indeed, the gap between the two countries in terms of the size of government spending has narrowed from nearly 40 per cent in 1991 and 1992 to just 2.3 per cent in 2008. The gap increased slightly in 2009, although again the trend towards eliminating the gap is clear.[8]

Total Government Spending as a Share of GDP

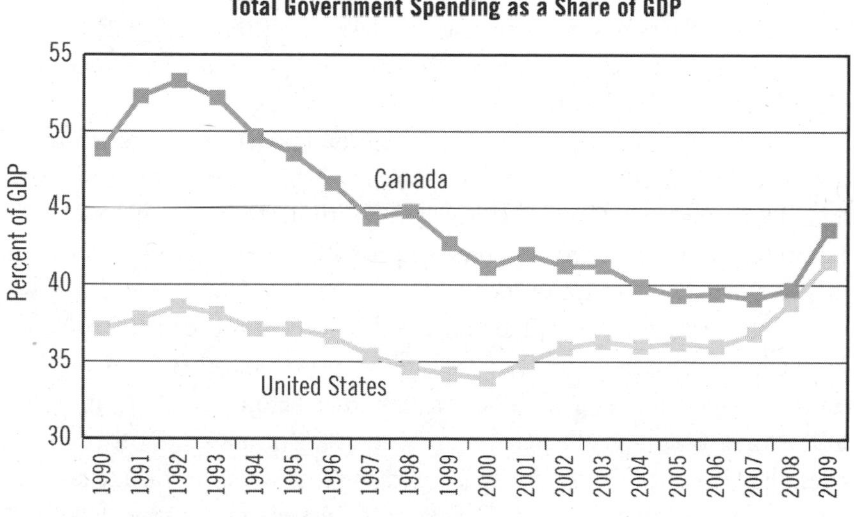

Source: OECD *Economic Outlook*, No. 86, November 2009 and No.83, June 2008

The trend line for spending in the United States is going in one direction and one direction only—up. It is easily foreseeable that in the next few years, the size of government, and thus the burden of government (i.e., taxes, including deficits) will be *less* in Canada than in the United States.

The Need to Remix the Tax Cocktail

Another important consideration is the mix of taxes used by the United States compared to other countries, particularly Canada. The reason this matters is that different taxes impose different costs on society. All taxes influence behaviour in one way or another.[9] The trick in designing tax policy is to minimize these costs. For example, studies have repeatedly shown that personal and corporate income taxes impose very high costs on society by reducing the incentives for work effort, entrepreneurship, saving, and investment, which are all beneficial activities to society. In other words, when countries rely on these types of taxes, they tend to get less work effort, entrepreneurship, savings, and investment than they otherwise would, which results in a less prosperous country. A less prosperous country is one with less employment opportunities, higher unemployment, lower levels of business investment, and less entrepreneurship. Everyone should agree that these are things we want more of and benefit extraordinarily from when they're present.

Other taxes, such as sales or consumption taxes, have far less destructive effects.[10] Indeed, the research investigating the differing costs of taxes, including research in Canada, is nearly unanimous that certain taxes, such as capital-based and income taxes, impose higher costs on society than others, such as consumption tax.[11]

A challenge for the United States is that it relies more heavily on corporate income taxes, which impose higher costs than other taxes and less on consumption taxes, which have much lower economic costs, in terms of the total revenues collected by government. Compared to other countries, the US collects more income taxes and less consumption taxes. For instance, according to the OECD, corporate income taxes represented 11.8 per cent of total tax revenues in 2006, the latest year for which information is available.[12] In fact, the proportion of US revenues contributed by corporate income taxes has been increasing since 1985, when they constituted 7.5 per cent of total revenues.[13] In addition, President Obama has expressed his interest in raising more revenues from businesses.[14]

The United States' nearly 12 per cent reliance on corporate income taxes is only slightly higher than Canada's 11 per cent and the OECD average of 10.7 per cent. However, the trend line in both Canada and many

OECD countries is to reduce reliance on corporate income taxes because of their damaging effects.

At the same time, the United States collected a mere 3.9 per cent of total taxes in the form of consumption taxes compared to 7.6 per cent for Canada and an OECD average of 10.5 per cent.[15] This is a critical consideration given the much lower costs imposed on citizens, workers, and the economy as a whole when consumption taxes are used to raise revenues.

In addition—and this is critical to understanding the dilemma the United States faces—most industrialized countries, including Canada, are dramatically reducing their corporate taxes, including the corporate income tax rate. The US, meanwhile, remains stuck in the status quo.[16] For example, while the United States' federal corporate income tax rate has remained at 35 per cent for years, Canada has reduced its federal corporate income tax rate from 28 per cent to 19 per cent, with further reductions to 15 per cent planned over the next two years. Most provinces have also reduced their corporate income tax rates, as the federal government and the provinces converge on a planned 25 per cent combined rate.[17] Indeed, the United States now has the second-highest statutory corporate income tax rate in the industrialized world.[18] This simply makes the US uncompetitive when it comes to the burden of business taxes, which has an influence on where businesses invest and expand. Countries with business taxes so far out of line with their competitors will inevitably pay a price in lower levels of investment, employment, and growth.

The recognition that the US maintains a much more complicated tax system than most countries, and certainly more complicated than Canada's, coupled with the acknowledgment that it relies too heavily on inefficient and thus economically costly taxes, results in a clear conclusion: the US needs major tax reform. Such reform would include simplifying the tax system but also changing the mix of taxes used.

Who Pays the Bill?

The deterioration of the US's tax advantage, its complicated tax rules, and its mix of taxes that rely too heavily on inefficient taxes are not the only structural problems present in the country's tax system. Unfortunately, there is another problem in the tax system that may actually be one of the biggest barriers to reform: the distribution of taxes.

The distribution of taxes simply refers to who pays the tax burden. The following analysis relies on data collected and organized by the CBO.[19] It analyzes income and taxes by breaking the population (households) into groups ("quintiles," each quintile representing one-fifth of all taxpayers) based on their income and then examines the amount and percentage of the tax burden each group pays.[20]

For the most recent year available, 2006, the bottom 20 per cent of households earned 4.7 per cent of total after-tax income. They incurred 0.8 per cent of the total federal tax burden. If only individual income taxes are analyzed, the bottom 20 per cent of households were actually net beneficiaries of the tax system. They got more in transfers than they paid in taxes. The analysis for the next 20 per cent of households is similar: they earned 9.5 per cent of total after-tax income in 2006 and incurred 4.1 per cent of the total federal tax burden.

A very different and indeed more pronounced situation exists for higher-income households. The top 20 per cent of households earned a little over half, 52.1 per cent, of all the after-tax income in 2006 but incurred 69.3 per cent of the total federal tax burden. In other words, their share of the federal tax burden exceeded their share of after-tax income by a little over a third. The results are even more stark when the top 1 per cent of households are examined: they earned 16.3 per cent of total after-tax income in 2006 but incurred 28.3 per cent of the total federal tax burden.[21]

Another way to look at these data is to consider the fact that only the top fifth of households incur a higher burden of federal taxes[22] than their share of after-tax income. In other words, the redistribution of income in the US is highly skewed from the top to the rest of the households. This effectively means that for at least four out of five households in the US, their share of taxes paid is less than their share of after-tax income.

This high degree of redistribution becomes even more pronounced once the provision of goods and services by government is accounted for. In other words, if we examine both the revenues raised by government—taxes—as well as the services those revenues are used to provide, the redistribution of resources from one group of Americans to another becomes even more pronounced. The Tax Foundation,[23] a non-partisan Washington, DC, research organization specializing in tax-related issues, completed a study in 2007 examining the tax burden and the benefits of government spending.[24] The study calculated the ratio of benefits received per dollar of taxes paid by US households. The calculations included federal, state, and local spending. The top 20 per cent of households received $0.41 in benefits per dollar paid in taxes. This compared to $8.21 in benefits received per dollar of taxes for the bottom 20 per cent of households.[25]

This imbalance between the share of income earned compared to the share of taxes paid and benefits received from government programs illustrates a major barrier to budget reform in the US. A clear and growing majority of Americans receive benefits, in some cases large benefits, from the government while contributing little, if anything, by way of taxes.[26] Such a dynamic, when it reaches these proportions of the population, makes it politically difficult to reverse the pattern of benefits and redistribution, at least in the short to medium term.[27]

The reason the pronounced imbalance between who pays and who benefits from government creates a barrier to change is that, to reform programs and services, politicians would have to propose reforms that adversely affected the majority of citizens, at least in the short run. Such a scenario makes it politically disadvantageous to pursue genuine and effective reform. It is much easier to extract resources from a minority of the population, in this case upper-income households, and redistribute the proceeds to the majority of households. This dynamic, therefore, is a serious barrier to reform, whether to specific programs like Social Security, Medicaid, or Medicare, or general government spending and taxes.

Conclusion

Just as Canada's reputation as a high-tax jurisdiction is increasingly undeserved, the United States' low-tax advantage has lingered in memory long after the reality has been eroded; moreover, the erosion will continue and perhaps accelerate as the pressures of current spending increases are coupled with the future onslaught of Social Security and Medicare/Medicaid spending. These pressures are only aggravated by the fact that the United States relies relatively more on high-cost taxes, such as corporate and individual income taxes, and not enough on lower-cost taxes, such as consumption or sales taxes. The extraordinarily complicated and confusing nature of the US tax code exacerbates this already troubling situation. Finally, the increasing imbalance between the shares of income earned by households, compared to their federal tax burden, will act as a barrier to reform now and in the future.

This imbalance actually acts to promote more and more demands on government in the US by more and more households because a majority now realize that they can demand services from government and have the costs passed on to others—whether high-income taxpayers today or future taxpayers when the bill for government debt falls due. These more structural issues are subtler and less apparent than the debt and deficit issue, but they impose real costs on the US economy and act as extra barriers to reform.

The reforms undertaken successfully by Canada in the Redemptive Decade have stood the country in good stead during turbulent and prosperous times alike. The United States has generally failed to achieve reforms that come even close to matching those achieved in Canada. The US is plagued by unrelenting deficits, mounting debt, and increasing interest costs that together weigh like a monumental anchor on the country's governments and their prospects to reform government programs and reduce taxes. These problems are only exacerbated by current proposals for even more government spending, larger deficits and debt, and expanded government programs.

Worse, the financial position of the United States will be eroded further as the obligations for Social Security, Medicare, and Medicaid come due over the next decade. Yet those who control the levers of power currently seem quite intent on continuing the ill-considered policies of the past eight years, namely more spending, taxing, deficits, debt, and unfunded obligations.

It is the failure of past reform efforts in the United States, together with the current appetite to extend these failed policies in the future, that creates an enormous, historical opportunity for Canada. If we follow Laurier's plan, we can succeed at long last in establishing a real, long-lasting and broadly based economic advantage over the United States and in so doing create a beacon of prosperity within North America.

part IV

The Future Belongs to Canada . . . If We Want It

LAURIER'S UNFINISHED SYMPHONY chapter nine

All the preceding chapters amply justify this book's premise: that when Canada follows the master plan that Laurier envisaged, its people prosper and it is a magnet for the best that the world has to offer. Moreover, Laurier's plan is not parochial but of broad application. When the world followed his prescriptions, as it largely was doing before World War I, it knew unprecedented prosperity. As we saw in Chapter Two, however, war, depression, and revolution all intervened to drag us down.

In the period immediately following World War II, however, Canada and the United States together trod Laurier's path—open societies that welcomed investment, people, goods, and services; that kept the tax burden tolerably light, the public debt on a downward course, and government relatively small; and that encouraged and rewarded work, savings, investment, and entrepreneurship while discouraging dependence.

In the sixties, Canada began a nearly thirty-year love affair with an aggressively expanding state, turning an increasingly deaf ear to the entreaties of those who still hewed to Laurier's line. Taxes may not have risen enormously, but they certainly overtook those in the United States and we lost the competitive tax advantage Laurier thought crucial to our success given the relative strengths of the economies on either side of the border.

But even higher tax rates than those in the US were not enough; our politicians knew that there was little appetite to pay taxes commensurate with those decades' huge rise in social welfare programs, unemployment insurance, transfers to the provinces, and more. They accordingly took the easy and politically expeditious route of running up the public debt. In 1960 it took roughly 28 per cent of GDP to pay for the cost of government at all levels.[1] At the peak of the expansion of government and burgeoning public debt in 1992, it was taking 53 per cent of GDP[2] to pay all the government's bills, including interest on the debt, and the *Wall Street Journal* was calling Canada an honorary Third World country. By 1990, borrowed money was the second-largest source of government revenue, second only to the personal income tax and double what was raised from corporate income taxes.[3]

In a paroxysm of nationalist fervour, we threw up barriers to the free flow of capital looking to invest in Canada. The big-government zeitgeist in the Western world embraced our growing unemployment and fear of Quebec nationalism; the offspring of this union was social welfare programs enriched to the point where we were having major problems with welfare dependency and strong growth in low-performance public employment.[4] Our productivity, the real key to rising standards of living, grew at a much slower rate than in America.[5] In short, we did everything that Sir Wilfrid thought would deny us success. The potential for the Canadian century slumbered quietly within us, always there, frequently visited with dreams of greatness, but never quite wakened.

America trod a different path over these decades, at least to the extent that it never embraced the growth of the state, the rise of taxation, and the growth of dependency on social programs to the degree that we did. They were reluctant; we were enthusiastic. The share of GDP devoted to government at its peak in Canada rose to 53 per cent; America has only just passed the threshold of 40 per cent. But their trend is up, while ours has been down. On current trends, they will overtake us in a few short years.

In fact, therefore, Canada's opportunity to fill the twenty-first century arises from two separate sources. On the one hand, Canada has unwittingly begun to find its way back to Laurier's plan, while on the other hand, America is increasingly losing the script, flubbing its lines at the crucial moments as the plot unfolds. If Canada puts in place all the elements of the Laurier plan, it will propel our population to the forefront of global prosperity and development. If, in addition, America continues on its current course, Canada will find itself without peer in North America as a magnet for investment, for immigrants, for innovation, and for growth. This is not to suggest that the US economy will stagnate but rather that Canada will become a markedly preferred location for investment, business development, and entrepreneurship within North America due to both its improved business climate as well as its preferential access to every North American market, including the US. Some of the wealthiest economies in the world, places like Switzerland, Holland, Luxembourg, Taiwan, Singapore and Hong Kong, are often small, nimble, disciplined societies that carefully manage their relationship with a neighbouring behemoth. The opportunity of the Canadian Century does not require that America stagnate; indeed a stagnant America would drag Canada down. What our opportunity does require is that Canada raise its game above America's, and, thereby reap a disproportionate share of growth in our shared continental economy.

Free trade with the United States and the GST, both the product of Conservative government in Ottawa, began the process of putting us back on the path of virtue defined by Laurier. This was followed by further difficult and historic reforms enacted federally and in many provinces during the 1990s, reforms to which every political party and every region of the country contributed, such as the NDP in Saskatchewan, the Tories in Alberta and Ontario, and the Liberals in Ottawa, British Columbia, and New Brunswick. This consensus on reform, which breached party divisions, ideological divides, and regional differences, moved Canada toward a smaller, smarter government and in so doing ushered in a period of heightened economic prosperity. The combination of spending reductions, balanced budgets, reduced debt, and lower interest costs, coupled with important tax relief, fundamentally changed Canada for the better. Those reforms continue to benefit the country enormously even as governments, both federally and provincially, have failed to an ever-increasing extent to meet the standard of these core fiscal principles by allowing spending to increase dramatically and beginning to run deficits again. Still, the Canada we look upon today remains in many ways markedly different than it was prior to the Redemptive Decade.

This opportunity is further amplified by the near-absolute inability of our neighbours to the south to reform and deal with many of their critical problems. In many ways, the United States sits where Canada did in the early 1990s.

The question for Canadians now is whether our governments have the fortitude and vision to replicate the successful reforms of the Redemptive Decade to solve our current problems and extend the reforms to accomplish Laurier's vision for a Canadian century. In other words, do we aspire to achieve the type of prosperity and prominence envisioned by Sir Wilfrid when he foresaw a Canada that would be a light unto the world? "For the next seventy-five years, nay the next hundred years, Canada shall be the star towards which all men who love progress and freedom shall come."[6]

We believe and hope Canada is prepared to muster the fortitude and sense of direction that enabled governments at all levels and of all political persuasions to enact meaningful and in many cases historic reforms in the 1980s and 1990s. This final chapter addresses what we believe Canada and the provinces must do to replicate and then complete the reforms so well begun in those decades. If we succeed in completing the plan while America continues to founder, our reward will be that we will leave America's shadow and enter into the Canadian century, fulfilling Laurier's dream for the country he believed would lead the world.

Two sets of reforms are discussed in this section. The first, which are presented in some detail, are those that naturally flow from our discussions of the Canadian reforms and what needs to be done to build on them to bring Canada back in line with Laurier's plan. In parallel with that discussion, we look at the lack of reform in some key areas in the United States over the past few decades and look at the scale of the challenge to America in getting its fiscal house in order. In both cases, the reforms we will discuss are largely fiscal in nature: government spending, taxes, fiscal discipline, and the overall size—role—of government in our society.

Importantly, though, achieving the prosperity envisioned by Laurier is not just about returning the size of government and the tax burden to levels compatible with economic growth and progress; rather, to paraphrase former federal finance minister and prime minister Paul Martin, it is about smaller and smarter government. There is a whole set of issues that this book can only touch on but that are none the less important components of reform. These issues will be mentioned with references for additional reading. In addition, it is the plan of the Macdonald-Laurier Institute, which has supported this book, to publish future works that deal with these issues more thoroughly in order to create a more detailed and comprehensive plan of reform over time.

Canada's Discipline Deficit: Back to the Future

Canada has not been immune from the economic downturn that has troubled most of the world, although in many ways Canada has been one of the least affected.[7] That is not to say that Canada has not suffered or that the situation has not evolved very rapidly. Consider, for example, that in the federal government's budget, tabled in January 2009, it indicated that it would incur a small deficit for 2008–09 of $1.1 billion and a much larger deficit for the fiscal year 2009–10 of $33.7 billion.[8] As discussed in more detail previously, that budget responded to the precipitous economic downturn observed globally, as well as to domestic political forces, by implementing so-called stimulus spending.[9] In addition to those deficit forecasts, Ottawa at that time expected to operate in deficit for the next three fiscal years, accumulating deficits slightly in excess of $50.1 billion.[10]

Throughout 2009, the federal government's fiscal situation deteriorated considerably.[11] The federal government now expects the 2009–10 deficit to reach $55.9 billion, representing 3.7 per cent of GDP, and expects deficits to persist through to 2014–15. As a result, the national debt is now expected to increase from $463.7 billion in 2008–09 to $628.1 billion by 2014–15, an increase of $164.4 billion.[12]

The provinces are in a similar situation. While the provinces enjoyed a slightly larger collective surplus of $10.8 billion in 2007–08 compared to the federal government's surplus of $9.6 billion, they are now also experiencing a slightly lower collective deficit.[13] Specifically, the aggregation of the various provincial budgets indicates that the provinces will run a collective deficit of $514 million for 2008–09 and a much larger $23.2-billion collective deficit for 2009–10.[14] Given the deterioration in federal finances, it is likely that the provincial finances have also deteriorated in the interim.

The result of deficit financing last year, currently, and for the next few years means more debt, both federally and provincially, as well as higher nominal interest charges. There are two paths facing Canada, which in many ways are reminiscent of the decisions facing our country in the early 1990s. The federal and provincial government can either implement spending reductions to bring their respective budgets back into balance, which was the basis of the economic success and prosperity enjoyed in the 1990s, or they can continue to spend beyond their current means, resulting in either continuing deficits or increased taxes.[15] The lessons outlined in this book, both in terms of the successes of Canadian reforms and the near-absolute failures observed in the United States, strongly favour reducing spending over the next several years to return to balanced budgets. In fact, the simple winding down of what was supposed to be temporary stimulus spending should make a quick return to balanced budgets relatively easy, although the timing of such a withdrawal must be the subject of careful planning.[16]

Government Spending: The Source of Budget Deficits

It is important to understand the source of current and projected future deficits. Clearly, there has been a slowdown in the Canadian economy that has reduced revenues to governments. For example, the federal government's spring 2009 budget predicted revenues would fall to $224.9 billion in 2009–10.[17] The 2009 fall economic update estimated that revenues for 2009–10 would in fact only reach $216.6 billion, a $19.8-billion decline from 2008–09.[18]

However, both the 2009 federal budget and the more recent fall economic update both indicated an expectation that revenues would rebound beginning in 2010–11.[19] Indeed, the fall economic update showed revenues growing strongly, by an average rate of 6.6 per cent, starting in 2010–11 through to 2014–15.[20] Normally, such strong revenue growth would allow for a speedier return to balanced budgets than indicated by the federal government.

The real explanation for the current and future deficits in Canada is the increase in government spending. Even before the start of the recession, governments in Canada were increasing spending at an alarming rate. For instance, between 2000–01 and 2008–09, the federal government increased program spending at an average annual rate of 6.1 per cent, almost twice the rate required to maintain real per capita spending, which is 3.3 per cent. In other words, the federal government was increasing real per person spending in Canada fairly aggressively well before the recession.

This increase in ordinary spending has been compounded by the increase in temporary government spending to combat the recession. Canada is not alone in implementing special, temporary spending in an attempt to combat the recession.[21] For example, federal program spending spiked from $207.9 billion in 2008–09 to an estimated $241.9 billion in 2009–10.[22] In addition, there are a number of programs, such as employment insurance[23] and provincial welfare,[24] which are specifically designed so that spending increases during economic downturns. So federal and provincial spending has increased due to a combination of temporary stimulus spending to counteract the recession, growing program spending over time, and a number of countercyclical programs like EI that automatically increase during recessions.

If the bulk of the spending increase observed over the past year or so was either temporary or linked to cyclically sensitive programs like EI, one would expect federal spending to fall back to pre-recession levels with the end of the downturn.

Not so. Over the next five years, the federal government plans to increase nominal (i.e., not adjusted for inflation) program spending from $241.9 billion to $261.4 billion in 2014–15.[25] In other words, the increase in federal government program spending put in place in 2009–10, ostensibly to combat the recession, looks likely to remain post-recession and perhaps indefinitely. Put more colloquially, there is nothing more permanent than temporary government spending. It is this more permanent spending that Canadians should be concerned with.[26]

Although the expected growth in federal program spending of 1.6 per cent over the next five years is not a high rate in itself, it comes after that extraordinary recession-fighting increase in program spending of 16.4 per cent in 2009–10. The federal government has made no case as to why we should simply absorb this temporary stimulus spending into the government's ordinary spending plans. And that big spike comes on the heels of a near-decade-long streak of rising program spending beginning in 2000–01, which consistently rose faster than inflation and population. In some cases, the increases were startling: program spending increased by over $22 billion, or almost 15 per cent, in 2004–05 alone!

Spending has ballooned out of control, not just in Ottawa but in many provincial capitals, including Toronto and Edmonton. The recession has now become simply an excuse for it to get even further out of control. These are exactly the circumstances that got us into the mess the Chrétien–Martin reforms rescued us from, and we cannot lose or squander such hard-won progress. Like the dramatic reforms of the 1990s, Canada must move to balance the federal budget as soon as possible with no sacred cows protected.[27] However, the federal government must go further, and indeed should look to the review process and results achieved during the Chrétien–Martin era as a blueprint to reduce spending while getting better results through reform instead of just trying to slow the growth of federal spending.[28]

This same process must be replicated at the provincial and indeed municipal levels. Spending must not only be reduced but reformed.[29] Provinces and municipalities must commit to bringing their spending in line with revenues through spending reforms that yield better results through innovation.

Budgeting and Debt

Disciplined budgeting of the type established during the Chrétien–Martin era is an admittedly mundane but extremely effective measure that promises to return us to sustained but manageable prosperity. For example, governments should be forbidden from adopting overly optimistic revenue assumptions when writing a budget. Economic assumptions should be based on the consensus of forecasts from the private sector. The remedy here is removing politics from the budget. Disciplined budgeting guarantees only good surprises, as opposed to the bad surprises we have had in the past few years. This means the risks associated with the budget's assumptions will largely exist on the upside rather than the downside. Governments should also return to the practice of creating cushions against unexpected events (such as contingency and economic risk accounts) in order to ensure balanced budgets.

Government needs to be put on a very short leash: strict limits need to be imposed on additional spending beyond that approved in the budget each year. Traditionally, governments approve extra year-end spending before a budget period comes to an end. The proverbial principle of spend it or lose it seems to dominate the capitals during these periods. Such wasteful and unplanned spending should be prohibited. Not only would this mechanism introduce much-needed transparency to the notoriously opaque orgy of year-end spending sprees that are undertaken annually by every federal, provincial, and municipal department, but it would—if conservative projections prove *too* conservative—reward a fiscally prudent government with unexpected year-end money to pay down debt, which creates permanent savings through lower interest expenses. Indeed, the authors favour this type of debt reduction strategy to formal, legislated debt reduction.[30]

Tax Relief

The benefits of returning to a balanced budget and beginning back on a path toward cutting our debt is only a first step in the process of achieving Laurier's vision for our country. Once the country's fiscal house is placed back in order, a multi-year plan for tax relief must be implemented. The success of Canadian reforms in the 1990s and the dearth of change observed in the US offer us an opportunity to create a meaningful tax advantage over the United States and most industrialized countries over the next five years, once the government's finances are again balanced. Yes, that is correct. We believe Canada can establish a lasting tax advantage over the United States, just as Laurier recommended.

A multi-year plan for tax reductions should be prepared and enshrined in law. In many areas, Canada has already achieved tax competitiveness with the US. The next steps are to amplify that advantage, if it exists, or establish it, if it doesn't.

Personal Income Taxes

The first, largest, and most important tax reduction must be to reduce personal income taxes. Personal income taxes have been proven to influence a wide range of economic decisions and behaviour, from work effort, to savings and investment, to risk-taking, to entrepreneurship. These are all activities Canada should want to encourage and attract. Unfortunately, Canadian personal income tax rates remain too high and apply to relatively low levels of income, particularly when compared to the American tax rates.[31]

Although important reductions have been implemented, particularly during the Chrétien–Martin era, additional reductions are needed to heighten Canada's attractiveness as a destination for the brightest, most ingenious, and entrepreneurial people around the world.[32] In our view, personal income tax relief can best be achieved over the next five years by eliminating the middle-income tax brackets, leaving only one rate for the majority of citizens and one higher rate for upper-income Canadians. In addition, the threshold of income at which the top rate applies should be increased substantially.

These same tax-cutting principles should be applied in the provinces. Some provinces, like Alberta, already have a single rate tax in place. Most provinces, however, still have multiple tax rates that kick in at fairly low levels of income.[33] Provinces should generally move toward eliminating middle-income tax brackets, resulting in one rate for the majority of taxpayers and possibly a second rate applicable only to upper-income taxpayers along the lines proposed for the federal rates and thresholds.

The combination of personal income tax relief at the federal and provincial levels would constitute the overwhelming bulk of the tax relief we propose, although we will suggest other important tax reductions a bit farther on. These changes, coupled with tax relief already implemented in Canada and the likelihood of increased taxes in the United States, mean that Canada would now offer workers, investors, and entrepreneurs lower taxes across the board compared to the United States. Put differently, Canada would reward activities that we want more of—work effort, savings and investing, and entrepreneurship—compared to the United States by allowing people to keep more of the gains they earn through such activities.

Business Tax Relief—Who Is the High-Tax Jurisdiction Now?

As indicated, the personal income tax reductions outlined previously represent the bulk of the tax cutting we propose. However, there are a series of smaller tax cuts that we also believe are critically important if Canada is to capitalize on the opportunity before us.

For example, the federal government and the provinces should further reduce business taxes[34] in order to make Canada not only tax competitive but indeed to create that tax advantage over our competitors, and especially the Americans, that Laurier urged. Laurier thought that such a tax gap in favour of Canada would provide potential investors and businesses yet another reason to consider Canada—and he was right. Canada has recognized the costly and damaging nature of high business taxes—lower levels of investment, business development, and entrepreneurship—and moved to reduce a host of business taxes over the past decade. But being competitive is different from creating a lasting advantage. Additional reductions in the corporate income tax rate for the federal government and the provinces would create and solidify a business tax advantage.

Another, smaller business tax issue that could yield real benefits to the Canadian economy would be the elimination of corporate capital taxes for all firms, including financial companies. Canada began using capital taxes more vigorously during the 1980s and '90s as a way to reduce deficits. Most jurisdictions have moved away from imposing a capital tax on general firms because of this tax's extraordinarily high cost and distorting affects.[35] Unfortunately, many still impose it on financial firms, more for political reasons than economic ones.

Canadian financial firms were largely immune from the type of financial implosions witnessed in the US and Europe. This creates opportunities for Canadian financial firms to become more dominant international players and indeed for Canadian financial centres, such as Toronto, to become more competitive. A sector-specific tax, like the corporate capital tax on financial firms, impedes both these opportunities and, again, provides very little revenue.

These changes, along with reforms of provincial sales taxes, discussed below, will create an advantage for Canada in business taxes, particularly compared to the United States.[36] Such an advantage could yield real benefits in the way of increased investment and business development, as well as entrepreneurship for Canada.

Smaller But Nonetheless Important Tax Changes

A host of smaller tax changes could also be implemented to further Canada's advantage and move toward the attainment of the Canadian century. For example, the capital gains tax, which taxes the nominal appreciation of assets, has been shown to impose fairly large economic costs while not generating all that much revenue.[37] Indeed, the Chrétien–Martin regime acknowledged the negative effects of the capital gains tax and reduced the tax twice. In addition, in 2008 the Conservative Party implemented a new tax-free savings plan, which allows Canadians to invest after-tax money with no additional taxes paid on earnings in the accounts.[38] The combination of tax-deferred savings accounts, such as Registered Retirement Saving Plans (RRSPs) and pensions, coupled with the new tax-free savings plan and the allowances for small businesses, mean that many if not most Canadians can now significantly reduce or even avoid capital gains taxes.[39] This raises the question, however, of why we would maintain a tax that distorts economic behaviour and imposes economic costs, doesn't raise that much revenue, and if people are organized about their savings, they can to some extent avoid. A signal to the international investment community that dramatic changes are occurring in Canada that would not cost government all that much in the way of direct revenues would be the elimination of the capital gains tax.[40]

Another tax issue that *is* being solved relates to the design of our sales taxes. Sales taxes, to be effective, should tax the purchase of final goods and services rather than inputs into the creation of those goods and services. The GST, while vilified by most Canadians, represents an important tax reform achievement by the Mulroney Conservative government. The GST essentially taxes the final consumption of goods and services. Unfortunately, many provinces maintained independent sales taxes, which meant both that businesses had to keep two sets of financial records for their two sales taxes, federal and provincial, and that the provincial sales taxes were being applied to business inputs, making it more expensive to invest and develop one's business.

Many provinces have moved to correct this design problem.[41] Three of the Atlantic provinces (Newfoundland and Labrador, Nova Scotia, and New Brunswick) have already harmonized their provincial sales taxes with the GST, which means simply that the provincial sales tax piggybacks on the federal GST.[42] Quebec chose a slightly different route but achieved much of the gains observed in Atlantic Canada.[43] Now both British Columbia[44] and Ontario[45] have signalled that they too will harmonize their sales taxes with the federal GST.[46] Now only Saskatchewan, Manitoba, and Prince Edward Island are left to fix this problem.[47]

Decentralization—Key to Getting More From Less

Creating a lasting Canadian advantage is not just a matter of taxes. As our earlier discussions have illustrated, decentralized programs that not only permit but encourage innovation and experimentation are far more likely to outperform centrally planned and administered programs. The experience of Canadian and US welfare reform bears out this result. Canada must, however, go further in decentralizing, and in particular decentralize the most important and pressing public policy issue facing the country: health care.

Health Care: The Courage to Act

Canada's health care system has become the third rail of Canadian politics but is none the less in need of fundamental and sweeping reform.

Canadians and their government have shown the fortitude to tackle difficult policy challenges in the past, such as reforming the Canada Pension Plan and provincial welfare systems. Indeed, it is our practical and highly successful experience with provincial welfare reform as part of the package of reforms in the 1990s that provides our country with a road map for reforming health care.

As discussed at length in the Canadian chapters, the federal government changed the provinces' financial incentives with respect to welfare by moving away from federal transfers based on federal–provincial cost-sharing programs to a block-grant approach in which the amount transferred by the federal government to the provinces did not depend on how much the province spent on the programs. In the early days, the total amount transferred was also reduced. That was the trade-off: in return for more autonomy and less federal interference, the provinces had to accept less money from Ottawa. This change unleashed a wave of creativity, innovation, experimentation, and reform among the provinces that made welfare more effective and less of a disincentive to work while reducing costs.

Unfortunately, Canadian governments have not applied the lessons from welfare and CPP reform to health care. Instead, Canadian governments have collectively thrown tens of billions of dollars at our health care problem.[48] And while Canada has one of the world's most expensive health care systems, these costs are not accompanied by high performance.[49]

The status quo is simply not acceptable. Canadians can and should look to the success of welfare reform as a model for solving our country's health care problems. The simple reality is that the federal government must allow for greater experimentation and innovation by the provinces in designing and ensuring high-quality universal health care, and it must make the provinces pay attention to the need for reform by capping transfers for health, just as it reformed the way it helped pay for welfare spending. The result was not misery and poverty but more efficient and lower-cost programs.

This requires the federal government to amend the Canada Health Act to allow for and indeed encourage provincial reforms within the confines of universal health care coverage.

We would expect to see reforms common to all the provinces as well as province-specific health care changes, much like the response to welfare reform.[50] National reforms are those that make sense regardless of the region, population, or specific health trends of the area. In welfare, these reforms tended to be bringing benefit levels back in line with comparable work earnings.

The specific health care reforms that might be unleashed will obviously depend on the provincial governments in power at the time and the specific circumstances they find themselves in. However, examples of reforms that will almost certainly move quickly onto the agenda for serious consideration would include greater private sector delivery within the public universal health care system. The fact that there is a great deal of innovation along these lines in several provinces today shows that experimentation is already in play to some extent. And the reason that these experiments are proceeding is the increasingly widespread view that greater private sector involvement is almost inevitable and would be highly productive in terms of providing capital and investment, private sector know-how on delivery, and innovation.[51]

A second reform that might well win favour in some provinces is the introduction of some system of co-payments for users—consumers—of the health care system. Such a change would improve the consumption of health care and the health care decisions being made by individuals across the country. Currently, too many Canadians view their health care decisions as separate and distinct from the resources required to finance health care. Introducing a small co-payment, from which lower-income Canadians would be exempt, requires health care consumers to make more financially informed decisions. Put differently, we as consumers make different and better-informed decisions when we face financial incentives—that is, having skin in the game. International evidence shows that when patients are responsible for some of the cost of their care, they use fewer resources and end up no worse off in health outcomes.[52]

While there may be additional standard reforms implemented across the country, we would also expect much more variation and experimentation across the provinces, just as we saw in welfare reform. For instance, more urbanized provinces will likely pursue different types of reforms than more rural provinces. What we would also expect is that provinces would learn from one another as each experimented with different approaches. This is well-established as the best pathway to discovering what works and what doesn't.

What is not an option is the status quo whereby Canadians spend billions of dollars on a system that is not delivering high-quality health care commensurate with its costs. Fundamental reforms that recognize the strengths of the private sector and allow provinces to experiment and innovate are the keys to health care reform and success.

The sum of these measures equals the completion of one part of Laurier's plan. The freedom of Canadians would be increased as governments take less of their income and reform important public programs such as health care and EI—just as successfully as we did with welfare and the CPP.

Not only would the tax burden borne by Canadians fall, but we would have restored the tax advantage of Canada vis-à-vis our southern neighbours. And it is to our relations with those neighbours, and the world, that we now turn.

Self-Confident Engagement with the Americans

Early in this book, in our account of Laurier's plan for Canada, we wrote:

> Canada could not shrink before the challenge posed by American dynamism and proximity, but instead Canada must meet them head-on, turning them as best we could to our own account . . . We were not strong enough to impose our will on America. Laurier believed, therefore, that we had to play cleverly and well the few cards that we had been dealt.

Those words apply just as much to our situation today as they did in Sir Wilfrid's day. They describe an enduring verity about Canada's place in the world. But what does it mean today to play our few cards cleverly and well?

Laurier would not have recognized the words we use today to describe the cross-border relationship with America, and he would have marvelled at the size of the exchanges between our two nations. What he would have felt entirely at home with, however, is the perennial nature of the challenge Canada faces in managing its complex and indispensable relationship with America. The advice that Laurier gave to Canadians throughout his career is just as apposite as it was a century ago: we can neither neglect nor retreat from our relationship with America. We can only move forward and seek to shape it to our purposes.

Canadians' anxiety about and fear of America is the stuff of legends. Laurier learned to his cost that the reasonableness of the idea of protecting Canada's interests by binding the US to rules governing our relationship was not self-evident to everyone. John Turner came close to sinking the free trade ship during the 1988 federal election with his aggressively nationalist stance, which clearly struck a chord with many.

On the other hand, Canada has more than twenty years of experience with free trade with America, and whatever else we may have learned, two lessons from that experience stand out.

First, the major complaint about the Free Trade Agreement (FTA) is that it doesn't go far enough in removing from America's hands the tools it has used so often in the past to harm Canada's interests. The logic of that lesson impels us not to retreat from free trade, which would simply loosen the inadequate bonds restricting America's destructive power. Rather, we need to press on and complete, to the extent that we can, the taming of our neighbour.

The second lesson is that free trade is in no way incompatible with a separate Canadian identity and choices that are different in Canada than in the US. Free trade did not result in the abolition of medicare or regional development subsidies, any more than it dragged us into the war in Iraq or compelled us to participate in America's plans for a missile shield (the Strategic Defense Initiative, or SDI). Whatever the merits of the various decisions we took on those issues, the undeniable fact is that we took different decisions than the Americans and the sky did not fall, despite the fact that our economic integration has reached impressive levels under the protection of the FTA.

Now our level of integration within the continental economy is, if anything, even deeper than it was in 1988. Moreover, twenty years' experience of free trade with America has underlined the limitations of our current binational institutions. Canadians are thus squarely where we have always least wanted to be: in need of further engagement with America. But Laurier's advice to us was to have the courage not to shrink before this necessity. Providence and history have placed us here in North America, and prudence and self-interest have made us increasingly throw in our economic lot with America. Our future, as Laurier so clearly saw, can only be protected and enriched by nurturing this relationship and putting it on an ever sounder institutional footing.

Indeed, if there is a theme that dominates the thinking of those charged with reflecting on and managing this vast and unwieldy relationship, it is that the institutional and legal framework that supports our economic partnership is outdated, patchy, and insufficient. It is not to be cast aside, but certainly requires modernization and expansion, not least to respond to the weaknesses revealed by the anti-trade sentiment (especially among the trade unions), protectionism, and Buy American policies the present recession has given rise to.

The consensus is also that the impetus for change will need to come from Canada; the US simply has too many other pressing challenges (e.g., two wars, the Middle East, terrorism, nuclear proliferation, health care, financial sector reform, and other domestic issues), while the relationship with Canada gets the usual benign neglect reserved for those we feel we can take for granted. To get the attention of our neighbours will require us to come forward with our own proposal, our own plan for engagement, what some call a Big Idea (e.g., new institutions, a common tariff or customs union, etc.).[53] It will also indubitably require us to agree to make trade-offs, such as a greater commitment from Canada on issues of common continental security in the face of terrorist and other threats, because giving Americans the chance to get something they want is how we get their attention for our issues. In other words, Canada will need to follow Laurier's example of self-confident engagement with the Americans.

There are those who look at the current state of American public and elite opinion and see no hope of finding there the tools with which to build further on our common institutions. But this is to miss the significance of Laurier's own experience, as well as that of those who came before and after. Laurier pursued the goal of reciprocity with the US throughout his political career, but like Macdonald before him, he despaired of ever finding partners on the other side of the border who would be willing to deal. Laurier endured a long period of American jingoism at the highest levels, and it was a surprise to him when the Americans, on a change of administration, suddenly signalled their interest in and willingness to make progress, and quickly. Eternal vigilance is the price

Canadians must pay for the successful management of our relationship with America. When they are ready to deal, we must already have our game plan ready to go.

The American political system is composed of many powerful and conflicting interests held together in a state of barely maintained equilibrium. Tiny shifts in circumstance, in opinion, and in political power can propel interests and policies to the forefront, only to see them dissolve again like the last snow of spring on a change of administration or even a midterm shift in congressional power. It was only because Canada repeatedly and doggedly made known to America its desire to improve relations and to build institutional buttresses for our binational relations that reciprocity unexpectedly came back on the table in 1911. Even when relations with America seem at their most hopeless, the guiding principle for Canadian policymakers should always be "This too shall pass."

Indeed, if Laurier's experience and ours is anything to go by, the greatest risk to Canada is of inaction, not action. Think only of the recent conflict with state and local governments in the US over Buy American policies.

The free trade agreement with Washington, later subsumed under the North American Free Trade Agreement (NAFTA), bound the American federal government, but not the states or municipalities, in their purchasing policies. The agreement made provision for these other levels of government to be brought within its ambit, but this required energy and determination on Canada's part. One thing was sure: these other governments were not going to sign on without being given some reason to do so. Instead, Canada closed its eyes and hoped for the best. By failing to engage the Americans then at this level, we found ourselves with little legal or institutional protection for our exports destined for the huge public procurement market at the state and local level at precisely the moment when stimulus spending is making that market smoking hot.[54] We should take no comfort from the fact that we were able in extremis to negotiate some exemptions from Buy American. Placing ourselves in the position of being most vulnerable to America when they are least likely to want to deal is asking for trouble in the long run. The next time Lou Dobbs may be president.

Canadians have no one to blame but themselves for not pushing their advantage when trade was popular with Americans, free traders occupied the Oval Office, protectionist trade unions were weak, and we had the momentum following the deal at the national level. But this is an example of how we can and must do better, and how we cannot wait until we need better legal and institutional protections to negotiate them. By then, it is often too late.

Retreating from deeper integration with the Americans is simply not available as a choice, at least not without a wrenching decline in our standard of living. The issue is not the usual statistics trotted out in favour of free trade, that goods and services worth $1.9 billion cross the border every day, that we export 40 per cent of what we produce, and of that, nearly 80 per cent goes to the Americans, representing roughly half the production of Canada's private sector. It is not that thirty-seven states have Canada as their largest international market, although this is true and significant.[55]

It is rather the depth of the integration within companies and industries that really matters now. Forty per cent of all exports from Canada to the US are so-called intra-company trade, meaning that companies carry on integrated production processes on both sides of the border, moving pieces of production to one country or the other depending on the availability of expertise and capacity.[56] And this very high degree of integration happens not just within companies but within industries as well, as Canada fills specific niches in larger industries such as chemicals, telecommunications, and transport. Our major railways use Canadian ports to service Canadian and American customers throughout the continent without distinction. American markets provide the investment and end users for many natural resources that our smaller local markets could never justify. Nova Scotia's offshore gas would likely never have been brought ashore, nor would a pipeline have been built, without the Boston market to support it. Electric generation capacity has similarly been spurred by easy access to American markets thanks to continentally integrated infrastructure.[57]

Contrary to the assertions of those who would turn back the clock, the integration of our two economies is not limited to dying automobile manufacturers, although the auto industry is certainly a major beneficiary.[58] The reality is that we do not, by and large, make finished products in Canada as a result of self-contained production processes. We contribute a piece of production in many companies and industries within vast continental supply and production chains. Our production is fitted to niches within that continental production.[59] In other parts of the world, production is configured differently; they have different supply, distribution, and retail chains. It is not impossible to shift some part of our production to other markets, but the effort to do so would be significant and the benefits meagre.

Even within our natural resources, we cannot sell our hydroelectricity to China, because electricity cannot be efficiently transmitted over such distances.[60] Our natural gas cannot easily go to Germany because natural gas tends to be a continental industry with connections via pipelines and it would be very expensive to build the infrastructure to liquefy our natural gas and put it in ships, although the very early stages of such an infrastructure are now being created. Even our few oil refineries that produce for export are conceived and built to cater to North American standards and market niches and could not easily shift production elsewhere. Yes, we can sell oil and diamonds and copper to the highest bidder anywhere, but a great deal of Canada's production is not of such interchangeable commodities but of highly specialized products that fit a continental market we have been stitching ourselves into for generations.[61] Yes, for strategic reasons Canada should consider increasing its bargaining power with the Americans by, for example, building pipelines to carry some of our oil sands production to the west coast, making it more available for export to other markets in China and elsewhere. An America preoccupied with energy security needs occasionally to be reminded that Canada has alternative markets for its oil, whereas America's alternatives to Canada come from far less congenial parts of the globe.

The complex intertwining of our economies touches every part of what Canada does and makes. Canada does not make space shuttles—our economy is too small. We could and did, however, design and make the Canadarm, a state-of-the-art robotic arm that is a crucial part of the space shuttle. Without the Americans making space shuttles, though, the market for Canadarms would hardly exist. And if the Canadarm manufacturer is bought by Americans, other opportunities quickly arise to take their place and other niches are filled by our entrepreneurial effort. Canada cannot afford a military to match America's, but we can and do make BlackBerrys that sit in the pocket of every American military officer and provide a great deal of the information network on which the day-to-day operations of that huge organization depend.

It is for these reasons that all efforts by governments in Ottawa to "diversify" our economy away from dependence on US markets are doomed to make little headway. We are not the separate closed economy of the economic nationalists' dreams, able to shift our production of a wide range of finished products to customers anywhere in the world. In fact, official statistics undoubtedly understate the extent of our exports to other countries because so many of our exports lie buried inside products and services sold to others by companies based in the United States. We are a deeply integrated part of a continental economy, and the border represents perhaps the single greatest threat to our ability to seize the opportunity represented by the Canadian century.

To summarize what needs to happen to engage the Americans constructively, we should listen to Canada's former ambassador to the US, Allan Gotlieb, who advises:

> For any initiative to succeed, it must meet a number of conditions. It must be bold; it must come from Canada and be espoused at the highest level. It must be comprehensive so as to allow trade-offs and broad constituencies to come into play. It must address the U.S. agenda as well as ours.[62]

In other words, the Big Idea must come from us because the Americans have their interests focused elsewhere and a proposal from them would in any case be regarded with suspicion in many quarters in Canada. The Big Idea is the lure that draws America's attention, the blueprint that obliges the Americans to engage. By being broad and bold, the Big Idea allows the kind of trade-offs across many areas of interest on both sides of the border that makes a deal possible.

Will the Americans play ball? It all depends on circumstances and the quality of the Canadian approach, but what we do know, according to trade expert Colin Robertson, is that

> American leadership responds best to big ideas that play to their agenda. By framing our own interests around the American preoccupation with national security, economic recovery and climate change we can advance our agenda.[63]

So yes, it is true, in the current recession, protectionist instincts have come to the fore in America and therefore the appetite for trade-opening measures is not great. Free trade agreements awaiting Senate approval are falling by the wayside. But not only should the current passing circumstances not be an excuse for taking our eye off the long-term goal, we must also take to heart the truth at the core of each of the pieces of advice above from long-term America watchers. Our approach to America cannot just be about us. It must also be about what America wants and needs. One former Canadian official in Washington tells the story of meeting Senator John McCain to brief him on some issue of pressing importance to Canadians. This powerful senator's response? "We never hear from you guys except when you want something."

Succeeding in making a breakthrough in Canada–US relations, then, requires us to think about what Americans want. Putting a broad range of interests on the table allows us to make trade-offs that are attractive to Americans. Being a dependable ally to an America seeking friends in global conflicts in the Middle East, Iran, North Korea, Afghanistan, and other conflict zones is part of it. That means not merely being willing to say the right things when Canada's interests and America's coincide, but being willing and able to risk blood and treasure when the circumstances call for it. Canada's willing participation in NATO missions in both the former Yugoslavia and Afghanistan won us important bargaining chips with America. Our sudden and unexplained withdrawal of our all-but-promised support for the Anti-Ballistic Missile System, by contrast, deeply damaged our standing and our credibility.[64]

America also wants to feel safer at home. A common North American security perimeter with shared standards around who is admitted to our continental space plus enhanced policing of potential or actual terrorism suspects and international organized crime would be a good start. It may be a frustrating reality that Americans persist in believing, mistakenly, that the 9/11 terrorists entered the US from Canada. The simple fact of the matter is that if such a connection ever became reality, if a major terrorist attack were ever found to have an important Canadian connection, border openness would fast become a distant memory. Best to engage the Americans as deeply as we can on establishing safe standards, sharing information, and building trust that we will do everything humanly possible to ensure that our territory can never be used to threaten America.

We have made significant progress under projects like the Security and Prosperity Partnership of North America, but we can carry this budding relationship to higher levels of cooperation and confidence-building.

And America too has a deep interest in keeping the border open. Members of Congress from border states are keenly aware of the significance of open borders for the success of their own economies. Many industries across America know that their production processes are spread on both sides of the border. They need certainty that open access will be maintained. Washington not only wants to worry less about the border, but it wants it to be easier to administer. And Washington wants to make sure that access to Canadian markets is kept as open as possible as well. All of these facts give us tools to work with.

Most of the ideas that Canada should be prepared to put on the table are already part of current public debate. What is lacking now is a Canadian government willing to take that indispensable lead that alone will give us any hope of moving our relationship with America to a new level of certainty, intimacy, and mutual confidence.

What to Ask For

At a minimum, Canada should be seeking:

A new treaty on continental security and a common external tariff. We already collaborate successfully with the Americans on continental air defence through NORAD (North American Aerospace Defense Command). What we want now is to establish a jointly administered perimeter around North America, one that has a common tariff on foreign goods. In an ideal world, we might also aim for agreed-to standards for admitting non–North American nationals, although America's current immigration angst may make that difficult. But the prize is worth having: by creating such a "perimeter border" around the continent, we move administrative and policing pressures from the choke points at the physical Canada–US border because issues involving third countries are handled and resolved elsewhere.

A new joint commission on border management. We already have an International Joint Commission tying Canada and the US together to manage transborder waters.[65] It has been a very successful innovation that could serve as a model for managing the border more generally. An autonomous organization given a mandate and a budget by both countries to resolve border infrastructure and administration issues would help cut through the bureaucratic and political fog that surround decision-making about the border, particularly in Washington, where so many congressional and administrative forces have a finger in the pie. It is taking decades simply to build a new crossing connecting Windsor and Detroit. Clearly, a powerful new institutional structure is required with a strong mandate to shoulder aside bureaucratic and other obstacles, and a budget to match.

This could also be the body that deals with establishing appropriate standards for regulatory harmonization on both sides of the border. At a minimum, this commission could issue reports about regulatory issues, such as truck weight, food inspection, waiting times at border crossings, and so forth, that could be considered by each government. The far more positive outcome, however, would be to empower this body to issue regulatory harmonization orders that would become effective on both sides of the border unless vetoed by one side or the other within ninety days. Similarly, where appropriate, it could issue orders for mutual recognition of existing regulatory standards in both countries.

A new joint committee of Congress and Parliament on Canadian–American issues. In Canada, we always lament our inability to get the attention of policymakers in Washington for issues critical to the Canada–US relationship. By creating a formal joint body, composed of equal numbers of members of both national legislatures, co-chaired by a Canadian and an American, required to meet regularly and frequently, and empowered to hold hearings, summon witnesses, and issue reports to the two originating bodies, we move continental issues into the heart of their decisions. We engage senators and representatives by giving them a forum to voice their concerns and get their issues on the table. And creating a body where important policymakers get to know one another and learn to cooperate across the border to advance their issues builds relationships that can only advance Canada's interests.

A nice twist would be to recognize that the prime minister of Canada is both our leading legislator and the effective head of our executive, whereas these two functions are separated in the American system. We make a mistake by focusing all prime ministerial attention on relations with the president, leaving the leaders of the legislature in Washington out of the conversation. Just as our prime minister has regular meetings with the president, he or she must have regular summits with the congressional leadership. These are the people who make many of the decisions where the stakes are high for Canada, and they act quite independently of the president. Canada, through the prime minister, needs to engage the Speaker of the House and the leadership of both parties in both houses on a regular basis.

A joint tribunal on issues that arise under our various cross-border agreements. Building the mutual confidence and trust that make joint decision-making possible requires a sense that whatever rules are agreed to will be enforced fairly and without regard to competing national interests. While the dispute settlement mechanism created by the original free trade agreement was a step in the right direction, and has often been unfairly maligned by its critics, that mechanism is clearly inadequate to deal with adjudication of the potential disputes that might arise within the broad array of agreements and institutions proposed here. Separation between those who make the rules and those who interpret and apply them is a cornerstone of institutional legitimacy. We need to make a new court, staffed by judges appointed by both sides and charged with the impartial application of all the new rules of continental cooperation.

The International Joint Commission (IJC) and NORAD are both working models of the principle we want to put into effect in the creation of new institutions between Canada and the US. Anyone can create binational institutions. The trick is to create institutions where Canada is not merely at the table with the US but is recognized by the US as an equal partner at that table, with equal weight in the decisions to be taken. That must always be the underlying objective of every negotiation we undertake. We have done it before, and we can do it again. But only if we do as Sir Wilfrid did and boldly take the lead.

Trade with the World

What about Mexico? Canadians charged with representing Canada's interests have increasingly come to regret allowing Mexico's clever manoeuvering in the 1990s to pull us into a three-cornered relationship with Washington and Mexico City.[66] The anxiety is growing that Canada's relationship with the US will be held hostage to the very different relationship with Mexico, on the grounds that Washington always has in the back of its mind that whatever is given to Canada must eventually be granted to Mexico.

Canada needs to remember, though, that we were first to the bilateral table with the FTA and that we have a great many other bilateral institutions, such as the IJC and NORAD, that do not involve Mexico. If America sees bilateral negotiations with Ottawa as a way to realize objectives they hold dear, they will not hesitate to sit down with us one on one. But neither should we reject out of hand making common cause with the Mexicans on issues where our combined negotiating power may help us win a better deal from America.

In fact, if we think back to the notion that successful negotiations will require that Canada must be able to show America that we can be part of the solution to their problems, then Mexico can be an opportunity as well as a distraction. Remember that Mexico looms large in the American political imagination right now. Mexican immigration, as well as movement of the American population closer to the Mexican border, means that Mexican issues will always get a lot of attention in Washington. Beyond that, however, the Americans are deeply concerned about the possibility of the emergence of a failed state on their southern border. This reason, perhaps more than any other, explains how Mexico ended up at the NAFTA table: the US administration thought that giving access to North American markets and prosperity today was a better solution than facing tens of millions of refugees from a failed state later.

We earned points and bargaining weight in Washington by being part of helping the US with its worries about Mexico. We saw another example recently when Prime Minister Harper offered financial assistance and police training to Guadalajara, to Mexico's delight and Washington's relief.[67] In other words, we must neither embrace nor reject involvement with Mexico indiscriminately. Where engagement with the Mexicans increases our bargaining power with Washington, we should engage. Where bilateralism with the Americans is more likely to protect and promote Canadians' interests, that should be our policy.

While Canada will benefit most from a deepening of the economic and institutional relationship within North America, this is no reason for Canada not to do everything it can to raze barriers to trade with every country in the world. Just because the bulk of our trade, especially in goods, must flow to the United States for some very practical reasons, those incremental increases in trade that we might achieve with, say, the BRIC nations—Brazil, Russia, India, and China—or the European Union

(EU) or the Asian Tigers are all highly desirable in themselves. They simply will not displace the primacy of the Canada–US trade relationship in any foreseeable future, at least in the field of trade in goods and products. But in terms of trade in services, the constraints on diversifying our markets are much less binding, and we should pursue growth in those areas as aggressively as we possibly can. This too is part of the Laurier Plan: recognize America's dominance, and do everything within our power to tame it, but don't use the close ties between the two countries as an excuse not to pursue opportunities wherever they may be found. As Laurier himself underlined the point, "Our policy has been, is and will be . . . to seek markets wherever markets are to be found."[68]

That means that Canada must be an active participant in all the usual international forums seeking to liberalize international trade. The World Trade Organization's Doha Round of negotiations on the world trading system is a good case in point. Canada has foolishly and wastefully squandered its international bargaining power and prestige in those negotiations in a vain effort to protect our antiquated and antediluvian marketing board system.[69] Other major Western agricultural exporters, countries such as Australia and New Zealand, have shown that it is possible to use these negotiations to advance the interests of their farmers without sacrificing those of consumers or progress on international trade liberalization. Laurier would not have approved of Canada's giving up the search for markets wherever they are to be found to placate a few selfish and noisy domestic producers.

And if, despite coming back to the table with a positive negotiating position within the WTO, progress is still blocked by the intransigence of others, Canada should not hesitate to take the second-best route of working out other bilateral deals with countries, as we have done with Chile, for example, or with other trading blocs, such as the EU.[70] Canada's future lies in the freest trade possible with as many willing partners as we can find.

Other Issues

Another area of focus for reform, and one which to some extent has been facilitated by the recent stimulus spending by the federal government, is infrastructure—namely highways, bridges, border crossings, etc. The federal government recently accelerated and expanded investment in infrastructure by $12 billion over the next two years, 2009–10 and 2010–11. It is critical that these resources be devoted to projects that enhance productivity and economic growth. To do so, the focus for investment should be on increasing the easy movement of goods and people to the greatest extent possible.[71] Economies, to be successful, must be able to transport their goods and services from production to sales to consumption in a timely and efficient manner. A number of analysts have raised concerns over the years regarding the state of Canada's infrastructure.[72] Canada should focus resources on improving transportation times between major cities both within Canada and, equally as important, internationally. Indeed, one of the areas we would focus on is border infrastructure, to reduce the time it takes to cross the border.

We know that Laurier thought that investment in genuine infrastructure was a core responsibility of government in general and of Ottawa in particular. For a long time, Canada outdid the US in terms of its public investments in transport and communications,[73] building the productivity of Canadians by giving them better tools to work with. Laurier also saw that borrowing to finance such genuine infrastructure was a perfectly reasonable and sound policy because it allowed governments to spread the cost of such investments over their useful life while ensuring that everyone who benefited from them contributed to their cost, and not just those who happened to be paying taxes in the year they were built.

When public spending got out of control in Canada and deficits rose, however, it was not to finance productivity-enhancing infrastructure but to pay for consumption, civil servants' salaries, visits to the doctor, pensions, and the like. That is not meant to imply that these are not worthy things to spend tax dollars on—only that such expenditures, consumed in the year they are made, should also be paid for in that year, by taxes raised in that year. When we started to borrow to finance current expenditure, we crowded out a lot of genuine investment. As we return to more disciplined finances under Laurier's plan, we should not end borrowing but make sure that we borrow only for genuine infrastructure while hewing to the bedrock principle that today's consumption of public services should be paid for out of today's taxes.

Finally, there are a host of other issues worthy of note that should and will be pursued in the future as part of the Macdonald-Laurier Institute's commitment to the Canadian Century project, of which this book represents a first step. Issues including the inadequate protection of the rights of Canadians to live, work, invest, and sell their goods and services everywhere in the country; how Canada regulates its labour markets, with particular emphasis on employment insurance; immigration; independent monetary policy; and education, both K-12 and post-secondary are areas where additional research and education will be pursued in the future. The aim is to build on the framework developed in this book to create a more comprehensive and detailed plan to achieve the Canadian century that is clearly within our grasp.

This book tells of a great Canadian success story, one that is little known and even less appreciated by Canadians.

Through the wisdom and foresight of some of our greatest early leaders, and especially of Sir Wilfrid Laurier, Canadians inherited a plan for the future based on deep insights into our origins, our character, our circumstances, and our practical opportunities. Laurier promised us that the twentieth century would be ours if we had the discipline to follow it and the imagination to see where it would lead.

And indeed, when we have followed that plan, we have prospered. When we shrugged off the self-restraint on which the plan was premised—when we binged on debt and expensive and poorly designed social programs and self-indulgent petty nationalism—we lost our way.

The story told here is of how Canadians in all regions, in all political parties, woke up to our predicament and began to rediscover the wisdom in what we had so lightly discarded. Free trade, the GST, provincial and federal reforms of taxes, spending, and borrowing—all of these were elements of that reawakening.

These good beginnings, however, were only that. People in all regions and of all political persuasions have equally participated in the past few years in a dissipation of the momentum created in the Redemptive Decade. That's the thing about redemption: it is not a permanent state and the possibility of falling afresh is ever-present. The work of putting Canada firmly back on the path Laurier sketched out for us remains unfinished, yet the opportunity is doubled by America's confusion and loss of direction.

The question now is whether Canadians will take up Laurier's challenge and finish the job.

notes

Chapter One
Laurier's Plan for Canada

1 Laurier was our seventh prime minister and the first French Canadian to occupy this post; he is widely regarded as a towering figure in Canadian politics whose "sunny ways" no doubt helped him enormously in his task of shaping the early Dominion. He was also an ardent free trader, an anti-clerical liberal rouge, a doughty defender of individual and minority rights. For more on Laurier and his political career, see Réal Bélanger, "Sir Wilfrid Laurier," in Ramsay Cook and Réal Bélanger, *Canada's Prime Ministers, Macdonald to Trudeau: Portraits from the Dictionary of Canadian Biography* (Toronto: University of Toronto Press, 2007), pp. 149–192.

2 Robert Craig Brown and Ramsay Cook, *Canada, 1896–1921: A Nation Transformed* (Toronto: McClelland and Stewart, 1974), p. 50; and W.A. Mackintosh, *The Economic Background of Dominion-Provincial Relations* (Ottawa: Royal Commission on Dominion-Provincial Relations, first published in 1939), p. 40.

3 See, for instance, P.B. Waite, *Canada, 1874–1896: Arduous Destiny* (Toronto: McClelland and Stewart, 1971).

4 Robert Bothwell, Ian Drummond, and John English, *Canada, 1900–1945* (Toronto: University of Toronto Press, 1987), p. 60.

5 Between 1896 and 1914, the number of American residents moving north came closer to equalling the number of residents of Canada heading south. The exact figures are elusive because contemporary Canadian and US government statistics of annual immigrant arrivals disagree dramatically with the decennial censuses. But according to two noted historians, Canada's net outmigration to the US was less than 200,000 during this period, a figure they rightly note "was a spectacular improvement over the preceding half-century." See John Herd Thompson and Stephen J. Randall, *Canada and the United States: Ambivalent Allies* (Athens: University of Georgia Press, 1994), pp. 80–81.

6 After Saskatchewan became a province in 1905, the population surged with settlers lured by cheap land and the vision of Saskatchewan as the breadbasket of Canada. By the 1931 census, Saskatchewan had more than 922,000 people and was the third-largest province in Canada. But the

Great Depression and the Dirty '30s hit the province's agriculture-based economy like a hammer, and by 1951 Saskatchewan's population had dropped to 832,000. See James Woods, "Boom and Bust: Sask. Population Dip Stirs Debate over Future," *Star-Phoenix* (Saskatoon), July 1, 2006, A1.

7 The closing of the American frontier for homesteading by the end of the nineteenth century left Canada with the "last best west"; combined with Sifton's aggressive homestead policies, it helped "to make the prairies one of the most ethnically diverse and economically dynamic regions in the country." See Franca Iacovetta (ed.), *A Nation of Immigrants: Women, Workers, and Communities in Canadian History, 1840s–1960s* (Toronto: University of Toronto Press, 1998), pp. 115–117.

8 Joseph Schull, *Laurier: The First Canadian* (Toronto: Macmillan, 1965), p. 455.

9 For just one example, see H.V. Nelles's work on Ontario's expansionary impulse, *Politics of Development: Forests, Mines, and Hydro-Electric Power in Ontario, 1849–1941*, 2nd ed. (Montreal and Kingston: McGill-Queen's University Press, 2005), pp. 52–57.

10 Robert Bothwell, Ian Drummond, and John English, *Canada, 1900–1945* (Toronto: University of Toronto Press, 1987), p. 63.

11 Joseph Schull, *Laurier: The First Canadian* (Toronto: Macmillan, 1965), p. 457.

12 Robert Bothwell, Ian Drummond, and John English, *Canada, 1900–1945* (Toronto: University of Toronto Press, 1987), p. 63.

13 Robert Bothwell, Ian Drummond, and John English, *Canada, 1900–1945* (Toronto: University of Toronto Press, 1987), p. 63.

14 Robert Craig Brown and Ramsay Cook, *Canada, 1896–1921: A Nation Transformed* (Toronto: McClelland and Stewart, 1974), p. 99.

15 Robert Craig Brown and Ramsay Cook, *Canada, 1896–1921: A Nation Transformed* (Toronto: McClelland and Stewart, 1974), p. 91.

16 Nobel Prize–winning economist Douglass North has shown that the presence of these economic and social "institutions" are fundamental to economic outcomes. See Douglass North, *The Role of Institutions in Economic Development—Gunnar Myrdal Lecture* (New York: United Nations, 2003); and North, *Institutions, Institutional Change, and Economic Performance* (Cambridge: Cambridge University Press, 1990). See also Nathan Rosenberg and L.E. Birdzell Jr., *How the West Grew Rich: The Economic Transformation of the Industrial World* (New York: Basic Books, 1986).

17 Robert Bothwell and J.L. Granatstein, *Our Century: Canadian Journey* (Toronto: McArthur and Company, 2000), p. ix.

18 Robert Bothwell, Ian Drummond, and John English, *Canada, 1900–1945*

(Toronto: University of Toronto Press, 1987), p. 75.

19 Doug Owram, *The Government Generation: Canadian Intellectuals and the State, 1900–1945* (Toronto: University of Toronto Press, 1986), p. 35.

20 For an account of the sort of community-based institutions that responded to these needs without any intervention by the state, consult David Beito's *From Mutual Aid to the Welfare State: Fraternal Societies and Social Services, 1890–1967* (Chapel Hill: University of North Carolina Press, 2000); or Beito, Peter Gordon, and Alexander Tabarrok, *Voluntary City: Choice, Community, and Civil Society* (Ann Arbor: University of Michigan Press, 2002).

21 David B. Perry, *Financing the Canadian Federation, 1867 to 1995: Setting the Stage for Change* (Toronto: Canadian Tax Foundation, 1997), p. xiii.

22 See, for instance, Jeffrey Simpson, "A Very Scary PM: 'I Don't Believe Any Taxes Are Good Taxes,'" *Globe and Mail*, July 14, 2009, A13.

23 Quoted in W. Irwin Gillespie, *Tax, Borrow and Spend: Financing Federal Spending in Canada, 1867–1990* (Ottawa: Carleton University Press, 1991), p. 48.

24 Robert Bothwell, Ian Drummond, and John English, *Canada, 1900–1945* (Toronto: University of Toronto Press, 1987), p. 75.

25 More than 1.5 million immigrants came to Canada between 1871 and 1901, but emigration, most of it to the United States, exceeded immigration in this period. Only in the first decade of the twentieth century was the balance redressed as 2.5 million immigrants arrived on Canadian shores to balance the more than 1 million people who left the country between 1901 and 1911. See Reg Whitaker, *Canadian Immigration Policy Since Confederation* (Ottawa: Canadian Historical Association, 1991), Tables 1 and 2.

26 W. Irwin Gillespie, *Tax, Borrow and Spend: Financing Federal Spending in Canada, 1867–1990* (Ottawa: Carleton University Press, 1991), p. 51.

27 W. Irwin Gillespie, *Tax, Borrow and Spend: Financing Federal Spending in Canada, 1867–1990* (Ottawa: Carleton University Press, 1991), p. 56.

28 American duties on most imported goods exceeded 50 per cent for much of the first half of the twentieth century. See Michael Hart, *A Trading Nation: Canadian Trade Policy from Colonialism to Globalization* (Vancouver: UBC Press, 2002), pp. 92–93.

29 The Dominion Income War Tax Act obtained royal assent in 1917. The basic personal exemption in 1917 was $1,500, or close to $25,000 in current dollars, according to a recent analysis by Jack Mintz. See Mintz, "After 87 Years, It Is Time to Fix the Income Tax Act," *C.D. Howe Institute E-Brief*, September 20, 2004, p. 1.

30 As several scholars have shown, customs duties remained the principal

source of federal revenues from Confederation to the introduction of the first federal income tax in 1917. See Michael Hart, *A Trading Nation: Canadian Trade Policy from Colonialism to Globalization* (Vancouver: UBC Press, 2002), pp. 62–63; and Richard Pomfret, *Economic Development of Canada* (Toronto: Routledge Press, 2006), p. 79.

31 David Bercuson (ed.), *Canada and the Burden of Unity* (Toronto: Gage, 1980).

32 For one of the best examples, see Ben Forster, *A Conjunction of Interests: Business, Politics, and Tariffs, 1825–1879* (Toronto: University of Toronto Press, 1986).

33 A customs union is a trade bloc composed of a free trade area with a common external tariff.

34 Laurier said: "For my part personally—I have told you before—I am not disposed to change at all except to go forward. I would be ready tomorrow to go to the length of Commercial Union, including a common tariff and pooling of the revenue: in fact applying to this continent the German *Zollverein*. We would undoubtedly raise a storm, but as I am satisfied the future lies in that direction I would not mind the storm at all, nor the consequences. But in this the party would not follow me, and therefore there is no use thinking of it." Quoted in Joseph Schull, *Laurier: The First Canadian* (Toronto: Macmillan, 1965), p. 263.

35 J.W. Dafoe, *Laurier: A Study in Canadian Politics* (Toronto: McClelland and Stewart, 1963), p. 81.

36 Quoted in Joseph Schull, *Laurier: The First Canadian* (Toronto: Macmillan, 1965), p. 344.

37 In the Laurier years, there were four years of budget surpluses, seven years of deficits of less than 1 per cent of GDP, and three years of slightly larger deficits. See W. Irwin Gillespie, *Tax, Borrow and Spend: Financing Federal Spending in Canada, 1867–1990* (Ottawa: Carleton University Press, 1991), p. 271.

38 Using just one example, between 1903 and 1911, when Laurier was defeated in a general election, railway track mileage increased by about 40 per cent, from just over 18,000 miles to 25,400 miles, much of it financed with some government support. See Joe Martin, *"Irrational Exuberance": The Creation of the CNR, 1917–1919*, Rotman School of Management case study (2006), p. 5.

39 Quoted in W. Irwin Gillespie, *Tax, Borrow and Spend: Financing Federal Spending in Canada, 1867–1990* (Ottawa: Carleton University Press, 1991), p. 53.

40 According to Gillespie, "Dominion governments pursued an active policy

of extensive borrowing and debt enlargement, in order to keep taxes low and to engage in spending on 'great public works.'" See W. Irwin Gillespie, *Tax, Borrow and Spend: Financing Federal Spending in Canada, 1867–1990* (Ottawa: Carleton University Press, 1991), p. 71.

41 The most obvious example of private sector investment with public sector backing during the Laurier years was the railways. For more on the public–private financing of the railways, see Donald MacKay, *The People's Railway, A History of Canadian National* (Vancouver: Douglas and McIntyre, 1992); and G.R. Stevens, *History of the Canadian National Railways* (New York: Macmillan, 1973).

42 This balancing act was a major preoccupation for the Laurier government. As one scholar explains, "The Dominion government's strong demand for debt finance resulted in a search for low interest rates and a concern to preserve the 'good credit standing' of the Dominion. In turn, this desire to maintain a good credit rating, in order to have access to international capital funds at low interest rates, constrained the government's borrowing power. The revenue policy problem of Dominion governments involved the choice between incurring additional debt, if it could be lodged without seriously damaging the credit ratings, and imposing additional high indirect taxation, with the associated political costs of discouraging immigration and encouraging emigration." See W. Irwin Gillespie, *Tax, Borrow and Spend: Financing Federal Spending in Canada, 1867–1990* (Ottawa: Carleton University Press, 1991), p. 51.

43 As two noted Canadian historians write, "The nub of the Alaska issue was access through its long, narrow southern 'panhandle' to Canada's Yukon gold fields. If the American claim was upheld, Canada would own none of the water routes inland . . . The judgment stung because Canada seemed alone in the world, bullied by the United States, abandoned by Great Britain." See Norman Hillmer and J.L. Granatstein, *Empire to Umpire* (Toronto: Irwin, 2000), pp. 25–26.

44 Joseph Schull, *Laurier: The First Canadian* (Toronto: Macmillan, 1965), p. 470.

45 See Edmund Morris, *The Rise of Theodore Roosevelt* (New York: Modern Library, 2001), p. xvi.

46 In 1896, when Laurier assumed office, 57 per cent of Canada's exports went to Britain, while 34 per cent were going to the United States, an imbalance due in part to the Americans' punitive tariff regime. That gap would continue to close, however, and by 1920 exports to the US rose dramatically over the value going to Britain and would remain higher for the rest of the century with the exception of a few aberrant years. See Michael

Hart, *A Trading Nation: Canadian Trade Policy from Colonialism to Globalization* (Vancouver: UBC Press, 2002), p. 73; John Herd Thompson and Stephen J. Randall, *Canada and the United States: Ambivalent Allies* (Athens: University of Georgia Press, 1994), p. 202; and Bruce Muirhead, *The Development of Postwar Canadian Trade Policy: The Failure of the Anglo-European Option* (Montreal and Kingston: McGill-Queen's University Press, 1993), p. 183.

47 The Conservative Party, unlike its Liberal opposition, was by the late 1870s conscious of the business community's growing proclivity for tariff protection and refrained from any public flirtations with continental free trade, preferring to excoriate the opposition Liberals for their "dangerous" policy of free trade. See Ben Forster, "The Coming of the National Policy: Business, Government and the Tariff, 1876–1879," in Douglas McCalla (ed.), *The Development of Canadian Capitalism: Essays in Business History* (Toronto: Copp Clark Pitman, 1990); and Michael Bliss, *The Evolution of Industrial Policies in Canada: An Historical Survey* (Ottawa: Economic Council of Canada, 1982).

48 Canada, House of Commons, *Debates*, March 7, 1911, pp. 4740–4824.

49 As Robert Borden's biographer puts it, "The Conservatives, to a man, were stunned. There had never been such a challenge to their National Policy; there had never been a proposal so calculated to win the support of the vast majority of Canada's farmers, fishermen, lumbermen, and industrial workers. Laurier's party, though old, tired, and slipping badly in its organizational prowess, seemed assured of another sweeping victory; Borden's men faced a fifth deeply humiliating defeat." Ramsay Cook and Réal Bélanger (eds.), "Sir Robert Laird Borden," in *Canada's Prime Ministers: Portraits from the Dictionary of Canadian Biography* (Toronto: University of Toronto Press, 2007), p. 205.

50 J.L. Granatstein, "Freer Trade and Politics," in Norman Hillmer (ed.), *Partners Nevertheless: Canadian-American Relations in the Twentieth Century* (Toronto: Copp Clark Pitman, 1989), p. 68.

51 J.L. Granatstein, "Freer Trade and Politics," in Norman Hillmer (ed.), *Partners Nevertheless: Canadian-American Relations in the Twentieth Century* (Toronto: Copp Clark Pitman, 1989), p. 70.

52 For just one example, see Mel Hurtig, *The Betrayal of Canada*, (Toronto: Stoddart, 1992), p. 3.

53 In fact, some scholars have gone back to the 1911 election and are now challenging the view that Laurier's election defeat was about free trade at all. See, for instance, Eugene Beaulieu and J.C. Herbert Emery, "Pork Packers, Reciprocity, and Laurier's Defeat in the 1911 Canadian General

Election," *Journal of Economic History* 62, no. 4 (December 2001): 1083–1101.

54 Soon after arriving in the united provinces in 1847, Governor General Lord Elgin, with the support of key figures in the Legislative Assembly, made reciprocity the main focus of the colony's commercial policy. As Hart chronicles in extensive detail, Elgin expended remarkable personal effort on reaching an agreement. It took him more than five years to negotiate a satisfactory agreement and assemble a congressional majority in the United States, "using artful bribes and entertainment effected through a confidential agent hired for the purpose." See Michael Hart, *A Trading Nation: Canadian Trade Policy from Colonialism to Globalization* (Vancouver: UBC Press, 2002), pp. 49–52.

55 Paul Johnson, *The Birth of the Modern: World Society 1815–1830* (New York: Harper Perennial, 1999), pp. 321–323.

56 See W.T. Easterbrook and Hugh G.J. Aitken, *Canadian Economic History* (Toronto: University of Toronto Press, 1990), pp. 350–377; and W.L. Morton, *The Critical Years: The Union of British North America, 1857–1873* (Toronto: McClelland and Stewart, 1968), pp. 203–222.

57 Rae Murphy, *Canadian History since 1867: The Post-Confederation Nation* (Piscataway, NJ: Research and Education Association, 1993), p. 44.

58 Michael Hart, *A Trading Nation: Canadian Trade Policy from Colonialism to Globalization* (Vancouver: UBC Press, 2002), p. 64. Emphasis added.

Chapter Two
A Country and a Century Derailed

1 For more on Borden, including his tenure as the leader of a Unionist government, see R.C. Brown, "Sir Robert Borden," in Ramsay Cook and Réal Bélanger, *Canada's Prime Ministers, Macdonald to Trudeau: Portraits from the Dictionary of Canadian Biography* (Toronto: University of Toronto Press, 2007), pp. 193–224.

2 The 1921 census put Canada's population at an impressive 8.78 million people. For more on the rapid growth of the first twenty years of the twentieth century, see Robert Craig Brown and Ramsay Cook, *Canada, 1896–1921: A Nation Transformed* (Toronto: McClelland and Stewart, 1974).

3 Fuelled by its growing economic relationship with the United States, Canada's economy grew significantly in the 1920s. In fact, according to two noted economic historians, "only the period 1900–1910 saw a greater growth in real GNP per capita." See Kenneth Norrie and Doug Owram, *A History of the Canadian Economy* (Toronto: Harcourt, Brace and Jovanovich, 1991), p. 471. See also John Herd Thompson and Allen Seager, *Canada, 1922–1939: Decades of Discord* (Toronto: McClelland and Stewart,

1985), pp. 76–103.

4 Kenneth Norrie and Doug Owram, *A History of the Canadian Economy*, (Toronto: Harcourt, Brace and Jovanovich, 1991), p. 303.

5 Britain's economic decline invariably strengthened Canada's close economic relationship with the United States. For most, at least at first, this was seen as an inevitable if not desirable development. For others, such as historian Donald Creighton, Canada's diminishing relationship with the United Kingdom was lamentable. See Creighton's famous polemic—and last book—*The Forked Road: Canada, 1939–1957* (Toronto: McClelland and Stewart, 1976).

6 Michael Bliss, *Right Honourable Men: The Descent of Canadian Politics from Macdonald to Chrétien* (Toronto: HarperCollins, 2004), p. 177.

7 David Frum, "Three Dangers and an Opportunity," *C2C Journal*, June 22, 2009, p. 2.

8 Richard M. Bird, *The Growth of Government Spending in Canada* (Toronto: Canadian Tax Foundation, July 1970), p. 47.

9 According to one eminent postwar scholar, "The [St-Laurent] government's policy can be summed up as 'managing prosperity,' through regular budgetary surpluses and modest improvements to social welfare programs. The provinces had blocked any progress toward a comprehensive welfare state and St-Laurent had no ambition to go farther for the time being . . . Taxes remained low, certainly by comparison with Britain, the rest of Europe, and the United States, which in the 1950s had a more extensive social welfare system as well as a greater burden for defence." See Robert Bothwell, "Louis-Stephen St-Laurent," in Ramsay Cook and Réal Bélanger, *Canada's Prime Ministers, Macdonald to Trudeau: Portraits from the Dictionary of Canadian Biography* (Toronto: University of Toronto Press, 2007), p. 344.

10 Quoted in P.E. Bryden, *Planners and Politicians: Liberal Politics and Social Policy 1957–1968* (Montreal and Kingston: McGill-Queen's University Press, 1997), p. 22.

11 Kari Levitt's *Silent Surrender* became the clarion call for the postwar nationalist movement that sought to end the purported Americanization of the Canadian economy. Historian Stephen Azzi has documented the nationalists' efforts, including the emergence of the Waffle Group within the New Democratic Party and Liberal MP Walter Gordon's failed attempts to impose a nationalist agenda on Laurier's old party. See Levitt, *Silent Surrender: The Multinational Corporation in Canada* (Montreal and Kingston: McGill-Queen's University Press, 2002); and Azzi, *Walter Gordon and The Rise of Canadian Nationalism* (Montreal and Kingston:

McGill-Queen's University Press, 1999).

12 For more on the international influence of Keynesianism, see Daniel Yergin and Joseph Stanislaw, *The Commanding Heights: The Battle for the World Economy* (New York: Simon and Schuster, 1998). For the Canadian experience with Keynesianism, see Stanley L. Winer and J. Stephen Ferris, "Searching for Keynesianism," *European Journal of Political Economy* 24 (2008): 294–316; Robert M. Campbell, *Grand Illusions: The Politics of the Keynesian Experience in Canada, 1945–1975* (Peterborough, ON: Broadview Press, 1987); and H. Scott Gordon, "A Twenty Year Perspective: Some Reflections on the Keynesian Revolution in Canada," in *Canadian Economic Policy since the War: A Series of Six Public Lectures in Commemoration of the Twentieth Anniversary of the "White Paper" on Employment and Income of 1945* (Ottawa: Carleton University, 1965), pp. 23–46. For more on the technocratic underpinnings of the new "mixed economy" model, see Sean C. Speer, *J.J. Deutsch: A Keynesian in Canada, 1911–1976* (unpublished Ph.D. thesis, University of Ottawa, forthcoming in 2011).

13 Nixon's decision to impose price and wage controls was promptly imitated by France, Italy, and ultimately Canada. His famous assertion seemed to sum up the economic thinking of the era: "We are all Keynesians now." See David Frum, *How We Got Here: The '70s* (New York: Basic Books, 2000), p. 313; and Daniel Yergin and Joseph Stanislaw, *The Commanding Heights: The Battle for the World Economy* (New York: Simon and Schuster, 2002), pp. 42–43.

14 See Brian Lee Crowley, *Fearful Symmetry: The Fall and Rise of Canada's Founding Values* (Toronto: Key Porter Books, 2009).

15 While many countries had larger governments as a percentage of GDP, no major industrialized country, as Dennis Mueller shows, grew as significantly during the period from 1960 to the early 1990s, when Canada's government as a percentage of GDP peaked at 53 per cent. See Mueller, *Public Choice Approach to Politics* (Northampton, MA: Edward Elgar, 1993), p. 367. Comparative data from the OECD largely confirm this account. Only a handful of small industrialized countries saw government growth during this period that rivalled Canada's, while Canada surpassed every other major industrialized country. For the primary data, see *OECD Economic Outlook*, December 1985 to June 2008.

16 See Chris Schafer, Joel Emes, and Jason Clemens, *Surveying U.S. and Canadian Welfare Reform* (Vancouver: Fraser Institute, 2001), available at http://fraserinstitute.org; Kenneth J. Boessenkool; *Back to Work: Learning from the Alberta Welfare Reform Experience* (Toronto: C.D. Howe Institute, April 1997), p. 3; and William Watson, John Richards, and David Brown,

The Case for Change: Reinventing the Welfare State (Toronto: C.D. Howe Institute, 1994), p. 3.

17 Employment figures reveal that about 27 per cent of the Canadian workforce was employed in government and the broader public sector (e.g., health and education). As a share of total employment, public sector employment in Canada is about 30 per cent higher than in the US and the OECD average. See Joseph B. Rose, Gary N. Chaison, and Enrique de la Garza, "A Comparative Analysis of Public Sector Restructuring in the US, Canada, Mexico and the Caribbean," *Journal of Labor Research* 21, no. 4 (Fall 2000): 601–625; and P.B. Beaumont, "Public Sector Industrial Relations in Europe," in Dale Berman, Morley Gunderson, and Douglas Hyatt (eds.), *Public Sector Employment in a Time of Transition* (Madison, WI: Industrial Relations Research Centre, 1996), pp. 283–307.

18 Data from *OECD Economic Outlook* 84 (December 2008) and 83 (June 2008).

19 Andrew Coyne, "Social Spending, Taxes, and the Debt: Trudeau's Just Society," in Andrew Cohen and J.L. Granatstein (eds.), *Trudeau's Shadow: The Life and Legacy of Pierre Elliott Trudeau* (Toronto: Vintage Canada, 1999), p. 226.

20 See William Watson, *Globalization and the Meaning of Canadian Life* (Toronto: University of Toronto Press, 1998), p. 42; and Robert Lawson and Michel Kelly-Gagnon, *The Scope of Government and the Wealth of Quebecers*, Economic Note, Montreal Economic Institute (February 2001): 1–2.

21 Federal government debt grew from 51.7 per cent of GDP in Canada in 1960 to 75.6 per cent of GDP in 1996. In the US, government debt grew from 56 to 67.3 per cent of GDP over this period. See Statistics Canada, *National Economic and Financial Accounts*, CANSIM tables 380-0007 and 385-0014, available at http://cansim2.statcan.gc.ca; and Statistics Canada, *Canadian Economic Observer, Historical Statistical Supplement 1995/96*, Catalogue No. 11-210-XPB (1996).

22 As one scholar writes, "The Canadian content [regulations] coming out of Trudeau's model of Canadianization was highly mixed in quality, reception, and impact, and it did not necessarily do much to promote a sense of national place. This consequence should come as no surprise, of course, as cultural industrialism works better for bureaucrats and a cultural worker than it does for those whose primary concern is the opening of systems of communication to greater domestic discourse." See Ryan Edwardson, *Canadian Content: Culture and the Quest for Nationhood* (Toronto: University of Toronto Press, 2008), pp. 220–222.

23 For more on the divergence in Canadian and American unemployment

rates and the policy factors, see Peter Kuhn and Chris Riddell, "The Long-Term Effects of a Generous Income Support Program: Unemployment Insurance in New Brunswick and Main, 1940–1991" (Cambridge, MA: National Bureau of Economic Research, NBER Working Paper No. 11932, January 2006); and David A. Green and W. Craig Riddell, "The Economic Effects of Unemployment Insurance in Canada: An Empirical Analysis of UI Disentitlement," *Journal of Labor Economics* No. 1, Part 2: U.S. and Canadian Income Maintenance Programs (January 1993): S96–S147.

24 *Immigration Statistics: 1980* (Ottawa: Employment and Immigration Canada, 1982), p. 11.

25 Total taxes as a percentage of GDP in Canada increased from 25.7 per cent in 1965 to 35.6 per cent in 1995. In the US, total taxes as a percentage of GDP increased from 24.7 per cent to 27.9 per cent of GDP over this period. Taxes include those on income and profits, payroll, property, and consumption, as well as compulsory contributions to social security programs. See OECD, *Revenue Statistics, 1965–2007*, available at www.oecd.org.

26 A review of Canada's poor productivity record over the past forty years is well documented in Brian Lee Crowley, *Fearful Symmetry: The Fall and Rise of Canada's Founding Values* (Toronto: Key Porter Books, 2009). For a more recent analysis, see Andrew Sharpe's "Lessons for Canada from International Productivity Experience," *International Productivity Monitor* 14 (Spring 2007): 1–18.

27 John Fayerweather, *Foreign Investment in Canada: Prospects for a National Policy* (Toronto: Oxford University Press, 1974), p. 8.

28 Gordon Laxer, *Open for Business: The Roots of Foreign Ownership in Canada* (Toronto: Oxford University Press, 1989), p. 12.

29 Michael Bliss, "American Investment," in Norman Hillmer (ed.), *Partners Nevertheless: Canadian-American Relations in the Twentieth Century* (Toronto: Copp Clark Pitman Ltd., 1989), p. 261.

30 Stephen Azzi, *Commentary on Laura Richie Dawson's "The Evolution of Canadian FDI Policy in the Post-War Era,"* p. 1, available at www.carleton.ca/ctpl/pdf/conferences/tradeinvestment_azzi_comments.pdf.

31 Harry G. Johnson, *The Canadian Quandary: Economic Problems and Policies* (Toronto: McClelland and Stewart, 1977), p. 12.

32 Nixon's protectionist initiative and his unwillingness to grant Canada its historical exemption stunned the Trudeau government. Despite diplomatic efforts by Canadian officials, the American government remained adamant that the import surcharge contained in the NEP would be universally applied. As the historian Bruce Muirhead notes, "The Canadians

continued to be perplexed as to why they did not fit into a special category as they had in the past, especially as their condition vis-à-vis the U.S. had not changed since the 1960s." See Muirhead, "From Special Relationship to Third Option: Canada, the U.S. and the Nixon Shock," *American Review of Canadian Studies* 34, no. 3 (Spring 2004): 439.

33 See Dimitry Anastakis, *Auto Pact: Creating a Borderless North American Auto Industry, 1960–1971* (Toronto: University of Toronto Press, 2005).

34 Bruce Muirhead, *Dancing Around the Elephant: Creating a Prosperous Canada in an Era of American Dominance, 1957–1973* (Toronto: University of Toronto Press, 2005), pp. 41–42.

35 Bruce Doern and Brian Tomlin, *Faith and Fear* (Toronto: Stoddart, 1991), p. 20.

36 Mitchell Sharp, "Canada-US Relations: Options for the Future," *International Perspectives*, Special Issue (Autumn 1972): 1–24; and Paul Wonnacott, *The United States and Canada: The Quest for Free Trade: An Examination of Selected Issues* (Washington, DC: Institute for International Economics, 1987), p. 16.

37 Robert Bothwell, "Canadian-United States Relations: Options for the 1970s," *International Journal* 58, no. 1 (Winter 2002–03): 74.

38 Michael Bliss, *Northern Enterprise: Five Centuries of Canadian Business* (Toronto: McClelland and Stewart, 1987), p. 551.

39 The degree of economic integration is really unprecedented. According to most studies, more than 70 per cent of our trade is *intra-industry*, while close to 40 per cent is *intra-corporate*. This is particularly true in the auto and auto parts industries. Additionally, about one-third of Canada's exports to the US are composed of goods that have been previously imported from the United States. See Someshwar Rao, *North American Economic Integration: Opportunities and Challenges for Canada* (Montreal: Institute for Research on Public Policy, Working Paper Series No. 2004-09a, 2004), pp. 1–14; and Michael Kergin and Brigit Matthiesen, *A New Bridge for Old Allies* (Toronto: Canadian International Council, November 2008).

40 Michael Bliss, *Northern Enterprise: Five Centuries of Canadian Business* (Toronto: McClelland and Stewart, 1987), p. 551.

41 William Johnson, "'Leap of Faith': Canada Must Act on Free Trade, Macdonald Says," *Globe and Mail*, November 19, 1984, A1.

42 The idea of sectoral free trade—that is, free trade arrangements limited to specific sectors of the economy—was endorsed by the Trudeau government's review of Canada's trade policy in August 1983. In particular, the review discussed the possibilities for freer trade in four product areas: steel, farm equipment, urban mass transit equipment, and computer serv-

ices. For more on the 1983 review and the government's pursuit of sectoral free trade, see Michael Hart, *Some Thoughts on Canada–United States Sectoral Free Trade* (Montreal: Institute for Research on Public Policy, 1985).

43 This quotation was later reprinted in Peter C. Newman, *The Secret Mulroney Tapes: Unguarded Confessions of a Prime Minister* (Toronto: Vintage Canada, 2006), pp. 181–182; and Linda Deibel, "Long Battle over Free Trade Coming to an End," *Toronto Star*, December 24, 1988, A1.

44 For a fuller discussion of the outcome of the Tokyo Round, see Michael Hart, *A Trading Nation: Canadian Trade Policy from Colonization to Globalization* (Vancouver: UBC Press, 2002), pp. 308–338.

45 Bruce Doern and Brian Tomlin, *Faith and Fear* (Toronto: Stoddart, 1991), p. 17.

46 See Stephen Clarkson, "The Liberals: Disoriented in Defeat," in Alan Frizzell, Jon H. Pammett, and Anthony Westell (eds.), *The Canadian General Election of 1988* (Ottawa: Carleton University Press, 1989), p. 34.

47 Peter Maser, "On the Hustings," in Alan Frizzell, Jon H. Pammett, and Anthony Westell (eds.), *The Canadian General Election of 1988* (Carleton University Press, 1989), p. 59.

48 Linda Deibel, "Long Battle over Free Trade Coming to an End," *Toronto Star*, December 24, 1988, A1.

49 Stephen Azzi, "Debating Free Trade," *National Post*, January 14, 2006, A18.

50 Bilateral trade growth is the best measure of the benefits of the free trade agreement. Two-way trade in goods crossing the Canada–US border is now valued at $1.9 billion per day. In 2008, thirty-five US states had Canada as their number one merchandise export market. The US exports more goods and services to Canada than to any individual country—more than to Japan and Mexico combined. According to one researcher, "If anything, Canada has seen the strongest gains [of the three NAFTA countries]." See, for example, Lee Hudson Teslik, "NAFTA's Economic Impact," Council on Foreign Relations backgrounder, July 7, 2009.

51 W. Irwin Gillespie, *Tax, Borrow and Spend: Financing Federal Spending in Canada, 1867–1990* (Ottawa: Carleton University Press, 1991), p. 7.

52 See Karin Treff and David B. Perry, *Finances of the Nation: A Review of Expenditures and Revenues of the Federal, Provincial, and Local Governments of Canada*, multiple series, 1985–90 (Toronto: Canadian Tax Foundation), available at www.ctf.ca.

53 See Bruce Bartlett, "Remembering Reagan's Tax Cuts," *Human Events* 62, no. 27 (August 14, 2006): 1–5.

54 Increasingly, in the post-stagflation era, economists in both Canada and elsewhere began to recognize the folly of an uncompetitive tax regime.

For a Canadian perspective, see Harry G. Johnson, *The Canadian Quandary: Economic Problems and Policies* (Toronto: McClelland and Stewart, 1977). See also Victor A. Canto, Douglas H. Joines, and Arthur B. Laffer, *Foundations of Supply-Side Economics—Theory and Evidence* (New York: Academic Press, 1982).

55 W. Irwin Gillespie, *Tax, Borrow and Spend: Financing Federal Spending in Canada, 1867–1990* (Ottawa: Carleton University Press, 1991), pp. 202–203.

56 See Thomas Courchene, "Tax Reform: Impact on Individuals," in E.A. Carmichael (ed.), *Tax Reform: Perspectives on the White Paper* (Toronto: C.D. Howe Institute, 1988), pp. 11–48.

57 W. Irwin Gillespie, *Tax, Borrow and Spend: Financing Federal Spending in Canada, 1867–1990* (Ottawa: Carleton University Press, 1991), pp. 202–203.

58 As one study put it, "Canada's manufacturers' sales tax had long been widely recognized as one of the worst sales taxes levied by any advanced country." See Charles E. McLure Jr., "What Can the United States Learn from the Canadian Sales Tax Debate?" in John B. Shoven and John Whalley, *Canada-U.S. Tax Comparisons* (Chicago and London: University of Chicago Press, 1992), p. 304.

59 The federal government's plan of comprehensive tax reform was outlined in the *White Paper on Tax Reform, 1987* (Ottawa: Minister of Finance, June 1987).

60 The original name for the new tax was to be the blended sales tax, but for some reason something called the BS tax proved a hard sell.

61 A C.D. Howe Institute study by economist Michael Smart shows that not only did the Atlantic provinces' harmonization of sales tax reduce their administrative costs but it also stimulated an increase in private sector investment compared to those provinces that maintained a separate retail sales tax. See Smart, *Lessons in Harmony: What Experiences in the Atlantic Provinces Show about the Benefits of a Harmonized Sales Tax* (Toronto: C.D. Howe Institute, Commentary No. 253, July 2007), p. 19.

62 See Michael Smart, *Lessons in Harmony: What Experiences in the Atlantic Provinces Show about the Benefits of a Harmonized Sales Tax* (Toronto: C.D. Howe Institute, Commentary No. 253, July 2007), pp. 1–28. Economist Jack Mintz has also done extensive research in this field. See, for instance, Mintz, "New Brunswick Rising: A Wide-Ranging *Tax* Revolution Is Set to Turn New Brunswick into a 'Have' Province, and a *Tax* Haven for Business," *National Post*, July 30, 2008, FP15; Mintz and Duanjie Chen, *Ontario's Fiscal Competitiveness in 2004* (Toronto: Institute for Competitiveness and Prosperity, November 8, 2004), p. 9; and Mintz, "Here's a Stimulus Plan: Fix the PST," *Financial Post*, February 20, 2009.

Chapter Three
From Basket Case to World Beater: Canada Shows the Way

1 *OECD Economic Outlook* 85 (June 2009), available at www.oecd.org. The G7 includes Canada, France, Germany, Italy, Japan, the United Kingdom, and the United States.

2 It is important to note that other macroeconomic policies contributed to Canada's robust economic performance. For example, Canada's monetary policy promoted price stability—low inflation—which reduced the impact of inflation on economic decisions made by Canadians. See http://www.bankofcanada.ca/en/ragan_paper/index.html.

3 Several studies have empirically measured the inefficiencies of governments and highlighted the repeated cases of government failure (i.e., waste, mismanagement, incompetence). For example, economists Ludger Schuknecht and Vito Tanzi estimated that there is approximately 25 per cent waste in Canada's public sector. See "Public Sector Efficiency: An International Comparison," *Public Choice* 123 (2005): 321–347. In addition, a review of auditor general reports from 1997 to 2004 found 305 examples of government cost overruns, unnecessary spending, improperly managed programs, and other examples of government failure. It is estimated that these failures cost Canadian taxpayers between $99 billion and $125 billion from 1992 to 2006. See Jason Clemens, Charles Lammam, Milagros Palacios, and Niels Veldhuis, *Government Failure in Canada, 2007 Report: A Review of the Auditor General's Reports, 1992–2006* (Vancouver: Fraser Institute, 2007).

There are several reasons we see and indeed should expect to continue to see case after case of government failure. First, as we note, governments spend other people's money, not their own. And to paraphrase the great economist Milton Friedman, people rarely spend other people's money as wisely as their own. Further, governments typically operate in situations in which there is little if any competition. Without competitive forces at play, there is little incentive to reduce costs and improve service. Perhaps most importantly, political decisions about the allocation of resources are not made to maximize their economic returns; rather, the calculus in the political marketplace involves making decisions to maximize votes (politicians) or power and influence (bureaucrats). An entire branch of economics, referred to as public choice, has developed to better understand the government sector and how it operates. For further information on public choice economics, please see William Mitchell and Randy Simmons, *Beyond Politics: Markets, Welfare, and the Failure of Bureaucracy*

(Oakland, CA: The Independent Institute, 1994), chapters 2, 3, and 4.; and Gordon Tullock, Arthur Seldon, and Gordon L. Brady, *Government Failure: A Primer in Public Choice* (Washington, DC: Cato Institute, 2002), Chapter 1: The Theory of Public Choice.

4 "Canada's New Spirit," *The Economist*, September 25, 2003, available at www.economist.com.

5 By "economic growth" we are talking about inflation-adjusted gross domestic product (GDP), or the total value of goods and services produced in a country.

6 Please see Alberto Alesina and Silvia Ardagna, "Large Changes in Fiscal Policy: Taxes Versus Spending" (Cambridge, MA: National Bureau of Economic Research, NBER Working Paper No. 15438, October 2009), available at www.nber.org/papers/w15438; Alberto Alesina, Roberto Perotti, Francesco Giavazzi, and Tryphon Kollintzas, "Fiscal Expansions and Fiscal Adjustment in OECD Countries," *Economic Policy* 10, no. 21 (October 1995): 207–248; and Alberto Alesina and Roberto Perotti, "Fiscal Adjustments in OECD Countries: Composition and Macroeconomic Effects" (Cambridge, MA: National Bureau of Economic Research, NBER Working Paper No. 5730, August 1996), available at www.nber.org/papers/w5730.

7 Data in this section are from *OECD Economic Outlook* 85 (June 2009), Statistical Annex, tables 1 and 5, available at www.oecd.org/document/61/0,3343,en_2649_34573_2483901_1_1_1_1,00.html; and OECD.Stat extracts for 2009, available at http://stats.oecd.org/index.aspx.

8 While Canada performed relatively well with respect to economic growth from 1997 to 2007, we performed poorly on productivity growth, particularly compared with our southern neighbour, the United States. This is especially true with respect to labour productivity—the average value of output produced per hour worked, measured by GDP—the most common and widely understood measure of productivity. Specifically, in 2007 Canada's GDP per hour worked was 79.1 per cent of that in the US, down from 85 per cent in 1997. See Statistics Canada, *Labour Force Historical Review 2008*, Catalogue No. 71F0004XCB (CD-ROM, 2009); Statistics Canada, Provincial Economic Accounts Data Tables (2009), available at www.statcan.gc.ca/bsolc/olc-cel/olc-cel?catno=13-018-X&lang=eng; US Bureau of Economic Analysis, National Income and Product Accounts Tables (2009), available at www.bea.gov; and US Department of Labor, Bureau of Labor Statistics, Regional and State Unemployment, 2008 Annual Averages (2009), available at www.bls.gov/lau.

Productivity growth is critically important, as it ultimately determines future living standards. A country with significant productivity growth is able to produce more output—goods and services—with a given set of inputs. This will be especially important as Canada's population ages in coming years and we will increasingly rely on a smaller working population.

There is little question that without the fiscal reforms at the federal and provincial levels, Canada's productivity record would have been much worse. As discussed elsewhere in this section, when governments borrow—run deficits—they ultimately compete with and displace other borrowers in the private sector, which reduces the amount of investment and capital available—one of the main drivers of productivity. This is precisely why Canada needs to replicate the successful reforms of the Redemptive Decade to solve our current problems and extend the economic benefits.

In addition, it is important to note that Canada has performed poorly on productivity growth for reasons unrelated to our fiscal situation. These reasons include our industrial structure—and government policies that help maintain that structure—an undervalued currency for much of the period, and a long-term record of weak innovation by Canadian business. For more information on the reasons for and solutions to Canada's productivity performance, see Andrew Sharpe, *Three Policies to Improve Productivity Growth in Canada* (Ottawa: Centre for the Study of Living Standards, 2007), available at www.csls.ca/reports/csls2007-05.PDF; Sharpe, *Lessons for Canada from International Productivity Experience* (Ottawa: Centre for the Study of Living Standards, 2006), available at www.csls.ca/reports/csls2006-02.pdf; Brian Lee Crowley, *Fearful Symmetry: The Fall and Rise of Canada's Founding Values* (Toronto: Key Porter Books, 2009); *In Search of Well Being: Are Canadians Slipping Down the Economic Ladder?* (Toronto: TD Bank, TD Economics, 2005), available at www.td.com/economics/topic/bc0105_wellbeing.pdf; *Who's To Blame for Canada's Productivity Woes?* (Toronto: TD Bank, TD Economics, 2005), available at www.td.com/economics/topic/cg0605_prod.pdf; and the Council of Canadian Academies, Expert Panel on Business Innovation, *Innovation and Business Strategy: Why Canada Falls Short* (2009), available at www.scienceadvice.ca/documents/(2009-06-11)%20Innovation%20Report.pdf; Niels Veldhuis and Jason Clemens (2006). *Productivity, Prosperity, and Business Taxes.* Vancouver, B.C.: The Fraser Institute. Available at http://www.fraserinstitute.org/commerce.web/product_files/Productivity ProsperityBusinessTaxes.pdf.

9 Statistics Canada, *Income in Canada, 2006*, Catalogue No. 75-202-X (2008), available at www.statcan.gc.ca/pub/75-202-x/75-202-x2006000-eng.pdf.

10 Statistics Canada measures the portion of Canadians with "low income" by measuring the percentage of Canadians who devote a larger portion of their income to food, shelter, and clothing than the average Canadian family. Specifically, Statistics Canada calculates the percentage of families that spend more than 63 per cent of their incomes—20 percentage points more than the average family in Canada—on basic necessities: food, shelter, and clothing. That is, the average Canadian family spends 43 per cent of its income on these basic necessities. Statistics Canada, *Income in Canada, 2007*, Catalogue No. 75-202-X (2009), available at www.statcan.gc.ca/pub/75-202-x/75-202-x2007000-eng.pdf.

11 Statistics Canada, *Income in Canada, 2007*, Catalogue No. 75-202-X (2009), available at www.statcan.gc.ca/pub/75-202-x/75-202-x2007000-eng.pdf.

12 Poverty rates measure the percentage of the population that does not have sufficient income to meet basic needs such as a nutritious diet, satisfactory housing, clothing, health care, public transportation, household insurance, telephone service, and a host of other items. In other words, poverty rates differ from low-income rates in that poverty counts the percentage of individuals or families who cannot afford basic necessities rather than the percentage of those who are less well off than their neighbours (i.e., are low-income).

13 Chris Sarlo, *Poverty in Canada: 2006 Update* (Vancouver: Fraser Institute, 2006), available at www.fraserinstitute.org/commerce.web/product_files/PovertyinCanada2006.pdf.

14 Investors, typically foreign investors, would stop financing the government's debt because they have lost confidence in the Canadian government's ability to meet its interest and principal obligations. In addition, investors may become weary of a depreciating foreign exchange, which would reduce the value of their investment over time. Put differently, government bonds become too risky in the eyes of lenders.

15 The data used in this historical section are from Statistics Canada, National Economic and Financial Accounts, CANSIM tables 380-0007 and 385-0014, available at http://cansim2.statcan.gc.ca. National accounts data are used for historical purposes and presented on a calendar year basis. Historical data on a fiscal year basis are preferable, but unfortunately a consistent time series is not available. The primary source of financial

data on a fiscal year basis is from the federal government's public accounts. Unfortunately, there is a break in public accounts data following the introduction of full accrual accounting—data from 1983–84 on are not directly comparable with earlier years.

16 See Statistics Canada, Public Institutions Division, *Financial Management System* (electronic data, 1998 and 1999); *Public Accounts of Canada, 1997–98* (Ottawa: Ministry of Public Works and Government Services, 1999); and the 1999 public accounts for each province and territory. Calculations by the authors.

17 In the ten years preceding 1993, the federal government investment in fixed capital and existing assets averaged 2.5 per cent of total spending. See Statistics Canada, Provincial and Territorial Economic Accounts: Data Tables, 2008 Preliminary Estimates, Vol. 2, no. 2, Catalogue No. 13-018-XWE, Table 7 (2009), available at www.statcan.gc.ca/pub/13-018-x/2009002/tab-eng.htm.

18 "Canada Bankrupt?" *Wall Street Journal* editorial, January 12, 1995. The editorial was attributed to John Fund. See Michael Walker, "Wall Street Journal Sounds Warning," *Fraser Forum*, February 1995.

19 Data presented in this section are from Statistics Canada, National Economic and Financial Accounts, CANSIM tables 380-0007 and 385-0014, available at http://cansim2.statcan.gc.ca. National accounts data are used for historical purposes and presented on a calendar year basis. Historical data on a fiscal year basis are preferable but unfortunately not available. The primary source of financial data on a fiscal year basis is from the federal government's public accounts. Unfortunately, there is a break in public accounts data following the introduction of full accrual accounting—data from 1983–84 onward are not directly comparable with earlier years.

While federal involvement in health care funding was initiated in 1948, it was greatly expanded in 1961 and 1968. The Hospital and Construction Grants Program (HCGP) of 1948 facilitated growth in the number of hospital beds and led to significant increases in health care costs. By 1961, the federal government's funding of health care had been expanded to include 50:50 cost sharing of universal medical insurance for hospital and physicians' services with the provinces. The Medical Care Act—universal health care, or medicare—was enacted by the federal government in 1968 to ensure provincial adherence to a publicly funded health care system. Under the Medical Care Act, the federal government split the costs of hospital and physicians' services equally with the provinces, which in part led to the increase in federal spending post-1968. See http://laws.justice.gc.ca/en/C-6/index.html for the Medical Care Act; and Philippe Cyrenne, *Private Health Care in the OECD: A Canadian Perspective* (Toronto: University of Toronto, Centre for Public Management, Monograph Series No. 13, 2004), available at www.renoufbooks.com/showbook.asp?selID=56955&stream=c&navID=38366.4601388889. A summary of the study is available in the Notes section of the website for the Frontier Centre for Public Policy, www.fcpp.org/publication.php/1012. See also Daniel Eriksson and Arne Björnberg, *Euro-Canada Health Consumer Index 2009* (Winnipeg, MB: Frontier Centre for Public Policy, Series No. 61, May 2009), available at www.fcpp.org/images/publications/61.%202009%20Euro-Canada%20Health%20Consumer%20Index.pdf; David Gratzer, *Code Blue: Reviving Canada's Health Care System* (Toronto: ECW Press, 1999); and William McArthur, Cynthia Ramsay, and Michael Walker, *Healthy Incentives: Canadian Health Reform in an International Context* (Vancouver: Fraser Institute, 1996), available at www.fraserinstitute.org/commerce.web/product_files/Healthy_Incentives.pdf.

20 For a broad and accessible summary of the research on the impact of government spending on economic growth, please see Daniel Mitchell, *The Impact of Government Spending on Economic Growth* (Washington, DC: Heritage Foundation, Backgrounder No. 1831, 2005), available at www.heritage.org/research/budget/upload/bg_1831.pdf. For a more academic discussion of how government spending affects economic performance, please see Alberto Alesina, Silvia Ardagna, Roberto Perotti, and Fabio Schiantarelli, "Fiscal Policy, Profits, and Investment," *American Economic Review* 92, no. 3 (2002): 571–589; Vito Tanzi and Ludger Schuknecht. "Reconsidering the Fiscal Role of Government: The International Perspective," *American Economic Review* 87 (1997): 164–168; and Alberto Alesina, Roberto Perotti, Francesco Giavazzi, and Tryphon Kollintzas, "Fiscal Expansions and Fiscal Adjustment in OECD Countries," *Economic Policy* 10, no. 21 (October 1995): 207–248. Finally, for a scholarly examination of how government spending influences social progress, please see Vito Tanzi and Ludger Schuknecht, "The Growth of Government and the Reform of the State in Industrial Countries," in Andres Solimano (ed.), *Social Inequality* (Ann Arbor: University of Michigan Press, 1998); and Vito Tanzi and Ludger Schuknecht, "Reforming Government: An Overview of the Recent Experience," *European Journal of Political Economy* 13 (1997): 395–417.

21 For a review of the literature on the impact of different types of taxes on behaviour, see Jason Clemens, Niels Veldhuis, and Milagros Palacios, *Tax*

Efficiency: Not All Taxes Are Created Equal (Vancouver: Fraser Institute, 2007), available at http://www.fraserinstitute.org/researchandpublications/publications/3178.aspx.

22 Statistics Canada, National Economic and Financial Accounts, CANSIM tables 380-0007 and 385-0014, available at http://cansim2.statcan.gc.ca. Much of the increase in the size of the federal government occurred under Prime Minister Pierre Trudeau, who held office from 1968 to 1979 and again from 1980 to 1984. Between 1968 and 1984, the size of the federal government increased by more than 40 per cent—from 16 per cent to 22.7 per cent of GDP. Under the Progressive Conservatives (1984 to 1993), led by Prime Minister Brian Mulroney, the size of the federal government initially decreased but ended up slightly larger than when the Conservatives first took office.

23 The website of the Centre for the Study of Living Standards has a research area devoted to studying productivity, www.csls.ca/sectors/productivity.asp, where a wealth of research on productivity in Canada and internationally is available. In particular, please see Andrew Sharpe, *Three Policies to Improve Productivity Growth in Canada*, www.csls.ca/reports/csls2007-05.pdf; and *Lessons for Canada from International Productivity Experience*, www.csls.ca/reports/csls2006-02.pdf. The Economics Department of the Toronto Dominion Bank has also published several readily accessible studies of Canadian productivity, such as *In Search of Well Being: Are Canadians Slipping Down the Economic Ladder?* (Toronto: TD Bank, TD Economics, 2005), available at www.td.com/economics/topic/bc0105_wellbeing.pdf; and *Who's To Blame for Canada's Productivity Woes?* (Toronto: TD Bank, TD Economics, 2005), available at www.td.com/economics/topic/cg0605_prod.pdf. For a discussion of productivity and business taxes, please see Niels Veldhuis and Jason Clemens, *Productivity, Prosperity, and Business Taxes* (Vancouver: Fraser Institute, 2006), available at www.fraserinstitute.org/commerce.web/product_files/ProductivityProsperityBusinessTaxes.pdf; and Niels Veldhuis, "What is Fiscal Policy? Is Government Spending a Source of Stability or Instability?" in Hassan Bougrine and Mario Seccareccia (eds.), *Introducing Macroeconomic Analysis: Issues, Questions, and Competing Views* (Toronto: Emond Montgomery, 2009).

24 Gross debt is the total stock of securitized liabilities owed by the government. This differs from net debt, which refers to the total stock of securitized liabilities owed by a government minus its financial assets. Gross debt is used in this section, as the government's interest payments are determined by the amount of gross debt held.

25 Statistics Canada, Provincial and Territorial Economic Accounts: Data Tables, 2008 Preliminary Estimates, Vol. 2, no. 2, Catalogue No. 13-018-XWE, Table 7 (2009), available at www.statcan.gc.ca/pub/13-018-x/2009002/tab-eng.htm.

26 Specifically, the impact of this cycle can be seen on the effective interest rate, measured as total interest costs relative to the federal debt. The effective interest rate increased significantly, from 5 per cent in 1974 to 7 per cent in 1993, an increase of nearly one-third.

27 As indicated above, the data in this section are from Statistics Canada, National Economic and Financial Accounts, CANSIM Tables 380-0007 and 385-0014, available at http://cansim2.statcan.gc.ca.

28 For election results, see www2.parl.gc.ca/Sites/LOP/HFER/hfer.asp?Language=E&Search=G.

29 Newly appointed minister of finance Paul Martin delivered the Liberals' first budget in February 1994 with a rather bold statement: "It is now time for the government to get its fiscal house in order . . . For years, governments have been promising more than they can deliver, and delivering more than they can afford. That has to end. We are ending it . . . The era of tax and spend government is gone." See Paul Martin, *Budget Speech* (Ottawa: Department of Finance, 1994), pp. 2–3.

30 The budget proposed an increase in program spending from $121.8 billion in 1993–94 to $122.6 billion in 1994–95 and $122.7 in 1995–96. In addition, revenues were forecasted to increase, and substantially, from $114.7 billion in 1993–94 to $123.9 billion in 1994–95 and $132 billion in 1995–96. The forecasted increases in revenue were based on expected increases in GDP growth, which was expected to provide a significant increase in personal income tax revenue as the result of the non-indexation of the tax system and corporate income tax revenues as the result of improved corporate profits. The budget also contained an increase in capital gains taxes, through the elimination of the personal capital gains exemption, and several corporate tax changes that increased revenue. As a result of the spending and revenue initiatives, the budget projected a decrease in the deficit from 6.4 per cent of GDP in 1993–94 to 5.4 per cent in 1994–95 and 4.2 per cent in 1995–96. Given this projection, the Liberals were leaving the largest reductions to the final year, 1996–97, making their goal unlikely without delivering tougher future budgets in the next two years or GDP growth increasing significantly. Please note that the deficit figure for 1993–94 differs slightly from those presented in the previous section, as they are based on the federal government's public accounts, which are on a fiscal year basis, rather than Statistics Canada's national economic and

fiscal accounts, which are on a calendar year basis.

31 Paul Martin, *Budget Speech* (Ottawa: Department of Finance, 1994), p. 13.

32 The Bank of Canada's key rate, the bank rate, upon which most other interest rates in the private market are based, increased from 3.9 per cent in January 1994 to 8.4 per cent in January 1995. See Statistics Canada, CANSIM Table 176-0043 (2009). Financial market statistics are as of the past Wednesday unless otherwise stated, and the monthly per cent bank rate is also available at statcan.gc.ca. For additional information on the impact of increased interest rates on the budget, see John Richards, *Now That the Coat Fits the Cloth . . .* (Toronto: C.D. Howe Institute, Commentary No. 143, June 2000), available at www.cdhowe.org/pdf/rich-4.pdf.

33 In its economic and fiscal update released in October 1994, the federal government indicated that higher-than-expected interest rates threatened to derail its deficit pledge and that further action would be required to achieve its targets. See *Economic and Fiscal Update* (Ottawa: Department of Finance, October 1994).

34 See Donald J. Savoie, *Governing from the Centre: The Concentration of Power in Canadian Politics* (Toronto: University of Toronto Press, 1999).

35 John Richards, *Now That the Coat Fits the Cloth . . .* (Toronto: C.D. Howe Institute, Commentary No. 143, June 2000), available at www.cdhowe.org/pdf/rich-4.pdf.

36 "Canada Bankrupt?" *Wall Street Journal* editorial, January 12, 1995.

37 Donald J. Savoie, *Governing from the Centre: The Concentration of Power in Canadian Politics* (Toronto: University of Toronto Press, 1999), p. 178.

38 Eric Beauchesne, "Reduce Debt Faster, Canada Told: Meeting Existing Target Is a Strict Minimum, OECD Warns," *Vancouver Sun*, December 6, 1994.

39 Paul Martin, *Budget Speech* (Ottawa: Department of Finance, 1995), p. 2.

40 Paul Martin, *Budget Speech* (Ottawa: Department of Finance, 1995), p. 6.

41 While employment insurance (EI) benefits were cut, the government was slow to bring down the contribution rates. The notional "surplus" with respect to employment insurance contributed significantly to the elimination of the deficit.

42 Data contained in these sections are from the federal government's 1995 budget. See *Canadian Federal Budget 1995* (Ottawa: Department of Finance, 1995), available at www.fin.gc.ca/toc/1995/buddoclist95-eng.asp.

43 While approximately 6,000 of the jobs would be transferred to the private sector, in particular in transportation, most would not. To help ease the transition, the government offered an early retirement incentive for employees aged fifty or over with ten or more years of employment, and a

cash-based early departure incentive for departments designated by Treasury Board as "most affected" because they are unable to meet their reductions through existing or workforce adjustment mechanisms.

44 The program review encompassed about $52 billion worth of spending, excluding only statutory federal government transfers to Canadians: $37.7 billion in 1994–95, consisting of elderly benefits, unemployment insurance, and veterans' allowances. Major transfers to other level of governments—$26.9 billion in 1994–95—underwent a separate restructuring, discussed below.

45 Transport Canada would shift its role of owning, operating, and/or subsidizing large parts of the transportation system to focusing instead on developing policy and regulations and enforcing safety standards. Specifically, changes included in the budget included transferring airports to local authorities, commercializing the air navigation system, eliminating transport-related subsidies for farmers and transportation companies, and improving the efficiency of the Coast Guard.

46 Specifically, the budget proposed reducing federal support of safety nets by 30 per cent over three years, reducing subsidies to milk producers by 30 per cent over two years, reducing federal resources devoted to inspection and regulation, closing seven research facilities, and terminating the feed freight assistance transportation subsidy.

47 The remaining assistance was to be largely in the form of loans and repayable contributions. Specifically, the budget eliminated the annual $560-million subsidy to the railways; eliminated the $99-million per year subsidy to the Atlantic region for freight assistance; reduced cultural subsides, including those to book publishing programs and postal subsidies to Canadian books and magazines; and changed the role of regional agencies from providing subsidies to granting loans and repayable contributions.

48 Specifically, the budget put in place the expenditure management system (EMS) to ensure that the scrutiny provided by the program review would become permanent. The EMS would require departments to prepare three-year business plans, including evaluation criteria that would link the performance of the department to the budget process. Program evaluation in particular was to be enhanced through the publication of audits and service standards.

49 The federal government also transfers money through the equalization program, which provides unconditional transfers to less-well-off provinces to provide reasonably comparable levels of public services as is provided in more prosperous provinces. The 1995 budget proposed no

changes to equalization. Territories were dealt with through territorial formula financing, which reduced by approximately 8 per cent from 1994–95 to 1995–96 and was frozen for 1996–97.

50 Direct federal spending on social programs includes the following departments: Citizenship and Immigration, Health, Human Resources Development, Indian Affairs and Northern Development, Canada Mortgage and Housing, and Veterans Affairs.

51 That is, there was no requirement that the EPF transfers must be spent on health and education; rather, provinces were free to spend the transfers on their own priorities. In essence, "health" and "post-secondary" were simply notional labels.

52 Under CAP, the provinces designed and delivered social services subject to federal standards, i.e., that the programs were provided with work and residency requirements.

53 Cost-sharing and national standards had substantial implications for the accountability of costs and quality of social programs—both in a negative direction. As finance minister Martin noted in his budget speech, "The restrictions attached by the federal government to transfer payments in areas of clear provincial responsibility should be minimized . . . they limit innovation . . . [and] increase administrative costs." See Paul Martin, *Budget Speech* (Ottawa: Department of Finance, 1995), p. 17.

54 The Canada Social Transfer (CST) was renamed the Canada Health and Social Transfer (CHST) in the 1996 budget.

55 While the Canada Social Transfer was a block transfer in the sense that the provinces could determine where the money was spent, it was not completely unconditional. To receive the transfer, the provinces had to abide by the principles set out in the Canada Health Act and provide social assistance without any minimum residency requirements. Money would be withheld by the federal government to enforce compliance with these requirements.

56 See Paul Martin, *Budget Speech* (Ottawa: Department of Finance, 1995), p. 7.

57 Specifically, the 1995 budget reduced the deduction limits for RRSP contributions and money purchase pension plans; introduced an additional tax on investment income received by Canadian-controlled private business; increased the corporate capital tax, Canada's most damaging tax, by 12.5 per cent; increased the corporate surtax by a third, from 3 to 4 per cent; increased the capital tax on financial institutions; increased tobacco taxes; and increased gasoline taxes. All told, the tax increases contained in the 1995 budget amounted to an additional $940 million in tax revenue in 1995–96 and $1.28 billion in 1996–97.

58 In 1995–96 spending reductions amounted to $4.3 billion compared to $940 million in tax increases, and in 1996–97 spending reductions amounted to $6.1 billion compared to $1.275 billion in tax increases.

59 Data contained in this section are from the government of Canada's 2008 public accounts and 2009 budget. See Department of Finance Canada, Fiscal Reference Tables (October 2009), available at www.fin.gc.ca/pub/frt-trf/index-eng.asp; and *Canada's Economic Action Plan: Budget 2009* (Ottawa: Department of Finance, 2009), available at http://www.budget.gc.ca/2009/home-accueil-eng.asp.

60 When the economy grows and incomes rise, the tax burden of Canadian families tends to increase to a greater extent than income. The reason for this accelerated increase in the tax burden compared to income is the progressive nature of the Canadian tax system. That is, many Canadians get bumped into higher tax brackets and are therefore forced to pay higher tax rates. The same applies for business income. As a result, revenues can grow more quickly than GDP even though the tax rate structure remains constant. This phenomenon is often called the fiscal drag of the tax system.

61 See Alberto Alesina, Silvia Ardagna, Roberto Perotti, and Fabio Schiantarelli, "Fiscal Policy, Profits, and Investment," *American Economic Review* 92, no. 3 (2002): 571–589; and Alberto Alesina, Roberto Perotti, Francesco Giavazzi, and Tryphon Kollintzas, "Fiscal Expansions and Fiscal Adjustment in OECD Countries," *Economic Policy* 10, no. 21 (October 1995): 207–248.

62 *OECD Economic Outlook* 85 (June 2009), available at www.oecd.org.

63 Lump-sum or head taxes, which require adults to pay an equal amount every year, are not distortionary because there is no way in which people can reduce their tax bill by changing their economic activities, i.e., work effort, consumption, or investment.

64 For a review of the literature on the economic cost of taxation, see Jason Clemens, Niels Veldhuis, and Milagros Palacios, *Tax Efficiency: Not All Taxes Are Created Equal* (Vancouver: Fraser Institute, 2007), available at www.fraserinstitute.org/researchandpublications/publications/3178.aspx.

65 Specifically, the 1994 budget eliminated the $100,000 lifetime capital gains exemption. See *The Budget Plan* (Ottawa: Department of Finance, February 1994), p. 42.

66 *The Budget Plan* (Ottawa: Department of Finance, February 1994); and *The Budget Plan* (Ottawa: Department of Finance, February 1995).

67 All Canadian federal government budgets from 1995 to 2009 are available at www.fin.gc.ca/access/budinfo-eng.asp.

68 Karin Treff and David Perry, *Finances of the Nation* (Toronto: Canadian Tax Foundation, 1997). The 2007 federal budget is available at www.fin.gc.ca/access/budinfo-eng.asp. The corporate income surtax—another tax on capital—was eliminated in 2008. See the 2009 federal budget at www.fin.gc.ca/access/budinfo-eng.asp.

69 *The Budget Plan 2006: Focusing on Priorities* (Ottawa: Department of Finance, 2006), available at www.fin.gc.ca/budtoc/2006/budlist-eng.asp. It is important to note that only the general corporate capital tax was eliminated, while the capital tax on financial institutions was modified but not eliminated in the 2006 budget. For more information on Canadian corporate capital taxes, see Peter E. McQuillan and E. Cal Cochrane, *Capital Tax Issues* (Ottawa: Department of Finance, Technical Committee on Business Taxation, Series 1996–8), available at www.collectionscanada.gc.ca/webarchives/20071124204903; www.fin.gc.ca/taxstudy/wp96-8e.html; http://www.collectionscanada.gc.ca/webarchives/20071205172430/http://www.fin.gc.ca/taxstudy/wp96-8e.pdf; *Capital Taxes in Canada: The Beginning of the End of an Era?* (Toronto: TD Bank, TD Economics, 2007), available at www.td.com/economics/special/pg0607_tax.pdf; and Jason Clemens, Joel Emes, and Rodger Scott, *Corporate Capital Tax: Canada's Most Damaging Tax* (Vancouver: Fraser Institute, 2002), available at www.fraserinstitute.org/researchandpublications/publications/2651.aspx.

70 Specifically, in 1997 federal personal income taxes were 17 per cent on income below $29,590; 26 per cent on income from $29,591 to $59,180; and 29 per cent on income above $59,181. Federal personal income taxes also included a general surtax calculated as a percentage of basic federal tax. For 1997 the general surtax rate was 3 per cent. In addition, a 5 per cent high-income surtax was applied to basic federal tax in excess. See Karin Treff and David Perry, *Finances of the Nation* (Toronto: Canadian Tax Foundation, 1997); and Canada Revenue Agency, www.cra-arc.gc.ca/tx/ndvdls/fq/txrts-eng.html. By 2009, the federal personal income taxes had decreased to 15 per cent on income below $40,726; 22 per cent on income from $40,726 to $81,452; 26 per cent on income between $81,452 and $126,264; and 29 per cent on income over $126,264.

71 It is also important to note that capital gains are taxed through the personal income tax system. When personal income tax rates decline, so too does the tax rate on capital gains. In addition, the tax rate on capital gains was not technically altered because, as described, the applicable tax rate is the personal income tax rate. Rather, the amount of a capital gain included in one's income to be taxed, referred to as the inclusion rate, was decreased twice: first from 75 per cent to 66 per cent and then again to 50

per cent. For a primer on capital gains taxes, please see Stephen Moore and John Silvia, *The ABCs of the Capital Gains Tax* (Washington, DC: Cato Institute, 1995), available at www.cato.org/pub_display.php?pub_id=1101; *Capital Gains Tax Cuts: Myths and Facts* (Heritage Foundation, WebMemo 47, 2001), available at www.heritage.org/Research/Taxes/wm47.cfm. For a detailed summary of the economic costs of capital gains taxes, see Niels Veldhuis, Keith Godin, and Jason Clemens, *The Economic Costs of Capital Gains Taxes* (Vancouver, BC: Fraser Institute, Studies in Entrepreneurship and Markets No. 4, 2007), available at www.fraserinstitute.org/commerce.web/product_files/EconomicCostsCapitalGainsTax.pdf. For a discussion of the economic benefits of eliminating capital gains taxes, please see Herbert Grubel (ed.), *Unlocking Canadian Capital: The Case for Capital Gains Tax Reform* (Vancouver: Fraser Institute, 2000), available at http://oldfraser.lexi.net/publications/books/capital_gains/section_05.html. For an interesting discussion on how best to treat capital rollover investments, please see Jack Mintz and Thomas Wilson, *Removing the Shackles: Deferring Capital Gains Taxes on Asset Rollovers* (Toronto: C.D. Howe Institute, 2006), available at www.cdhowe.org/pdf/backgrounder_94.pdf.

72 For more information on tax-free savings accounts, see www.tfsa.gc.ca.

73 *Fall Economic and Fiscal Statement* (Ottawa: Department of Finance 2008), available at www.fin.gc.ca/ec2008/ec-eng.html.

74 The opposition parties were also incensed about the change in election financing rules contained in the *Fall Economic and Fiscal Statement.* For details, see www.fin.gc.ca/ec2008/EC/ectoc-eng.html.

75 James M. Flaherty, *The Budget Speech 2009* (Ottawa: Department of Finance, 2009), available at www.budget.gc.ca/2009/pdf/speech-discours-eng.pdf.

76 The budget contained $11.8 billion in infrastructure spending, a $4-billion bailout for the auto industry, and a $1-billion community adjustment fund for rural towns.

77 See Jason Clemens and Niels Veldhuis, *GST Cut is the Least Beneficial.* (Vancouver, Fraser Institute, 2006), available at www.fraseramerica.org/Commerce.web/article_details.aspx?pubID=3614.

78 *Update of Economic and Fiscal Projections* (Ottawa: Department of Finance, September 2009), available at http://www.fin.gc.ca/ec2009/pdf/bac-eng.pdf.

Chapter Four
Fiscal Reform: Unsung Provincial Heroes

1 The provincial data presented in this section are consolidated, meaning that the financial accounts of all Canadian provinces and territories are combined (for brevity, we refer to provinces only throughout the chapter although territories are included). Put differently, provincial data are presented as if all provincial and territorial governments acted as one unit. While increases in government spending, use of deficits, and increased debt were more pronounced in some provinces, all individual Canadian provinces followed the same general trend, as indicated by the data presented.

2 The introduction of Canada's government-run health care system is at least partially responsible for the increase in provincial spending. The Medical Care Act, or medicare, was enacted by the federal government in 1968 to ensure provincial adherence to a publicly funded health care system. Under the Medical Care Act, the federal government split the costs of hospital and physicians' services equally with the provinces, which in part led to the increase in federal spending post-1968. See http://laws.justice.gc.ca/en/C-6/index.html for the Medical Care Act; and Philippe Cyrenne, *Private Health Care in the OECD: A Canadian Perspective* (Toronto: University of Toronto, Centre for Public Management, Monograph Series No. 13, 2004), available at www.renoufbooks.com/showbook.asp?selID=56955&stream=c&navID=38366.4601388889 (a summary of the study is available in the Notes section of the website for the Frontier Centre for Public Policy, www.fcpp.org/publication.php/1012); Daniel Eriksson and Arne Björnberg, *Euro-Canada Health Consumer Index 2009* (Winnipeg, MB: Frontier Centre for Public Policy, Series No. 61, May 2009), available at www.fcpp.org/images/publications/61.%202009%20Euro-Canada%20Health%20Consumer%20Index.pdf; David Gratzer, *Code Blue: Reviving Canada's Health Care System* (Toronto: ECW Press, 1999); and William McArthur, Cynthia Ramsay, and Michael Walker, *Healthy Incentives: Canadian Health Reform in an International Context* (Vancouver: Fraser Institute, 1996), available at www.fraserinstitute.org/commerce.web/product_files/Healthy_Incentives.pdf.

3 This measure indicates both the extent to which the government extracts resources from the economy and directs the resources of an economy.

4 The consolidated provincial government deficit reached a peak of 3.7 per cent of GDP in 1992 before declining to 2.9 per cent in 1993.

5 Specifically, the provinces accounted for 22 per cent of the cumulative federal and provincial government deficits from 1980 to 1993.

6 Gross debt is the total stock of securitized liabilities owed by the government. This differs from net debt, which refers to the total stock of securitized liabilities owed by a government minus its financial assets. Gross debt is used in this section because the government's interest payments are determined by the amount of gross debt held. Consolidated gross debt figures for provincial governments are not available prior to 1970.

7 Consolidated provincial and territorial government debt is not available back to 1961. The data source for debt, Statistics Canada's financial management system, differs from the other provincial and territorial fiscal data presented elsewhere in the paper, which are derived from Statistics Canada's national economic and financial accounts.

8 Specifically, interest costs on provincial government debt increased from 5.6 per cent of all provincial revenues in 1970 to 14.5 per cent in 1993.

9 Donald J. Savoie, *Governing from the Centre: The Concentration of Power in Canadian Politics* (Toronto: University of Toronto Press, 1999).

10 Paul Martin, *Budget Speech* (Ottawa: Department of Finance, 1995), p. 2.

11 Department of Finance Canada, Fiscal Reference Tables (October 2009), available at www.fin.gc.ca/pub/frt-trf/index-eng.asp.

12 Ed Tchorzewski, *Budget Address: Rebuilding Saskatchewan Together* (Regina: Saskatchewan Finance, 1992), p. 1.

13 Ed Tchorzewski, *Budget Address: Rebuilding Saskatchewan Together* (Regina: Saskatchewan Finance, 1992), pp. 5, 9.

14 Ed Tchorzewski, *Budget Address: Rebuilding Saskatchewan Together* (Regina: Saskatchewan Finance, 1992), p. 9.

15 Specifically, the 1992 budget increased the corporate income tax rate from 16 to 17 per cent; increased the corporation capital tax surcharge rate from 2 to 3 per cent; and increased the corporate capital tax on financial institutions from 3 to 3.25 per cent. The budget decreased the small business income tax rate from 10 to 9 per cent. Ed Tchorzewski, *Budget Address: Rebuilding Saskatchewan Together* (Regina: Saskatchewan Finance, 1992), pp. 32–33.

16 Ed Tchorzewski, *Budget Address: Rebuilding Saskatchewan Together* (Regina: Saskatchewan Finance, 1992), pp. 27–41.

17 Specifically, 0.7 per cent in 1995–96 and 2.2 per cent in 1996–97.

18 Funding for hospitals was set to decrease by 3 per cent in 1993–94 and 2.8 percent in 1994–95; funding for K-12 and university education was set to decrease by 2 per cent in 1993–94 and 4 percent in 1994–95; and funding for urban and rural municipalities was set to decrease by 5 and 3.3 per

cent, respectively, in 1993–94 and 8 per cent for both in 1994–95. Ed Tchorzewski, *Budget Address: Rebuilding Saskatchewan Together* (Regina: Saskatchewan Finance, 1992), p. 14.

19 Specifically, the 1993 budget increased the corporate capital tax resource surcharge rate from 3 to 3.6 per cent; increased fuel taxes by 2 cents a litre; and increased the sales tax rate from 8 to 9 per cent. Ed Tchorzewski, *Budget Address: Rebuilding Saskatchewan Together* (Regina: Saskatchewan Finance, 1992), p. 16.

20 Simon Fraser University professor John Richards investigated the degree to which the provinces relied on revenue increases versus spending cuts to balance their budgets. Professor Richards found that both Saskatchewan and Alberta cut program spending in multiple years, resulting in a "peak-to-trough reduction of 10 percent in Saskatchewan (fiscal years 1990–91 to 1993–94) and 21 percent in Alberta (1992–93 to 1995–96)." However, in terms of increases in revenues, Saskatchewan revenues increased much faster as the result of tax increases, while Alberta's revenue increased solely as a result of economic growth: "Saskatchewan increased its own-source revenues by 41 percent and Alberta by 23 percent." See John Richards, *Now That the Coat Fits the Cloth . . .* (Toronto: C.D. Howe Institute, Commentary No. 143, June 2000), available at www.cdhowe.org/pdf/rich-4.pdf.

21 *Annual Report* (Edmonton; Government of Alberta, 2006), available at www.finance.alberta.ca/publications/annual_repts/govt/ganrep06/execsumm.pdf.

22 Quoted in Herbert Emery and Ronald D. Kneebone, *Will It Be Déjà Vu All Over Again?* (University of Calgary, School of Public Policy, SPP Briefing Papers 2, Issue 1, April 2009), available at http://policyschool.ucalgary.ca/files/publicpolicy/SPP%20Briefing%20Paper%20-%20Kneebone%20&%20Emery%20FINAL%20(Apr%2009).pdf.

23 Quoted in Herbert Emery and Ronald D. Kneebone, *Will It Be Déjà Vu All Over Again?* (University of Calgary, School of Public Policy, SPP Briefing Papers 2, Issue 1, April 2009), available at http://policyschool.ucalgary.ca/files/publicpolicy/SPP%20Briefing%20Paper%20-%20Kneebone%20&%20Emery%20FINAL%20(Apr%2009).pdf.

24 *Annual Report* (Edmonton; Government of Alberta, 2006), available at www.finance.alberta.ca/publications/annual_repts/govt/ganrep06/execsumm.pdf.

25 In fact, oil prices, which peaked in 1983, inflation-adjusted, would not reach that level again until 2005.

26 *Informing Albertans: Message from the Premier* (Edmonton, AB: Ministry of Finance and Enterprise, 1993).

27 The job cuts are presented on a full-time equivalent basis.

28 *A Financial Plan for Alberta: Budget '93* (Edmonton, AB: Ministry of Finance and Enterprise, 1993), p. 11.

29 Kenneth J. Boessenkool, *Back to Work: Learning from the Alberta Welfare Experiment* (Toronto: C.D. Howe Institute, 1997), available at www.cdhowe.org/pdf/Kbkool.pdf.

30 Statistics Canada, Financial Management System, Public Institutions Division (2002).

31 Jim Dinning, *Budget Speech* (Edmonton, AB: Ministry of Finance and Enterprise, 1993), p. 2.

32 *A Better Way: Budget '94* (Edmonton, AB: Ministry of Finance and Enterprise, 1994).

33 Interestingly, Alberta finance minister Jim Dinning contrasted his plan with the federal government's 1994 budget: "The [federal] Liberal Government is putting off the inevitable in the hopes that things will simply get better: going slow, making small changes, launching task forces and studies and in the meantime increasing spending . . . and increasing the horrendous debt burden for all of us. Going slow may be comforting to some, but it's a house of cards built on false hopes. There is no way of avoiding the tough decisions . . . Next year when the studies are done and those tough decisions are still facing the federal government, we in Alberta will be only the smallest step away from the best announcement we're going to make: a balanced budget in 1996/97." *Alberta Hansard*, February 24, 1994, p. 257.

34 In achieving these five core functions of government, Alberta finance minister Jim Dinning highlighted numerous specific initiatives: "Firstly, investing in people and ideas. That means education for our children and adults. It means research and development. Secondly, building a strong, sustainable, prosperous province. That means building on the Alberta advantage to generate wealth and job growth. Thirdly, providing essential services for the health and well-being of Albertans. That's quality health care for Albertans and basic family and social services support. Fourth is maintaining a quality system of roads and highways, telecommunications and utilities. That means maintaining our infrastructure and preparing for a high-tech future of information superhighways and fibre optics. Fifth and last is providing law, order and good government. That means protecting the safety and the security of Albertans, providing a positive working environment, and open, accountable government. Those are the essentials. All of government's efforts will be focused on those five core businesses." *Alberta Hansard*, February 24, 1994, p. 255.

35 The 1994 budget noted that recovering costs for services through user fees would not apply to essential services (i.e., health, education, social services). See *A Better Way: Budget '94* (Edmonton, AB: Ministry of Finance and Enterprise, 1994), p. 15.

36 The data in this section are from the government of Alberta's 2008–09 annual report, available at www.finance.alberta.ca/publications/annual_repts/govt/index.html.

37 The accumulated debt was eliminated, as the government had set aside enough cash for future debt payments.

38 Department of Finance Canada, Fiscal Reference Tables (October 2009), available at www.fin.gc.ca/pub/frt-trf/index-eng.asp.

39 Statement by Mike Harris, premier of Ontario (1995), available at www.fin.gov.on.ca/english/budget/fallstatement/1995.

40 *1995 Fiscal and Economic Statement* (Toronto: Ministry of Finance, 1995).

41 For information on the welfare reforms enacted in Ontario, please see the Canadian Social Research summary, available at www.canadiansocialresearch.net/onwelf.htm; Marc Frenette and Garnett Picot, *Life After Welfare: The Economic Well Being of Welfare Leavers in Canada during the 1990s* (Ottawa: Statistics Canada, Business and Labour Market Analysis No. 192, 2003), available at www.statcan.gc.ca/pub/11f0019m/11f0019m2003192-eng.pdf; and Todd Gabel, Jason Clemens, and Sylvia LeRoy, *Welfare Reform in Ontario: A Report Card* (Vancouver: Fraser Institute, 2004), available at www.fraserinstitute.org/COMMERCE.WEB/product_files/WelfareReformInOntario.pdf.

42 While welfare benefits were reduced by 22 per cent, Ontario welfare benefits remained about 10 per cent above the national average. See Todd Gabel, Jason Clemens, and Sylvia LeRoy, *Welfare Reform in Ontario: A Report Card* (Vancouver: Fraser Institute, 2004), available at www.fraserinstitute.org/COMMERCE.WEB/product_files/WelfareReformInOntario.pdf.

43 The balanced budget plan was first introduced in the government's fall 1995 fiscal and economic statement, available at www.fin.gov.on.ca/english/budget/fallstatement/1995. The 1996 budget cut a number of different taxes. The two largest reductions were a 30 per cent cut in Ontario's personal income tax rate over three years—a $4.8-billion reduction in revenue per year—and a reduction in the employer health tax through a new $400,000 exemption, a $260-million reduction in revenue per year. The budget also contained many other smaller tax changes and reductions. See *Ontario Budget 1996* (Toronto: Ministry of Finance, 1996), available at www.fin.gov.on.ca/en/budget/ontariobudgets/1996.

44 Capital spending refers to spending on items with a useful life of more

than one year (i.e., schools, hospitals, and transportation infrastructure)

45 In 1996, Ontario's personal income tax system was based on federal personal income taxes paid. For the 1996 taxation year, the Ontario income tax rate was reduced to 56 from 58 per cent of basic federal tax. Fully phased in, the Ontario income tax rate would be reduced to 40.5 per cent of basic federal tax.

46 It is important to note that seven of ten Canadian provinces save for Ontario, Saskatchewan, and Alberta were still in deficit in 1999–2000. Indeed, the impressive reversal from large consolidated provincial deficits in 1993 to a small surplus in 1999 was largely the result of the austerity reforms enacted by these three provinces. Department of Finance Canada, Fiscal Reference Tables (October 2009), available at www.fin.gc.ca/pub/frt-trf/index-eng.asp.

47 Karin Treff and David Perry, *Finances of the Nation* (Toronto: Canadian Tax Foundation, 1995); Canada Revenue Agency, Corporation Tax Rates (2008), available at www.cra-arc.gc.ca/tx/bsnss/tpcs/crprtns/rts-eng.html; and Canada Revenue Agency, What Are the Income Tax Rates in Canada for 2008? (2008), available at www.cra-arc.gc.ca/tx/ndvdls/fq/2008_rt-eng.html.

48 In addition to reductions in corporate income tax rates, many provinces have or are in the process of eliminating their general corporate capital taxes, perhaps the most economically damaging type of tax on capital. Unfortunately, most provinces still maintain capital taxes on financial institutions.

49 Newfoundland, New Brunswick, and Nova Scotia harmonized in 1997. Ontario and British Columbia both recently announced intentions to harmonize their sales taxes with the GST. See new releases from the respective Ministry of Finance in BC and Ontario's ministries announcing the implementation of an HSTwww2.news.gov.bc.ca/news_releases_2009-2013/2009PREM0017-000141.htm; and www.rev.gov.on.ca/en. Note that Quebec maintains a provincial sales tax that is essentially harmonized in that the tax bases are nearly the same. With Alberta not having sales taxes, only Manitoba and Saskatchewan maintain independent provincial sales taxes.

50 For a summary analysis of the HST, see Jason Clemens and Niels Veldhuis, *GST Harmonization: Not Sexy, But Smart* (Vancouver: Fraser Institute, 2008), available at www.fraserinstitute.org/Commerce.web/product_files/GSTHarmonization.pdf.

Chapter Five
Reforming Canada's Entitlements—Glass Two-Thirds Full

1 The Peter G. Peterson Foundation (see www.pgpf.org) has done a great deal of analysis and education on the US's entitlement programs and their increasing problems. The OECD's Pensions at a Glance project (see http://ideas.repec.org/p/pra/mprapa/16349.html) gathers and organizes information on pension programs around the world. The Fraser Institute has for more than a decade accumulated and organized debt and liabilities information for the federal, provincial, and local governments in Canada. Please see Milagros Palacios, Niels Veldhuis, and Kumi Harischandra, *Canadian Government Debt 2008: A Guide to the Indebtedness of Canada and the Provinces* (Vancouver: Fraser Institute, 2008), available at www.fraserinstitute.org/commerce.web/product_files/CanadianGovernmentDebt2008.pdf.

2 For information on Quebec's parallel public pension plan, please see the Government of Quebec's website www.rrq.gouv.qc.ca/en/programmes/regime_rentes.

3 For information on the Canada Pension Plan, please see www.hrsdc.gc.ca/eng/isp/cpp/cpptoc.shtml.

4 For information on the Old Age Security program, please see www.servicecanada.gc.ca/eng/isp/oas/oastoc.shtml.

5 In 2009 the maximum OAS benefit for a single person was $516.96.

6 For the current and projected financial status of the OAS program, see Actuarial Report: Old Age Security, December 31, 2006, at www.osfi-bsif.gc.ca/osfi/index_e.aspx?DetailID=500.

7 For information on the Guaranteed Income Supplement, please see www.servicecanada.gc.ca/eng/isp/pub/oas/gismain.shtml.

8 In 2009, the maximum GIS benefit for a single individual was $652.51.

9 For past actuarial reports of the Canada Pension Plan, please see www.osfi-bsif.gc.ca/osfi/index_e.aspx?DetailID=499.

10 Quite misunderstood in Canada is the fact that the CPP is actually a provincial program administered and maintained by the federal government. Reforming the program therefore required the consent of the provincial governments.

11 For an excellent overview of the problems the CPP faced, as well as the reforms agreed to and implemented, please see *Canada Pension Plan Sixteenth Actuarial Report* (Ottawa: Office of the Superintendent of Financial Institutions, Office of the Chief Actuary, 1997), available at www.osfi-bsif.gc.ca/app/DocRepository/1/eng/oca/reports/cpp/cpp16_e.pdf.

12 For information on the CPP Investment Board, please see www.cppib.ca.

13 Previously, the exemption was calculated as 10 per cent of the earnings upon which the payroll tax was assessed, known as the year's pensionable earnings. While freezing the annual exemption at $3,500 may seem like a small change, it effectively led to a decrease in the value of the exemption every year relative to the average industrial wage. The result of the reduced value of the exemption in real terms meant providing less and less protection for low-income workers. As a result, more and more low-income workers were included in the pool of individuals contributing to the CPP. This was a fairly large change in terms of savings to the CPP: increased CPP contributions generated from this change almost equal the expected changes from *both* the accelerated increase in the payroll tax and the active investment of surplus funds outlined in reforms 1 and 2. See *Canada Pension Plan Sixteenth Actuarial Report* (Ottawa: Office of the Superintendent of Financial Institutions, Office of the Chief Actuary, 1997), available at www.osfi-bsif.gc.ca/app/DocRepository/1/eng/oca/reports/cpp/cpp16_e.pdf.

14 Life expectancy at age 65 for both men and women has increased significantly between 1966, when the CPP and QPP were created, and 2007, the most recent year for which data are available. Specifically, life expectancy at age 65 has increased from 13.8 years in 1966 to 18.2 years in 2007 for men and from 16.8 years to 21.2 years for women. See *23rd Actuarial Report on the Canada Pension Plan* (Ottawa: Office of the Superintendent of Financial Institutions, Office of the Chief Actuary of the Superintendent, 2007), available at www.osfi-bsif.gc.ca/app/DocRepository/1/eng/oca/reports/CPP/cpp23_e.pdf. It is important to recognize that many countries, including the United States, are already in the process of increasing their age of retirement. See the US Social Security Administration website at www.ssa.gov.

15 For example, there have calls for introducing stringent "ethical" and regional investment policies that would reduce the focus on maximizing rates of return at the CPPIB. See, for example, an article on the introduction of social responsibility measures into the investment guidelines of the CPPIB by Jason Clemens and Niels Veldhuis, *The CPP's Next Big Challenges* (Vancouver: Fraser Institute, 2005), available at www.fraserinstitute.org/researchandpublications/publications/3089.aspx.

16 Actuarial reports by the chief actuary in the Office of the Superintendent of Financial Institutions (OSFI) are available at www.osfi-bsif.gc.ca/app/DocRepository/1/RA/0809/eng/8.0_e.html.

17 *23rd Actuarial Report on the Canada Pension Plan* (Ottawa: Office of the

Superintendent of Financial Institutions, Office of the Chief Actuary, 2006), available at www.osfi-bsif.gc.ca/app/DocRepository/1/eng/oca/reports/CPP/cpp23_e.pdf.

18 See the financial result of the CCPIB, available at http://cppib.ca/Results/Financial_Highlights.

19 Specifically, the CCPIB notes that, "Despite the recent unprecedented market downturn, we remain confident that our investment strategy will deliver the returns required to help sustain the plan for decades and generations. The CPP Fund is broadly diversified and designed for a long investment horizon and multi-generational mandate." See www.cppib.ca/faqs.html.

20 In 1990, some 1.9 million Canadians, including dependants, or 7 per cent of the population, were receiving welfare benefits from government. Provincial and local spending on welfare reached $8.6 billion (inflation-adjusted 1996 dollars) in 1990–91. The combination of the 1991 recession and a general trend toward greater dependency resulted in the number of Canadians receiving welfare benefits reaching 3.1 million in 1994, representing an astonishing 10.7 per cent of the population. Real spending on welfare by local and provincial governments hit $14.3 billion in 1993–94. The growth in dependency by the Canadian population, coupled with the increasing pressure on governments to balance their fiscal affairs, set the stage for reform. See Ross Finnie, Ian Irvine, and Roger Sceviour, *Social Assistance Use In Canada: National and Provincial Trends in Incidence, Entry and Exit* (Ottawa: Statistics Canada, Analytical Studies Research Paper No. 245, Catalogue No. F0019M1E, May 2005), available at www.statcan.gc.ca/pub/11f0019m/11f0019m2005246-eng.pdf; F. Roy, *Social Assistance by Province, 1993–2003* (Ottawa: Statistics Canada, Catalogue No. 11-010, November 2004), available at www.statcan.gc.ca/pub/11-010-x/11-010-x2004011-eng.pdf; and Chris Schafer, Joel Emes, and Jason Clemens, *Surveying U.S. and Canadian Welfare Reform* (Vancouver: Fraser Institute, 2001), available at www.fraserinstitute.org/researchandpublications/publications/2559.aspx.

21 Professor John Richards of Simon Fraser University was instrumental in both raising awareness of the fundamental problems present in the country's welfare systems and offering possible solutions. For an excellent summary of his work, please see John Richards, *Retooling the Welfare State: What's Right, What's Wrong, What's to Be Done* (Toronto: C.D. Howe Institute, 1997). Also see the more recent *Reducing Poverty: What Has Worked, and What Should Come Next* (Toronto: C.D. Howe Institute, 2007), available at www.cdhowe.org/pdf/commentary_255.pdf.

22 While changes to the financing of social programs triggered significant welfare reforms in many provinces, a number of smaller reforms occurred prior to 1995. For example, in 1992 New Brunswick implemented a workfare program, New Brunswick Works, aimed at getting people off welfare and into jobs. See Harvey Sawler, *Frank McKenna: Beyond Politics* (Douglas and McIntyre, 2009) pp. 31–34.

23 With a block grant, the amount transferred by the federal government to the provinces does not depend on how much the province spends on the related program(s). On the other hand, cost-sharing grants are tied to the amount that provinces spend. For example, the Canada Assistance Plan (CAP) was a cost-sharing program in which the federal government paid up to half of provincial government spending on social services and social assistance. This meant that the federal government did not control its own spending. Perhaps more critically, the provinces made choices and then sent the federal government the bill for 50 per cent. As a result, the provinces were in the driver's seat and had little or at least reduced incentive to reform their social programs.

24 The increased flexibility and autonomy were not extended to the delivery and design of provincial health care systems, as the federal government continued to use the threat of reduced transfers to ensure that the provinces abided by the federal government's vision of health care as set out in the Canada Health Act.

25 An important experiment with respect to take-home income and employment incentives was completed in Canada. The Self-Sufficiency Project (SSP) was launched in 1992 by Human Resources Development Canada (HRDC). The project encouraged single-parent welfare recipients who had been on welfare for at least one year to find full-time employment by offering them up to three years of additional, or top-up, income. The supplemental income essentially doubled the average participant's earning compared to a minimum-wage job or welfare benefits. There have been disagreements about the longer-term implications of the study. For further information, please see Reuben Ford, David Gyarmati, Kelly Foley, and Doug Tattrie, *Can Work Incentives Pay for Themselves? Final Report on the Self-Sufficiency Project for Welfare Applicants* (Ottawa: Social Research and Demonstration Corp., 2003); Michalopoulos Card and Phillip Robins, *When Financial Incentives Pay for Themselves: Early Findings from the Self-Sufficiency Project's Applicant Study* (Ottawa: Social Research Demonstration Corp., 1999); and Todd Gabel and Sylvia LeRoy, *The Self-Sufficiency Project: No Solution for Welfare Dependency* (Vancouver: Fraser Institute, September 2003).

26 For an empirical examination of this issue during the 1990s, please see Joel Emes and Andrei Kreptul, *The Adequacy of Welfare Benefits in Canada* (Vancouver: Fraser Institute, 1999), available at http://oldfraser.lexi.net/publications/critical_issues/1999/welfare_benefits.

27 For a critical analysis of Saskatchewan welfare reform, please see Jason Clemens and Chris Schafer, *Welfare in Saskatchewan: A Critical Evaluation* (Vancouver: Fraser Institute, 2002), available at www.fraserinstitute.org/commerce.web/product_files/Welfarein Saskatchewan.pdf; and Garson Hunter, *Social Assistance Caseload Impact of the Building Independence Program in Saskatchewan: A Time-Series Analysis* (Regina: University of Regina, Social Policy Research Unit, 2004), available at http://dspace.cc.uregina.ca/dspace/bitstream/10294/926/1/oc-casional_paper_15.pdf. For a summary analysis, please see *The Triumph of Welfare Reform* (Winnipeg, MB: Frontier Centre for Public Policy Notes, September 1, 2004), available at www.fcpp.org/publication.php/809.

28 For a summary analysis of the reforms implemented in Alberta, please see Kenneth J. Boessenkool, *Back to Work: Learning from the Alberta Welfare Experiment* (Toronto: C.D. Howe Institute, 1997), available at www.cd-howe.org/pdf/Kbkool.pdf; and *Who's Better Off With Alberta's Welfare Reform?* (Winnipeg, MB: Frontier Centre for Public Policy Notes, November 3, 1997), available at www.fcpp.org/publication.php/122.

29 David Elton, *Where Are They Now? Assessing the Impact of Welfare Reform on Former Recipients, 1993–1996* (Calgary: Canada West Foundation, 1997). Please also see *Welfare Reform in Alberta: A Survey of Former Recipients* (Calgary: Canada West Foundation, 1997), available at www.cwf.ca/V2/files/199713.pdf. The claim that a large portion of Alberta's welfare recipients simply moved to British Columbia, which was often cited as an explanation, was found to be empirically unproven. For information, please see Kenneth J. Boessenkool, *Back to Work: Learning from the Alberta Welfare Experiment* (Toronto: C.D. Howe Institute, 1997), available at www.cdhowe.org/pdf/Kbkool.pdf.

30 For a discussion of the problems in the welfare system prior to reform, please see John Richards, *Retooling the Welfare State: What's Right, What's Wrong, What's to Be Done* (Toronto: C.D. Howe Institute, 1997). For a detailed examination of Ontario's welfare system, please see E. (Rico) Sabatini, *Welfare—No Fair: A Critical Analysis of Ontario's Welfare System (1985–1994)* (Vancouver: Fraser Institute, 1996).

31 F. Roy, *Social Assistance by Province, 1993–2003* (Ottawa: Statistics Canada, Catalogue No. 11-010 November 2004), available at www.statcan.gc.ca/pub/11-010-x/11-010-x2004011-eng.pdf.

32 Even before Ontario's focus on employment in 1998, Manitoba introduced work-focused programs for welfare recipients in 1996. The Making Welfare Work program was designed to assist employable recipients to make the transition from welfare to work. A number of targeted pilot programs were launched in the province, which made it a less ambitious and narrower program than pursued in Ontario.

33 See Ross Finnie, Ian Irvine, and Roger Sceviour, *Social Assistance Use In Canada: National and Provincial Trends in Incidence, Entry and Exit* (Ottawa: Statistics Canada, Analytical Studies Research Paper No. 245, Catalogue No. F0019M1E May 2005), available at www.statcan.gc.ca/pub/11f0019m/11f0019m2005246-eng.pdf; F. Roy, *Social Assistance by Province, 1993–2003* (Ottawa: Statistics Canada, Catalogue No. 11-010, November 2004), available at www.statcan.gc.ca/pub/11-010-x/11-010-x2004011-eng.pdf; Chris Schafer, Joel Emes, and Jason Clemens, *Surveying U.S. and Canadian Welfare Reform* (Vancouver: Fraser Institute, 2001), available at www.fraserinstitute.org/researchandpublications/publications/2559.aspx; and John Richards, *Reducing Poverty: What Has Worked, and What Should Come Next* (Toronto: C.D. Howe Institute, 2007), available at www.cdhowe.org/pdf/commentary_255.pdf.

The execution of the work-focused program was not, however, flawless. A number of problems were identified, including less-than-adequate work availability in the community portion of the program, insufficient funding for certain aspects of the program, and a number of ongoing administrative problems. See *The Battle against Exclusion: Social Assistance in Canada and Switzerland* (OECD, 1999). For an important analysis of the results of those leaving welfare, please see Marc Frenette and Garnett Picot, *Life After Welfare: The Economic Well Being of Welfare Leavers in Canada during the 1990s* (Ottawa: Statistics Canada, Business and Labour Market Analysis No. 192, 2003), available at www.statcan.gc.ca/pub/11f0019m/11f0019m2003192-eng.pdf.

34 For a summary and analysis of the reforms enacted in 2001, please see Jason Clemens and Chris Schafer, *Welfare Reform in British Columbia: A Report Card* (Vancouver: Fraser Institute, 2002), available at www.fraserinstitute.org/commerce.web/product_files/WelfareReforminBC.pdf.

35 Please note that as the deadline for the first two-year period in the five-year window of benefit eligibility approached, the regulations governing the penalties and deferrals were extended, which basically nullified the penalties and any sense of a real time limit on receipt of benefits. Please see Todd Gabel, Jason Clemens, Sylvia LeRoy, and Niels Veldhuis, *Staying the Course on Welfare Time Limits* (Vancouver: Fraser Institute, 2003),

available at www.fraserinstitute.org/commerce.web/product_files/Fraser-Forum_December2003.pdf.

36 Ross Finnie, Ian Irvine, and Roger Sceviour, *Social Assistance Use In Canada: National and Provincial Trends in Incidence, Entry and Exit* (Ottawa: Statistics Canada, Analytical Studies Research Paper No, 245, Catalogue No. F0019M1E, May 2005), available at www.statcan.gc.ca/pub/11f0019m/11f0019m2005246-eng.pdf; F. Roy, *Social Assistance by Province, 1993–2003* (Ottawa: Statistics Canada, Catalogue No. 11-010, November 2004), available at www.statcan.gc.ca/pub/11-010-x/11-010-x2004011-eng.pdf; Ross Finnie and Ian Irvine, *The Welfare Enigma: Explaining the Dramatic Decline in Canadians' Use of Social Assistance, 1993–2005* (Toronto: C.D. Howe Institute, 2008), available at www.cdhowe.org/pdf/commentary_267.pdf; and Chris Schafer, Joel Emes, and Jason Clemens, *Surveying U.S. and Canadian Welfare Reform* (Vancouver: Fraser Institute, 2001), available at www.fraserinstitute.org/researchandpublications/publications/2559.aspx.

37 For general information on Canada's health care system and the Canada Health Act, please see www.hc-sc.gc.ca/hcs-sss/medi-assur/index-eng.php.

38 While increased spending did purchase some additional health services, it also led to increased demand for those services. As a result, wait times actually increased despite the substantial increases in spending. Specifically, in 2009 wait times for medically necessary health services across Canada was 16.1 weeks, 73 per cent longer than it was back in 1993, the first year for which comparable national wait times data are available. Over this period, health spending per person in Canada increased by 41 per cent. See Nadeem Esmail, *Waiting Your Turn: Hospital Waiting Lists in Canada*, 19th ed. (Vancouver: Fraser Institute, 2009), available at www.fraserinstitute.org/commerce.web/product_files/WaitingYourTurn_2009.pdf. It is also important to note that increased health spending is often directed to areas that do not lead to increased health services (i.e., public sector wages and an expanded bureaucracy). A recent study by the Canadian Institute for Health Information (CIHI) found that despite an increase in inflation-adjusted health spending of 9 per cent per Canadian between 2004–05 and 2007–08, rates of surgery are about the same as they were in 2004–05, indicating little volume increase. Specifically, CIHI found that in 2007–08, "Age-standardized rates of surgery outside the priority areas [hip and knee replacements, cataract surgery, cardiac revascularization, and cancer surgery] are about the same as they were in 2004–05." Within the priority areas, rates of surgery climbed by 7 per cent between 2004–05 and 2005–06, and then essentially stopped growing to

2007–08. See *Surgical Volume Trends, 2009: Within and Beyond Wait Time Priority Areas* (Ottawa: Canadian Institute for Health Information, 2009).

39 Health expenditures in Switzerland were the same as those in Canada in 2005 on an age-adjusted basis.

40 Nadeem Esmail and Michael Walker, *How Good Is Canadian Health Care?* 2008 ed. (Vancouver: Fraser Institute, 2008), available at www.fraserinstitute.org/commerce.web/product_files/HowGoodisCanadianHealthCare2008.pdf. Please also see Philippe Cyrenne, *Private Health Care in the OECD: A Canadian Perspective* (Toronto: University of Toronto, Centre for Public Management, Monograph Series No. 13, 2004), available at www.renoufbooks.com/showbook.asp?selID=56955&stream=c&navID=38366.4601388889 (a summary of the study is available in the Notes section of the website of the Frontier Centre for Public Policy at www.fcpp.org/publication.php/1012); and Daniel Eriksson and Arne Björnberg, *Euro-Canada Health Consumer Index 2009* (Winnipeg, MB: Frontier Centre for Public Policy, Series No. 61, May 2009), available at www.fcpp.org/images/publications/61.%202009%20Euro-Canada%20Health%20Consumer%20Index.pdf.

41 Lawrence J. Kotlikoff and Christian Hagist, *Who's Going Broke? Comparing Healthcare Costs in Ten OECD Countries*, (Cambridge, MA: National Bureau of Economic Research, NBER Working Paper No. 11833, 2005).

42 Nadeem Esmail, *Waiting Your Turn: Hospital Waiting Lists in Canada*, 19th ed. (Vancouver: Fraser Institute, 2009), available at www.fraserinstitute.org/commerce.web/product_files/WaitingYourTurn_2009.pdf. Please also see Philippe Cyrenne, *Private Health Care in the OECD: A Canadian Perspective* (Toronto: University of Toronto, Centre for Public Management, Monograph Series No. 13, 2004), available at www.renoufbooks.com/showbook.asp?selID=56955&stream=c&navID=38366.4601388889 (a summary of the study is available in the Notes section of the website of the Frontier Centre for Public Policy at www.fcpp.org/publication.php/1012); and Daniel Eriksson and Arne Björnberg, *Euro-Canada Health Consumer Index 2009* (Winnipeg, MB: Frontier Centre for Public Policy, Series No. 61, May 2009), available at www.fcpp.org/images/publications/61.%202009%20Euro-Canada%20Health%20Consumer%20Index.pdf.

43 Nadeem Esmail, *Canada's Physician Supply* (Vancouver: Fraser Institute, 2008), available at www.fraserinstitute.org/commerce.web/product_files/FraserForum_November2008.pdf, pp 13–17. Little wonder, then, that nearly 1.7 million Canadians twelve or older in 2007, some 6 per cent of the population, reported being unable to find a regular doctor. See Statistics

Canada, Health Reports 2008002, Vol. 19, no. 2, available at www.statcan.gc.ca/bsolc/olc-cel/olc-cel?catno=82-003-X&chropg=1&lang=eng.

44 Nadeem Esmail and Michael Walker, *How Good Is Canadian Health Care?* 2008 ed. (Vancouver: Fraser Institute, 2008), available at www.fraserinstitute.org/commerce.web/product_files/HowGoodisCanadianHealthCare2008.pdf.

45 For a detailed explanation of the Canada Health Act, see *Canada Health Act Annual Report 2007–2008* (Ottawa: Health Canada, 2008), available at www.hc-sc.gc.ca/hcs-sss/pubs/cha-lcs/2008-cha-lcs-ar-ra/index-eng.php.

46 With respect to how the health care system is managed, governments across Canada have variously implemented, reorganized, or eliminated regional management models; focused on expanding the use of electronic health records; increased efforts to track and manage waiting lists; reorganized health care delivery to increase use of focused surgical centres; and announced wait time benchmarks and guarantees in select areas of care. The benchmarks apply specifically to joint replacement and repair, radiation therapy, cataract surgery, and heart surgery. The care guarantees apply in each province to any one of these areas but need not be the same length of time as the benchmark. See Nadeem Esmail, *Guaranteed Suffering* (Vancouver: Fraser Institute, May 2007), pp. 3–6. In terms of the incentives faced by providers of health care services, governments across Canada have variously outsourced a small number of health activities to private sector providers; purchased private surgical and diagnostic facilities; altered methods of compensation for providers; and altered scopes of practice. Finally, in attempting to control financial outlays, governments across Canada have variously reduced capacity; forcibly restricted health expenditures to contain budgets—spending restrictions at times led to cancellations of surgeries and reductions in the number of procedures being done at the health facility level; delisted health services; consolidated purchasing of health supplies; and eliminated or implemented new health taxes. A new health care tax was introduced in Ontario in 2004, while the health care tax in Alberta was eliminated in 2009. It should be noted that these reforms are not exhaustive but do provide a good guide for the changes that have, or perhaps more pertinently have not, been made over time.

47 Notable by their absence are substantial changes to the Canadian approach to universal health care insurance, such as a move away from first-dollar coverage of universally insured services or a substantial shift away from a monopolistic public hospital sector or from the public monopoly in health care insurance outside of Quebec, where the change was re-

quired by the Supreme Court of Canada. See *Chaoulli v. Quebec* (Attorney General) [2005] SCC35, available at www.canlii.org/en/ca/scc/doc/2005/2005scc35/2005scc35.html.

48 Readers should note that this reflects both an increase in health expenditures and a decrease in the size of government outlays relative to the size of the economy (see *OECD Health Data 2008*; calculations by the authors).

49 The rate of growth in health expenditures was contained by governments and actually fell on a real per capita basis during the early- to mid-1990s, during a period of economic rationalization intended to contain government spending after a long period of deficit spending.

Chapter Six
Where'd You Get That Suit? U.S. Buckles on Fiscal Straitjacket

1 Debt can also be accumulated when longer-term projects, which provide benefits to citizens over time, are financed with debt, such as bonds. This is an appropriate use of longer-term financing that better matches the costs over time with the benefits provided over time.

2 Deficits were certainly present and prominent prior to 1980; however, our period of analysis begins in 1980.

3 Please note that the fiscal year for the US federal government runs from October 1 to September 30.

4 The fiscal data presented in this section are a combination of historical data and expectations for the future compiled and calculated by the non-partisan Congressional Budget Office (www.cbo.gov). Specifically, historical data are available in CBO historical tables at www.cbo.gov/ftpdocs/100xx/doc10014/Historicaltables09Jun09web.XLS. The estimates for the future are based on a combination of the Congressional Budget Office's long-term analysis (see *The Budget and Economic Outlook: An Update* (Washington, DC: Congressional Budget Office, August 2009), available at www.cbo.gov/doc.cfm?index=10521); and the CBO's analysis of President Obama's proposed budget, *A Preliminary Analysis of the President's Budget and an Update of the CBO's Budget and Economic Outlook* (Washington, DC: Congressional Budget Office, March 2009), available at www.cbo.gov/doc.cfm?index=10014.

These series were selected to allow for a discussion and analysis of both historical and future expected budgets using a common economic definition. There are, however, important and relevant alternative sources of information, such as the Office of Management and Budget (www.omb.gov) and the Bureau of Economic Analysis's national economic accounts series, available at www.bea.gov/national.

5 There are a number of ways to view deficits, including their nominal and real (i.e., inflation-adjusted) dollar values as well as a percentage of government spending. While these measures are useful, we think the most instructive and informative way to examine deficits, and indeed a host of other government fiscal measures, is by comparing them to the overall economy (GDP).

6 More specifically, annual deficits as a share of the economy reached slightly more than 6 per cent of GDP in 1983, declined to 2.8 per cent of GDP by 1989, and then started increasing again, reaching almost 4.7 per cent of GDP in 1992.

7 See, for example, Thomas S. McCaleb, *Deficits and Taxes: Federal Budget and Fiscal Policy in the 1980s* (Washington, DC: Cato Institute, 1994), available at www.cato.org/pub_display.php?pub_id=911&full=1.

8 It is important to recognize that many of Clinton-era successes were achieved through a combination of the Republican-controlled Congress, both House and Senate, which controls the legislative side of the US government, and the president himself, who controlled the executive branch of the US government.

9 For more information on the Congressional Budget Office, please see www.cbo.gov.

10 It is worth noting that the US system of public finance is quite different from the parliamentary system Canadians are accustomed to. In our system, the governing party presents a budget in the spring for parliamentary approval and normally updates its finances in the fall. In other words, there are two discrete periods when the Canadian federal government and indeed the nation focus on government finances.

The US system of budgets is more fluid than the Canadian system. The executive branch of government—the president—presents a budget for consideration in the early spring, but it is the legislative branch—Congress—that actually crafts and approves a budget. In addition, the legislative branch must reconcile two versions, stemming from the House of Representatives and the Senate. It is not uncommon for budget proposals and updates to be published year-round.

11 The estimates for the future are based on a combination of the Congressional Budget Office's long-term analysis (see *The Budget and Economic Outlook: An Update* (Washington, DC: Congressional Budget Office, August 2009), available at www.cbo.gov/doc.cfm?index=10521); and the CBO's analysis of President Obama's proposed budget, *A Preliminary Analysis of the President's Budget and an Update of the CBO's Budget and Economic Outlook* (Washington, DC: Congressional Budget Office, March

2009), available at www.cbo.gov/doc.cfm?index=10014.

12 *A Preliminary Analysis of the President's Budget and an Update of the CBO's Budget and Economic Outlook* (Washington, DC: Congressional Budget Office, March 2009), available at www.cbo.gov/doc.cfm?index=10014.

13 *Mid-Session Review: Budget of the U.S. Government* (Washington, DC: Office of Management and Management, 2009), Table S1, page 25, available at www.whitehouse.gov/omb/assets/fy2010_msr/10msr.pdf. Importantly, though, both the CBO long-term estimate of expected accumulated deficits over the next ten years and the OMB update published on the same day were generally seen as overly optimistic. For instance, the CBO analysis assumed that all of the Bush-era tax cuts would be reversed, which no one, including the Obama administration, had proposed. Thus the revenues likely to accrue over the ten-year period would be less than assumed in the CBO analysis. Similarly, the OMB update assumed full revenues from the proposed cap-and-trade emissions permit system even though the bill passed by the House had reduced the expected revenues significantly and the bill was stalled in the Senate with passage unlikely in 2009. For further information on the overly optimistic nature of both economic updates, please see Jonathan Weisman and Deborah Solomon, "Decade of Debt: $9 Trillion.," *Wall Street Journal*, August 26, 2009, A1, available at http://online.wsj.com/article/SB125119686015756517.html.

14 William Ahern, *Can Income Tax Hikes Close the Deficit?* (Washington, DC: The Tax Foundation, No. 197, October 2009), available at www.taxfoundation.org/files/ff197.pdf.

15 *The Budget and Economic Outlook: An Update* (Washington, DC: Congressional Budget Office, August 2009), available at www.cbo.gov/doc.cfm?index=10521. Interestingly, though, the budget expectations at the time of writing actually included deficits that were less than originally proposed by the Obama administration in its 2010 budget submission. Under the budget proposal submitted by the Obama administration (for information on President Obama's proposed 2010 budget, please see the Office of Management and Budget at www.whitehouse.gov/omb/budget), deficits would have averaged 6 per cent of GDP over the ten-year period from 2010 to 2019. More specifically, deficits would have reached 13.1 per cent of GDP in 2009, would have declined to 4.1 per cent of GDP in 2013, and then begun increasing steadily, reaching 5.7 per cent in 2019. See *A Preliminary Analysis of the President's Budget and an Update of CBO's Budget and Economic Outlook* (Washington, DC: Congressional Budget Office, March 2009), available at www.cbo.gov/doc.cfm?index=10014.

16 Concerns about the deficits and accumulating debt spanned nearly the entirety of the political and economic spectrum. For instance, Dr. Alice Rivlin, first director of the Congressional Budget Office, deputy director of the Office of Management and Budget from 1993 to 1994, and director of the OMB from 1994 to 1996 under President Clinton, published a number of papers critical of the Reagan deficits—and Reagan economic policies more broadly—during the 1980s. See Alice Rivlin, "Why and How to Cut the Deficit," *Brookings Review* (1984). Similarly, organizations predisposed to smaller government, compared to the liberal Brookings Institution, also published studies critical of the deficits. See, for example, Thomas S. McCaleb, *Deficits and Taxes: Federal Budget and Fiscal Policy in the 1980s* (Washington, DC: Cato Institute, 1994), available at www.cato.org/pub_display.php?pub_id=911&full=1.

17 For example, a *Wall Street Journal*/NBC poll cited in the *Wall Street Journal* on June 18, 2009 (Laura Meckler, "Public Wary of Deficit, Economic Intervention," A1 and A14) showed that 58 per cent of respondents thought that the president and Congress should worry about "keeping the deficit down" compared to 35 per cent for "boosting the economy" and 7 per cent non-responsive. An increasing number of prominent economic and political commentators recognize the economic risks of the deficits being incurred and proposed in Washington. See, for example, Edmund L. Andrews, "Wave of Debt Payments Facing U.S. Government," *New York Times*, November 22, 2009, available at www.nytimes.com/2009/11/23/business/23rates.html?_r=2&th&emc=th; and Douglas Holtz-Eakin, "The Coming Deficit Disaster," *Wall Street Journal*, November 20, 2009, available at http://online.wsj.com/article_email/SB10001424052748704888404574547492725871998-lMyQjAxMDA5MDIwMjEyNDIyWj.html.

18 For more information on the Office of Management and Budget, please see www.whitehouse.gov/omb.

19 A number of other high-profile economists both in and outside of the administration have offered stark warnings about the economic effects of continuing and increasing deficits. For example, Federal Reserve chairman Ben Bernanke explicitly warned the US Congress of the deleterious effects of deficits in his regular testimony on June 3, 2009. See Jon Hilsenrath and Brian Blackstone, "Bernanke Urges Deficit Reduction, Sees Growth This Year," *Wall Street Journal*, June 4, 2009, A3, available at http://online.wsj.com/article/SB124403584900281215.html. In addition, economists with the more liberal-leaning Brookings Institution also recently warned of the negative effects of high and increasing deficits; see William G. Gale and Alan J. Auerbach, *An Update on the Economic and*

Fiscal Crises: 2009 and Beyond (Washington, DC: Brookings Institution, 2009), available at www.brookings.edu/papers/2009/06_fiscal_crisis_gale.aspx (a synopsis of the study is also available at www.brookings.edu/articles/2009/0730_deficit_gale.aspx). There are also, however, prominent economists who argue that large and increasing deficits should not be a source of concern; for example, see Paul Krugman, "Till Debt Does Its Part," *New York Times*, August 27, 2009, available at www.nytimes.com/2009/08/28/opinion/28krugman.html?_r=1.

20 *The Long-Term Economic Effects of Some Alternative Budget Policies* (Washington, DC: Congressional Budget Office, May 2008), p. 2, available at www.cbo.gov/ftpdocs/92xx/doc9216/05-19-LongtermBudget_Letter-to-Ryan.pdf.

21 The Congressional Budget Office reiterated these concerns yet again in its August 2009 economic and budget update. See *The Budget and Economic Outlook: An Update* (Washington, DC: Congressional Budget Office, 2009), available at www.cbo.gov/ftpdocs/105xx/doc10521/08-25-BudgetUpdate.pdf.

22 *The Long-Term Budget Outlook* (Washington, DC: Congressional Budget Office, June 2009), p. vii, available at www.cbo.gov/ftpdocs/102xx/doc10297/06-25-LTBO.pdf. Additional discussion of the economic costs of rising debt is available on pages 16 and 17.

23 *The Budget and Economic Outlook: An Update.* (Washington, DC: Congressional Budget Office, August 2009), available at www.cbo.gov/doc.cfm?index=10521.

24 Please recall the difference between debt and deficits. Deficits occur in any particular period, whether it is a quarter or annually, when government spending exceeds revenues. The shortfall in revenues compared to spending is covered through borrowing. Debt, on the other hand, is the accumulation of these deficits coupled with any other debt-financed projects.

25 The data used to analyze US federal debt is "debt held by the public." It is a narrower measure than gross federal debt, which stood at a little over $900 billion in 1980 compared to $711.9 billion in debt held by the public. The difference between the two measures is debt held in federal government accounts, principally the social security and other trust funds. Debt held by the public rather than gross federal debt was used in order to have a consistent series of debt over time; only debt held by the public is projected by the CBO in its analysis of the Obama administration's budget proposal.

26 Data for debt held by the public are a combination of historical information from the Congressional Budget Office data tables (Table F-2), available at www.cbo.gov/ftpdocs/100xx/doc10014/Historicaltables09Jun09web.XLS;

and estimates for the future based on the Congressional Budget Office's long-term forecast and their analysis of President Obama's budget proposal. See *The Budget and Economic Outlook: An Update* (Washington, DC: Congressional Budget Office, August 2009), available at www.cbo.gov/doc.cfm?index=10521; and *A Preliminary Analysis of the President's Budget and an Update of CBO's Budget and Economic Outlook* (Washington, DC: Congressional Budget Office, March 2009), available at www.cbo.gov/doc.cfm?index=10014.

27 Congressional Budget Office historical data tables (Table F-2), available at www.cbo.gov/ftpdocs/100xx/doc10014/Historicaltables09Jun09web.XLS.

28 *The Budget and Economic Outlook: An Update* (Washington, DC: Congressional Budget Office, August 2009), Table 1-2, p. 4, available at www.cbo.gov/doc.cfm?index=10521.

29 *The Budget and Economic Outlook: An Update* (Washington, DC: Congressional Budget Office, August 2009), Table 1-2, p. 4, available at www.cbo.gov/doc.cfm?index=10521.

30 *A Preliminary Analysis of the President's Budget and an Update of CBO's Budget and Economic Outlook* (Washington, DC: Congressional Budget Office, March 2009), Table 1-4, p. 10, available at www.cbo.gov/doc.cfm?index=10014.

31 For a discussion of the United States' longer-term debt problems, please see "America's Public Debt: Tomorrow's Burden," *The Economist*, October 22, 2009, available at www.economist.com/displaystory.cfm?story_id=14699754.

32 The United States quotes "net interest costs," which account for not only the borrowing costs incurred by the federal government but also the interest earned on social security and other trust assets. The "net" cost quoted is meant to reflect the actual, or net, cost of borrowing.

33 An alternative way to view interest costs and the way most other economic indicators are examined in this paper is by comparing them to the overall economy (GDP). Interest costs as a share of GDP were generally increasing from 1980 all the way through to 1995. Specifically, interest costs as a share of the economy stood at 1.9 per cent of GDP in 1980 and increased fairly steadily to reach a peak of 3.3 per cent of GDP in 1991. Interest costs then began to decline, from 3.2 per cent of GDP in 1995 to 1.2 per cent of GDP by 2009. (Please see Congressional Budget Office historical data tables (Table F-6), available at www.cbo.gov/ftpdocs/100xx/doc10014/Historicaltables09Jun09web.XLS). The Congressional Budget Office indicated that pre-budget fiscal policies would have increased interest costs as a share of the economy from 1.2 per cent in 2009 to 2.7 per

cent in 2019, more than doubling the economic burden of federal government interest costs. See *A Preliminary Analysis of the President's Budget and an Update of CBO's Budget and Economic Outlook* (Washington, DC: Congressional Budget Office, March 2009), Table 1-2, p. 3, available at www.cbo.gov/doc.cfm?index=10014.

34 Congressional Budget Office data tables F-1 and F-6, with calculations by the authors, available at www.cbo.gov/ftpdocs/100xx/doc10014/Historicaltables09Jun09web.XLS.

35 *The Budget and Economic Outlook: An Update.* (Washington, DC: Congressional Budget Office, August 2009), Table 1-2, p. 4, available at www.cbo.gov/doc.cfm?index=10521.

36 For a discussion of the specific attributes of entrepreneurial capitalism compared to other forms of capitalism, please see William J. Baumol, Robert E. Litan, and Carl J. Schramm, *Good Capitalism, Bad Capitalism, and the Economics of Growth and Prosperity* (New Haven, CT: Yale University Press, 2007). A summary of the book is available at http://sites.kauffman.org/capitalism.

37 *The Budget and Economic Outlook: An Update.* (Washington, DC: Congressional Budget Office, August 2009), Table 2, page XIII, available at www.cbo.gov/doc.cfm?index=10521.

38 In nominal terms, the US federal budget has grown from $590.9 billion in 1980 to almost $3 trillion in 2008, according to data from the OMB. See *Historical Tables: Budget of the United States Government* (Washington, DC: Office of the President of the United States, 2009), Table 1.1, p. 22, available at www.gpoaccess.gov/USbudget/fy06/pdf/hist.pdf.

39 For an interesting examination of fiscal stimulus, please see Alberto F. Alesina and Silvia Ardagna, *Large Changes in Fiscal Policy: Taxes Versus Spending* (Cambridge, MA: National Bureau of Economic Research, NBER Working Paper No. 15438, October 2009), available at www.nber.org/papers/w15438.

40 In addition to the $787-billion stimulus package passed in 2009 and approved by President Obama (details are available at www.recovery.gov), the US Congress also passed an additional $410-billion spending package for 2009, referred to as the omnibus spending bill (details are available at www.bloomberg.com/apps/news?pid=20601103&sid=aGcZFK6kDeQo&refer=us).

41 For example, it is not at all clear how certain portions of the health care, education and training, and tax relief measures included in the stimulus bill will be temporary. Indeed, a reading of the measures indicates that at least some portions of these aspects of the stimulus bill will constitute on-

going and perhaps even permanent new spending. See www.recovery.gov for more information on the stimulus bill.

42 *The Budget and Economic Outlook: An Update.* (Washington, DC: Congressional Budget Office, August 2009), Table 1-2, p. 4, available at www.cbo.gov/doc.cfm?index=10521.

43 *Historical Tables: Budget of the United States Government* (Washington, DC: Office of the President of the United States, 2009), Table 1.1, pp. 24, 25, available at www.gpoaccess.gov/USbudget/fy06/pdf/hist.pdf. Calculations by the authors.

44 Interestingly, though, the increases observed in the budget are less than those proposed by President Obama, who preferred to see federal government spending as a share of the economy reach 24.5 per cent by 2019. (See *A Preliminary Analysis of the President's Budget and an Update of CBO's Budget and Economic Outlook* (Washington, DC: Congressional Budget Office, March 2009), Table 1-4, p. 10, available at www.cbo.gov/doc.cfm?index=10014.

45 *The Budget and Economic Outlook: An Update* (Washington, DC: Congressional Budget Office, August 2009), Table 1-2, p. 4, available at www.cbo.gov/doc.cfm?index=10521. Calculations by the authors. For comparative purposes, President Obama's budget proposal called for spending as a share of the economy to reach 24.5 per cent by 2019. See *A Preliminary Analysis of the President's Budget and an Update of CBO's Budget and Economic Outlook* (Washington, DC: Congressional Budget Office, March 2009), Table 1-4, p. 10, available at www.cbo.gov/doc.cfm?index=10014.

46 For a concise discussion of the similarities between the Bush and Obama spending plans, see C. Edwards, *Obama's Budget Builds on Bush Precedents* (Washington, DC: Cato Institute, Tax and Budget Bulletins No. 55, March 2009), available at www.cato.org/pubs/tbb/tbb_0311_55.pdf.

47 *A Preliminary Analysis of the President's Budget and an Update of CBO's Budget and Economic Outlook* (Washington, DC: Congressional Budget Office, March 2009), available at www.cbo.gov/doc.cfm?index=10014.

48 For a recent study updating and analyzing the fiscal positions of the US states, please see *Beyond California: States in Fiscal Peril* (Washington, DC: Pew Center on the States, 2009), available at http://downloads.pewcenteronthestates.org/BeyondCalifornia.pdf; a summary and links are available at www.pewcenteronthestates.org/report_detail.aspx?id=56044.

49 Information is available from the US Census. A specific request for these data was submitted to and results received from Craig A. Langley, Public Accounting Specialist, United States Bureau of the Census. Calculations to convert the series to real dollars were completed by the authors.

50 Information is available from the US Census. A specific request for these data was submitted to and results received from Craig A. Langley, public accounting specialist, United States Bureau of the Census. Calculations to convert the series to real dollars were completed by the authors.

51 An alternative source of information on this series is available at the Federal Reserve Board, www.federalreserve.gov/releases/z1/Current/data.htm.

52 Information is available from the US Census. A specific request for these data was submitted to and results received from Craig A. Langley, Public Accounting Specialist, United States Bureau of the Census. Calculations to convert the series to real dollars were completed by the authors. Also, please note that the nominal increase in interest costs over this period was $20.5 billion to $97.2 billion. As a share of the economy, state and local interest costs have remained fairly stable at 0.7 per cent of GDP. Please recall that this stability is a function of two factors. The first is the general decline in interest costs beginning in the early 1990s. The second is the fairly robust US economy throughout the 1990s.

53 *National Income and Product Accounts Tables* (Washington, DC: U.S. Bureau of Economic Analysis, 2009), available at www.bea.gov. Calculations and analysis by the authors. An alternative source for state and local revenues and spending is the Census Bureau (www.census.gov). It shows similar trends but only covers up to 2005–06. For instance, the census data indicate that state and local government spending as a share of GDP increased from 13 per cent in 1980–81 to 16.2 per cent in 2005–06, which is before spending spikes in the 2008 and 2009 fiscal years due to the international recession.

54 For an interesting and provocative discussion of what many experts believe is an inevitable need for large-scale reform of state and local governments in the US, please see Mitch Daniels, "The Coming Reset in State Government," *Wall Street Journal*, September 4, 2009, A17, available at http://online.wsj.com/article/SB10001424052970204731804574390603114939642.html.

55 U.S. Bureau of Economic Analysis, National Income and Product Accounts Tables (2009), available at www.bea.gov. Calculations and analysis by the authors.

56 U.S. Bureau of Economic Analysis, National Income and Product Accounts Tables (2009), available at www.bea.gov. Calculations and analysis by the authors.

57 Robert Carling of Australia's Centre for Independent Studies recently published an analysis of the fiscal state of the United States, which is in many ways similar to our overall analysis. Please see Robert Carling, *Fiscal*

Shock and Awe in the United States (St. Leonards, NSW, Australia: Centre for Independent Studies, Vol. 1, No. 118, October 2009), available at www.cis.org.au/issue_analysis/IA118/IA118.pdf.

58 *The Long-Term Budget Outlook* (Washington, DC: Congressional Budget Office, June 2009), available at www.cbo.gov/ftpdocs/102xx/doc10297/06-25-LTBO.pdf.

59 See C. Edwards, *State and Local Government Debt Is Soaring* (Washington, DC: Cato Institute, Tax and Budget Bulletin No. 37, 2006), available at www.cato.org/pubs/tbb/tbb_0706-37.pdf.

Chapter Seven
Are Americans Entitled to Their Entitlements? Social Security and Medicare

1 For more information, please see the Social Security Administration website at www.ssa.gov.

2 For an excellent summary of the fiscal effects of Social Security and Medicare, please see *The Nation's Long-Term Fiscal Outlook: April 2008 Update* (Washington, DC: Government Accountability Office, 2008), available at www.gao.gov/new.items/d08783r.pdf; and *The Long-Term Budget Outlook* (Washington, DC: Congressional Budget Office, June 2009), available at www.cbo.gov/ftpdocs/102xx/doc10297/06-25-LTBO.pdf.

3 Please recall that Canada has largely solved its unfunded liability problems with respect to the Canada Pension Plan but not for our health care system. Thus the unfunded liabilities problem is more isolated and less broad-based in Canada than it is in the United States.

4 A leading organization in the education and promotion of reform regarding the US fiscal balance is the Peter G. Peterson Foundation. Information, including their widely heralded documentary, *I.O.U.S.A.*, is available at www.pgpf.org. David Walker, the former head of the US Government Accountability Office (GAO), was recently interviewed by the *Wall Street Journal* about the Peterson Foundation and its mission to educate Americans about the serious accumulation of debt; the interview is available at http://online.wsj.com/article/SB10001424052970203585004574392620693542630.html.

5 Please note that the normal age of retirement for those born after 1959 is being raised to 67.

6 The 12.4 per cent tax is technically split between employer and employee at 6.2 per cent each. The 6.2 per cent is actually further broken down to 5.3 per cent for old-age and survivors' benefits and 0.9 per cent for disability insurance.

7 Canada Pension Plan payments are augmented by Old Age Security benefits, with a maximum monthly benefit of $516.96, as well as a number of other smaller federal and provincial benefits.

8 *Annual Report of the Supplemental Security Income Program* (Washington, DC: Social Security Administration, May 2008), available at www.ssa.gov/OACT/ssir/SSI08/ssi2008.pdf.

9 See information available at www.servicecanada.gc.ca/eng/sc/oas/gis/guaranteeddincomesupplement.shtml.

10 Forty-five of the fifty states, with the exception of Arkansas, Kansas, Tennessee, Mississippi, and West Virginia, provide additional supplemental income on top of the federal benefit.

11 Reports are available at www.ssa.gov/OACT/TR/2009. Specifically, see the *2008 Annual Report of the Board of Trustees for the Federal Old-Age and Survivors Insurance and Federal Disability Insurance Trust Funds* (Washington, DC: Board of Trustees of the Federal Old-Age and Survivors Insurance and Federal Disability Insurance Trust Funds, 2008), available at www.ssa.gov/OACT/TR/2009/tr09.pdf; and *2008 Annual Report of the Board of Trustees of the Federal Hospital Insurance and Federal Supplementary Medical Insurance Trust Funds* (Washington, DC: Board of Trustees of the Federal Hospital Insurance and Federal Supplementary Medical Insurance Trust Funds, 2008), available at www.cms.hhs.gov/Reports TrustFunds/downloads/tr2009.pdf.

12 The term "notional assets" was used purposely because, while the funds are technically invested in special obligations from the Treasury, the real nature of the assets is to defray market borrowing by the federal government. In other words, the invested assets are essentially IOUs from American taxpayers to American taxpayers.

13 This is four years earlier than in the 2008 report, which predicted the funds would be exhausted in 2041, indicating an ongoing deterioration in the finances of Social Security.

14 *A Summary of the Status of the Social Security and Medicare Program* (Washington, DC: Social Security Administration, Trustees of Social Security and Medicare, 2009), available at www.ssa.gov/OACT/TRSUM/tr09summary.pdf.

15 See Neil Howe and Richard Jackson, *The Myth of the 2.2 Percent Solution* (Washington, DC: Cato Institute, 1997), available at www.cato.org/pubs/ssps/ssp11.html.

16 For an excellent summary of the longer-term challenges facing Social Security, please see "The Long-Term Outlook for Social Security," *The Long-Term Budget Outlook* (Washington, DC: Congressional Budget Office,

June 2009), Chapter 3, available at www.cbo.gov/ftpdocs/102xx/doc10297/06-25-LTBO.pdf.

17 The US Government Accountability Office (GAO) published an overview document of key issues in Social Security reform, *Social Security Reform: Answers to Key Questions* (Washington DC: Government Accountability Office, 2005), available at www.gao.gov/new.items/d05193sp.pdf. In addition, the Cato Institute (www.cato.org) has published an enormous amount of important and interesting research on Social Security issues, including reform options. Please see www.socialsecurity.org for additional information.

18 For example, see L. Jacob Rodriguez, "Chile's Private Pension System at 18: Its Current State and Future Challenges," The Cato Project on Social Security Privatization No. 17 (July 30, 1999), available at www.socialsecurity.org/pubs/ssps/ssp-17es.html.

19 For information on the GAO, please see www.gao.gov.

20 *The Nation's Long-Term Fiscal Outlook: April 2008 Update* (Washington, DC: Government Accountability Office, 2008), available at www.gao.gov/new.items/d08783r.pdf.

21 Detailed information about Medicare is available at www.medicare.gov as well as at www.ssa.gov/pgm/links_medicare.htm.

22 *The Long-Term Budget Outlook* (Washington, DC: Congressional Budget Office, June 2009), available at www.cbo.gov/ftpdocs/102xx/doc10297/06-25-LTBO.pdf. In particular, see Chapter 2, "The Long-Term Outlook for Medicare, Medicaid, and Total Health Care Spending."

23 For a concise discussion and comparison of the problems in Social Security versus Medicare, please see John R. Graham, "Why Consumer-Driven Health Care is Crashing on the Shoals of Medicare," *Health Policy Prescriptions* 6, no. 4 (2009), available at http://liberty.pacificresearch.org/docLib/20080408_HPPv6n4_0408.pdf.

24 Information about Medicaid is available at www.medicare.gov.

25 Dedicated revenues are expected to exceed anticipated costs one year sooner than calculated in a 2008 report and the notional fund is expected to be exhausted two years earlier than in last year's report, both highlighting the deteriorating nature of Medicare's financing.

26 *Summary of the Status of the Social Security and Medicare Program* (Washington, DC: Social Security Administration, Trustees of Social Security and Medicare, 2009), p. 2, available at www.ssa.gov/OACT/TRSUM/tr09summary.pdf.

27 *The Long-Term Economic Effects of Some Alternative Budget Policies* (Washington, DC: Congressional Budget Office, May 2008), p. 1, available

at www.cbo.gov/ftpdocs/92xx/doc9216/05-19-LongtermBudget_Letter-to-Ryan.pdf. More recently, the president's Council of Economic Advisers (www.whitehouse.gov/administration/eop/cea) released a paper examining health care in the United States, *The Economic Case for Health Care Reform*, available at www.whitehouse.gov/administration/eop/cea/TheEconomicCaseforHealthCareReform. The authors projected that costs of Medicare and Medicaid as a share of the economy would increase from roughly 6 per cent of GDP to 15 per cent by 2040, which is approximately three-quarters of current US federal government spending.

28 *The Long-Term Budget Outlook* (Washington, DC: Congressional Budget Office, June 2009), available at www.cbo.gov/ftpdocs/102xx/doc10297/06-25-LTBO.pdf.

29 *The Long-Term Economic Effects of Some Alternative Budget Policies.* (Washington, DC: Congressional Budget Office, May 2008), p. 10, available at www.cbo.gov/ftpdocs/92xx/doc9216/05-19-LongtermBudget_Letter-to-Ryan.pdf.

30 Available at www.pgpf.org.

31 This estimate is as of January 1, 2008, and includes all existing obligations and commitments as of that date. Information and the report are available at www.pgpf.org/about/nationaldebt.

Chapter Eight
Not What the Founders Had in Mind: Representation without Taxation

1 For an overview of recent studies examining tax compliance costs in the United States, please see *Tax Policy: Summary of Estimates of the Costs of the Federal Tax System.* (Washington, DC: Government Accountability Office, 2005), available at www.gao.gov/products/GAO-05-878. In addition, the Tax Foundation has published a number of studies on compliance costs in the United States; these studies are available at www.taxfoundation.org/research/topic/96.html. Finally, Ms. Nina Olson, the national taxpayer advocate at the IRS, recently argued for tax simplification in the United States; see "We Still Need a Simpler Tax Code," *Wall Street Journal*, April 10, 2009, A13, available at http://online.wsj.com/article/SB123933106888707793.html.

2 For example, François Vaillancourt and Jason Clemens have estimated total compliance costs for all taxes in Canada in 2005 at between $16.2 and $25 billion, representing between 1.2 and 1.8 per cent of GDP. See Vaillancourt and Clemens, "Compliance and Administrative Cost of Taxation in Canada," in Jason Clemens (ed.), *The Impact and Cost of Taxation in Canada* (Vancouver, BC: Fraser Institute, 2008), available at www.fraserinstitute.org/

researchandpublications/publications/5173.aspx. The Tax Foundation in the United States calculated tax compliance costs for federal income taxes at $265.1 billion for 2005. This represented approximately 2.1 per cent of GDP, and it ignores state and local taxes and federal taxes other than income taxes. See Total Federal Income Tax Compliance Costs, 1990–2015, available at www.taxfoundation.org/research/show/1962.html.

3 The 2006 federal budget in Canada created a whole set of new tax credits. For example, the budget created the new Canada employment credit, valued at up to $500 in employment income; a $2,000 tax credit for employers who hire apprentices; a $1,000 grant for first- and second-year apprentices; a new $500 tax deduction for tradespeople for tool costs in excess of $1,000; and a new tax credit for textbooks, to name just a few of the new credits and deductions created. See the section titled "Budget in Brief" in the 2006 Budget Summary for the Canadian Government at www.fin.gc.ca/budget06/brief/brief-eng.asp.

4 For a delineation and calculation of tax compliance costs in Canada, please see François Vaillancourt and Jason Clemens, "Compliance and Administrative Cost of Taxation in Canada," in Jason Clemens (ed.), *The Impact and Cost of Taxation in Canada* (Vancouver, BC: Fraser Institute, 2008), available at www.fraserinstitute.org/researchandpublications/publications/5173.aspx.

5 For a discussion of the costs of tax compliance costs in Canada, please see François Vaillancourt and Jason Clemens "Compliance and Administrative Cost of Taxation in Canada," in Jason Clemens (ed.), *The Impact and Cost of Taxation in Canada* (Vancouver, BC: Fraser Institute, 2008), available at www.fraserinstitute.org/researchandpublications/publications/5173.aspx. In addition, the Tax Foundation in the United States has done a great deal of work on tax compliance costs and related issues; please see their website for further information, www.taxfoundation.org/research/topic/96.html.

6 For example, please see *OECD Tax Statistics, Volume I: Revenue Statistics* (2009), available at www.oecd.org/document/51/0,3343,en_21571361_33915056_39142515_1_1_1_1,00.html#revenue.

7 OECD. Stats extract (2009), available at http://stats.oecd.org/index.aspx; and OECD Economic Outlook 85, (June 2009).

8 For comparative purposes, the total size of government, as measured by total government spending as a share of the economy (GDP), was 34.1 per cent in the United States in 1980 compared to 41.6 per cent in Canada, a difference of 22 per cent. In 1988, the last year of the Reagan administration, the difference in the size of government between the two countries

increased: government spending was 35.6 per cent of GDP in the US compared to 45.8 per cent in Canada. The size of government as a share of the economy reached its peak, 53.3 per cent, in Canada in 1992, the last year of the Bush administration, wherein government spending stood at 38.6 per cent of GDP. The gap between the two countries narrowed significantly during the Clinton administration: in 2000, for example, government spending as a share of the economy was 33.9 per cent in the US compared to 41.1 per cent in Canada. The gap in 2009 is slightly larger than it was in the previous few years. For example, in 2008, the gap was just 2.3-percentage points: 39.7 per cent in Canada compared to 38.8 per cent in the United States. Please see OECD. Stats extract (2009), available at http://stats.oecd.org/index.aspx; and OECD Economic Outlook 85 (June 2009).In addition, as discussed previously, the trend line for spending in the United States is going in one direction and one direction only—up. It is easily foreseeable that in the next few years, the size of government, and thus the burden of government (i.e., taxes, including deficits) will be less in Canada than in the United States.

9 The exception to this rule is a lump-sum tax, such as a head tax, which would have no incentive-based effect.

10 See Dale W. Jorgensen and Yun Kun-Young, "The Excess Burden of Taxation in the United States," *Journal of Accounting and Finance* 6 (1991): 487–508; Charles L. Ballard, John B. Shoven, and John Whalley, "General Equilibrium Computations of the Marginal Welfare Costs of Taxes in the United States," *American Economic Review* 75, no. 1 (1985): 128–138; Martin Feldstein, *The Effect of Taxes on Efficiency and Growth* (Cambridge, MA: National Bureau of Economic Research, NBER Working Paper No. 12201, 2006), available at www.nber.org/papers/w12201; and for an overview of studies examining tax compliance costs in the United States, Tax Policy: Summary of Estimates of the Costs of the Federal Tax System (Washington, DC: Government Accountability Office, 2005), available at www.gao.gov/products/GAO-05-878. For a more general discussion of this literature, please see Jason Clemens, Niels Veldhuis, and Milagros Palacios, *Tax Efficiency: Not All Taxes Are Created Equal* (Vancouver: Fraser Institute, 2007), available at www.fraserinstitute.org/researchandpublications/publications/3178.aspx.

11 For an overview and discussion of Canadian data on this topic, please see Jason Clemens, Niels Veldhuis, and Milagros Palacios, *Tax Efficiency: Not All Taxes Are Created Equal* (Vancouver: Fraser Institute, 2007), available at www.fraserinstitute.org/researchandpublications/publications/3178.aspx.

12 *Revenue Statistics, 1965–2007* (OECD, 2008), tables 12 and 13, p. 101.

General information is available at www.oecd.org and limited specific information about this particular study is available at www.oecd.org/document/4/0,3343,en_2649_34533_41407428_1_1_1_1,00.html.

13 *Revenue Statistics, 1965–2007* (OECD, 2008), tables 12 and 13, p. 101. General information available at www.oecd.org and limited specific information about this particular study is available at www.oecd.org/document/4/0,3343,en_2649_34533_41407428_1_1_1_1,00.html.

14 For information on President Obama's plans for corporate-based taxes as well as the larger business tax environment in the United States, please see www.taxfoundation.org/competeusa.

15 *Revenue Statistics, 1965–2007* (OECD, 2008) tables 26 and 27, p. 108. General information is available at www.oecd.org and limited specific information about this particular study is available at www.oecd.org/document/4/0,3343,en_2649_34533_41407428_1_1_1_1,00.html.

16 See *Corporate Income Tax Rates: International Comparisons* (Washington, DC: Congressional Budget Office, 2005), available at www.cbo.gov/ftpdocs/69xx/doc6902/11-28-CorporateTax.pdf; and Daniel J. Mitchell, *Corporate Taxes: America is Falling Behind* (Washington, DC: Cato Institute, Tax and Budget Bulletin No. 48, July 2007), available at www.cato.org/pubs/tbb/tbb_0707_48.pdf.

17 See Jack Mintz, *Cutting the Effective Corporate Tax Rate* (Washington, DC: Cato Institute, Tax and Budget Bulletin No. 50, October 2008), available at www.cato.org/pubs/tbb/tbb_1008-50.pdf.

18 Scott Hodge, "U.S. States Lead the World in High Corporate Taxes," available at www.taxfoundation.org/publications/show/22917.html.

19 Congressional Budget Office, Data on the Distribution of Federal Taxes and Household Income, April 2009, available at www.cbo.gov/publications/collections/taxdistribution.cfm.

20 The Congressional Budget Office uses the following process to categorize and organize households based on income: "Income categories are defined by ranking all people by their comprehensive household income adjusted for household size—that is, divided by the square root of the household's size. A household consists of the people who share a housing unit, regardless of their relationships. Quintiles, or fifths, contain equal numbers of people. Households with negative income (business or investment losses larger than other income) are excluded from the lowest income category but are included in totals." Further, the CBO defines income as, "Comprehensive household income equals pretax cash income plus income from other sources. Pretax cash income is the sum of wages, salaries, self-employment income, rents, taxable and nontaxable interest, dividends,

realized capital gains, cash transfer payments, and retirement benefits plus taxes paid by businesses (corporate income taxes and the employer's share of Social Security, Medicare, and federal unemployment insurance payroll taxes) and employee contributions to 401(k) retirement plans. Other sources of income include all in-kind benefits (Medicare, Medicaid, employer-paid health insurance premiums, food stamps, school lunches and breakfasts, housing assistance, and energy assistance)."

21 The Tax Policy Center recently published a new paper examining likely federal tax distributions over the 2009–12 period. Please see Rachael M. Johnson and Jeffrey Rohaly, *The Distribution of Federal Taxes, 2009–12* (Washington, DC: Tax Policy Center, 2009), available at www.taxpolicycenter.org/UploadedPDF/411943_distribution_federal.pdf.

22 The disparity between the shares of after-tax income and the burden of taxes becomes even more pronounced if individual income taxes are examined in isolation. Please see CBO data at www.cbo.gov/publications/collections/tax/2009/tax_liability_shares.xls for further information. Gerald Prante of the Tax Foundation (www.taxfoundation.org) recently completed an analysis of differences between income and income tax burdens. See Summary of Latest Federal Individual Income Tax Data, Fiscal Fact No. 183, available at http://taxfoundation.org/publications/show/250.html.

23 See www.taxfoundation.org.

24 Andrew Chamberlain, Gerald Prante, and Scott A. Hodge, *Who Pays America's Tax Burden, and Who Gets the Most Government Spending?* (Washington, DC: Tax Foundation, 2007), available at www.taxfoundation.org/files/sr151.pdf.

25 The distributional disparities are particularly stark when federal-only spending is examined. The top 20 per cent of households received $0.32 in benefits for each dollar paid in taxes, while the bottom 20 per cent of households enjoyed $14.76 in benefits per dollar of taxes paid. See Andrew Chamberlain, Gerald Prante, and Scott A. Hodge, *Who Pays America's Tax Burden, and Who Gets the Most Government Spending?* (Washington, DC: Tax Foundation, 2007), Figure 6, p. 9, available at www.taxfoundation.org/files/sr151.pdf.

26 The Tax Foundation study noted above calculated that the top 40 per cent of households received benefits that were less than $1 per dollar of taxes paid. Conversely, the bottom 60 per cent of households were calculated to receive benefits in excess of $1 per dollar of taxes contributed. Please see Andrew Chamberlain, Gerald Prante, and Scott A. Hodge, *Who Pays America's Tax Burden, and Who Gets the Most Government Spending?* (Washington, DC: Tax Foundation, 2007), Figure 6, p. 9, available at

www.taxfoundation.org/files/sr151.pdf. For an interesting non-technical discussion of this issue, please see Charles Murray, "Tax Withholding Is Bad for Democracy," *Wall Street Journal*, August 13, 2009, available at http://online.wsj.com/article_email/SB10001424052970204313604574328273572673730-lMyQjAxMDA5MDEwMzExNDMyWj.html.

27 For additional information on rent-seeking, or the seeking of benefits through the political system, please see any of the following: Jonathan Rauch, "Demosclerosis," *National Journal*, September 5, 1992, available at www.jonathanrauch.com/jrauch_articles/demosclerosis_the_original_article; Alexis de Tocqueville, *Democracy in America* (Chicago: University of Chicago Press, 2002); Mancur Olson, *The Rise and Decline of Nations: Economic Growth, Stagflation, and Social Rigidities* (New Haven, CT: Yale University Press, 1992); and William C. Mitchell and Randy T. Simmons, *Beyond Politics* (Oakland, CA: Independent Institute, 1994).

Chapter Nine
Laurier's Unfinished Symphony

1 Data from Statistics Canada, National Economic and Financial Accounts, 2009, available online at www.statcan.gc.ca/nea-cen/index-eng.htm.

2 Data from *OECD Economic Outlook* 84 (December 2008) and 83 (June 2008).

3 W. Irwin Gillespie, *Tax, Borrow and Spend: Financing Federal Spending in Canada, 1867–1990* (Ottawa: Carleton University Press, 1991), p. 7.

4 This line of thinking is further developed in Brian Lee Crowley, *Fearful Symmetry: The Fall and Rise of Canada's Founding Values* (Toronto: Key Porter Books, 2009).

5 Canadian productivity has lagged behind in the United States since the mid-1970s. See Richard Dion, "Interpreting Canada's Productivity Performance in the Past Decade: Lessons from Recent Research," *Bank of Canada Review* (Summer 2007): 19–32.

6 Quoted in Robert Bothwell and J.L. Granatstein, *Our Century: Canadian Journey* (Toronto: McArthur and Co., 2000), p. ix.

7 For example, in June 2009 the OECD calculated Canada's expected real (inflation-adjusted) GDP growth for 2009 as –2.6 per cent, which ranked Canada sixth best among the thirty OECD countries covered. The US was expected to record a slightly worse performance of –2.8 per cent real GDP growth for 2009. Canada ranked ninth for real GDP growth expectations for 2010. Please see *OECD Economic Outlook* 85 (June 2009), Annex Table 1, available at www.oecd.org/document/61/0,3343,en_2649_34573_2483901_1_1_1_1,00.html.

8 *Canada's Economic Action Plan: Budget 2009* (Ottawa: Department of Finance, 2009), Table 1.1, p. 29, available at www.budget.gc.ca/2009/pdf/budget-planbugetaire-eng.pdf.

9 Interestingly, the 2008 *Fall Economic and Fiscal Update* acknowledged the economic problems but approached them quite differently. Indeed, in many ways, the federal government's call for spending restraint and protecting the budget echoed the principles of the Chrétien–Martin era. For details, see *Fall Economic and Fiscal Statement* (Ottawa: Department of Finance, 2008), available at www.fin.gc.ca/ec2008/EC/ectoc-eng.html.

10 *Canada's Economic Action Plan: Budget 2009* (Ottawa: Department of Finance, 2009), Table 1.1, p. 29, available at www.budget.gc.ca/2009/pdf/budget-planbugetaire-eng.pdf. However, TD Economics' June 2009 updated forecast of federal finances suggested that the federal government would remain in deficit through 2013–14 as government finances continued to deteriorate throughout 2009. Specifically, TD Economics calculated that between 2010–11 and 2013–14, the federal government will run a cumulative deficit of $116.1 billion. Please see *5-Year Federal Fiscal Forecast* (Toronto: TD Bank, TD Economics, June 2009), available at www.td.com/economics/special/db0609_fiscal.pdf.

11 *Update of Economic and Fiscal Projections* (Ottawa: Department of Finance, 2009), available at www.fin.gc.ca/ec2009/ec-eng.asp. For an excellent summary of the fiscal situation facing the federal government, please see *The Coming Era of Fiscal Restraint* (Toronto: TD Bank, TD Economics, October 20, 2009), available at www.td.com/economics/special/db1009_fiscal.pdf.

12 *Update of Economic and Fiscal Projections* (Ottawa: Department of Finance, 2009), Table 1, p. 9, available at www.fin.gc.ca/ec2009/ec-eng.asp.

13 For succinct summaries and analysis of the provincial and federal budgets, please see TD Economics' Federal and Provincial Budget page at www.td.com/economics/gov_finances.jsp.

14 *Government Budget Balances and Net Debt* (Toronto: TD Bank, TD Economics, May 2009), available at www.td.com/economics/budgets/govt_budget_09.pdf.

15 Interestingly, the debate on how best to proceed with respect to fiscal policy (i.e., spending restraint to balance budgets versus ongoing deficits) is not unique to Canada. As well as the United States, a number of European countries are currently experiencing the same debate. See, for example, Kathryn Hopkins, "Britain Cannot Afford Any Further Fiscal Stimulus, King Warns," *Guardian*, March 24, 2009, available at www.guardian.co.uk/business/2009/mar/24/bankofenglandgovernor-banking; and Agnes

Crane, "New German Minister Rules Out Balanced Budget Paper," Reuters, October 25, 2009, available at www.reuters.com/article/bondsNews/idUSLP68293920091025.

16 For an interesting examination of fiscal stimulus, please see Alberto F. Alesina and Silvia Ardagna, *Large Changes in Fiscal Policy: Taxes Versus Spending* (Cambridge, MA: National Bureau of Economic Research, NBER Working Paper No. 15438, October 2009), available at www.nber.org/papers/w15438; and Niels Veldhuis, "What is Fiscal Policy? Is Government Spending a Source of Stability or Instability?" in Hassan Bougrine and Mario Seccareccia (eds.), *Introducing Macroeconomic Analysis: Issues, Questions, and Competing Views* (Toronto: Emond Montgomery, 2009).

17 *Canada's Economic Action Plan: Budget 2009* (Ottawa: Department of Finance, 2009), Table 1.1, p. 29, available at www.budget.gc.ca/2009/pdf/budget-planbugetaire-eng.pdf. Please note that 2008–09 revenues of $236.4 billion were already off markedly from the previous year's $242.4 billion.

18 *Update of Economic and Fiscal Projections* (Ottawa: Department of Finance, 2009), Table 1, p. 9, available at www.fin.gc.ca/ec2009/ec-eng.asp.

19 Critically, the assumption that revenues would recover fairly quickly was corroborated by TD Economics' June 2009 updated forecast of federal finances. Please see *5-Year Federal Fiscal Forecast* (Toronto: TD Bank, TD Economics, June 2009), available at www.td.com/economics/special/db0609_fiscal.pdf.

20 *Update of Economic and Fiscal Projections* (Ottawa: Department of Finance, 2009), Table 1, p. 9, available at www.fin.gc.ca/ec2009/ec-eng.asp.

21 Please note that the authors are not making a judgment on the efficacy of such "stimulative" spending. Rather, we are simply observing that some of the increase in spending, which has created sizable deficits, is the result of temporary spending.

22 *Update of Economic and Fiscal Projections* (Ottawa: Department of Finance, 2009), Table 1, p. 9, available at www.fin.gc.ca/ec2009/ec-eng.asp.

23 Please see www.servicecanada.gc.ca/eng/ei/menu/eihome.shtml for more information on Canada's employment insurance system. Apart from the cyclical increases in employment insurance benefits overall, the government expanded the program three separate times in 2009. First, the 2009 federal budget increased the generosity of EI by increasing the length of benefit period, or duration, easing the eligibility criteria, and expanding the availability of training. For details see *Canada's Economic Action Plan: Budget 2009* (Ottawa: Department of Finance, 2009), available at www.budget.gc.ca. More recently, the government again increased the

duration of EI benefits to a select group of unemployed workers, those who have contributed to the program in seven of the past ten years. For details, see the fact sheet at www.hrsdc.gc.ca/eng/employment/ei/fact_sheet.shtml. Finally, the government extended special benefits, including maternity, parental, sickness, and compassionate care benefits, to the self-employed; see the news release at http://news.gc.ca/web/article-eng.do?nid=493319. The federal government also froze premiums at the 2008–09 rates for the next two years. However, it also indicated that premiums will increase incrementally over the next five years to bring the EI account back into balance.

24 For information on Canada's welfare system, as well as the reforms implemented as part of the decentralization efforts of the federal government, which resulted in an explosion of provincial experimentation with welfare provision and design, please see Jason Clemens, Joel Emes, and Chris Schafer, *Surveying U.S. and Canadian Welfare Reform* (Vancouver: Fraser Institute, 2001), available at www.fraserinstitute.org/researchandpublications/publications/2559.aspx.

25 For example, spending on employment insurance benefits, which reacts strongly to the state of the economy and in particular the unemployment rate, was expected to increase from $14.3 billion in 2007–08 to a high of $19 billion by 2010–11 and then decrease to $17 billion by 2013–14. This increase, while sizable, does not explain the totality of the increase in government spending. Please see *Canada's Economic Action Plan: Budget 2009* (Ottawa: Department of Finance, 2009), Table 4.6, p. 225, available at www.budget.gc.ca/2009/pdf/budget-planbugetaire-eng.pdf.

26 For an interesting discussion of how government spending affects economic performance, please see Alberto Alesina, Silvia Ardagna, Roberto Perotti, and Fabio Schiantarelli, "Fiscal Policy, Profits, and Investment," *American Economic Review* 92, no. 3 (2002); 571–589; and Alberto Alesina, Roberto Perotti, Francesco Giavazzi, and Tryphon Kollintzas, "Fiscal Expansions and Fiscal Adjustment in OECD Countries," *Economic Policy* 10, no. 21 (October 1995): 207–248.

27 To some extent, the federal government has already shown a willingness, at least in words—but not necessarily actions—to review and assess existing spending with a focus on restraint and achieving better results. See *Canada's Economic Action Plan: Budget 2009* (Ottawa: Department of Finance, 2009), Annex 3, "Responsible Spending," p. 266–278, available at www.budget.gc.ca/2009/pdf/budget-planbugetaire-eng.pdf.

28 For information on the Chrétien–Martin-era spending reforms, please see the 1995 federal budget, available at www.fin.gc.ca/budget95/binb/BINB-

eng.asp; and *A New Framework for Economic Policy* (Ottawa: Department of Finance, 1994), available at www.fin.gc.ca/Archive/NFrmrkEcPol_e.pdf.

29 It is also interesting to note the work examining government efficiency internationally. In particular, the work of Dr. Vito Tanzi and his colleagues indicates that many countries, including Canada, could achieve better results while spending less money through program reforms. Please see Antonio Afonso, Ludger Schuknecht, and Vito Tanzi (2005), "Public Sector Efficiency: An International Comparison," *Public Choice* 123 (2005): 321–347.

30 There are several proven rules-based approaches to limiting increases in government spending. For example, pay-as-you-go, or PAYGO, requirements, which were extraordinarily successful in the United States under President Clinton, require that any new spending be financed by reductions in existing programs. For more information, see the statement of Peter R. Orszag before the Committee of the Budget, U.S. House of Representatives, July 25, 2007, *Issues in Reinstating a Statutory Pay-As-You-Go Requirement* (Washington, DC: Congressional Budget Office, 2007), available at www.cbo.gov/ftpdocs/83xx/doc8385/07-24-PAYGO_Testimony.pdf. In addition, many US states have implemented tax and expenditure limitations (TELs) laws, which are spending rules that constrain the spending and revenues of governments. For more information, see Jason Clemens, Todd Fox, Amela Karabegovic, Sylvia LeRoy, and Niels Veldhuis, *Tax and Expenditure Limitations: The Next Step in Fiscal Discipline* (Vancouver: Fraser Institute, October 2003), available at www.fraserinstitute.org/commerce.web/product_files/TaxandExpenditureLimitations.pdf.

31 Canada maintains one of the highest marginal personal income tax rates on middle- and upper-income earners among the G7 countries. For more information, see *The Budget Plan 2008: Responsible Leadership* (Ottawa: Department of Finance, 2008), available at www.budget.gc.ca.

32 Interestingly, the authors opposed the reduction in the GST from 7 to 5 per cent based not on an aversion to tax relief but rather the type of tax relief enacted. As discussed in the section on the structure of taxation in the US, some taxes are better than others—more accurately, some taxes impose less cost on society than others. The authors believe the GST should have been kept at 7 per cent and tax relief focused on personal and business income tax rates instead.

33 See Milagros Palacios, Niels Veldhuis, and Michael Walker, *Tax Facts 15* (Vancouver: Fraser Institute, 2008), available at www.fraserinstitute.org/researchandpublications/publications/5427.aspx.

34 For more information on business taxes in Canada generally, please see the Technical Committee on Business Taxation website at the federal

Department of Finance, www.fin.gc.ca/toc/1998/brie_-eng.asp; and the committee's final report at http://dsp-psd.pwgsc.gc.ca/Collection/F32-5-1998E.pdf. Also, the C.D. Howe Institute maintains an ongoing centre at www.cdhowe.org/display.cfm?page=taxCompetitive that provides important studies on Canada's business tax competitiveness.

35 For information on Canada's corporate capital tax, please see Jason Clemens, Joel Emes, and Rodger Scott, *The Corporate Capital Tax: Canada's Most Damaging Tax* (Vancouver: Fraser Institute, 2002), available at www.fraserinstitute.org/researchandpublications/publications/2651.aspx.

36 While less obvious, and to a great extent much more of an insider's issue, is reform of depreciation expenses. Few economists, let alone normal, sane people, spend time worrying about depreciation schedules. These are guidelines set out by the government for businesses to write off the expenses of capital purchases such as equipment and machinery. These schedules not only need to ensure that the writedowns are in line with the actual useful lives of the capital assets, but more importantly, they should be used to encourage, or at least not discourage, such investment. Indeed, a number of reports examining Canada's productivity challenges over the years have pointed to the need for more generous writedown allowances for such investment. See Duanjie Chen and Jack Mintz, *Still a Wallflower: The 2008 Report on Canada's International Tax Competitiveness* (Toronto: C.D. Howe Institute, 2008), available at www.cdhowe.org/pdf/ebrief_63.pdf; and Don Drummond, "The Economists' Manifesto for Curing Ailing Canadian Productivity," *International Productivity Monitor* 13 (Fall 2006): 21–26, available at www.csls.ca/ipm.asp.

37 For information on Canada's capital gains tax, please see Jason Clemens, Niels Veldhuis, and Keith Godin, *The Economic Costs of Capital Gains Taxes* (Vancouver: Fraser Institute, 2007), available at www.fraserinstitute.org/researchandpublications/publications/3193.aspx.

38 Please see www.tfsa.gc.ca for more information on these accounts. Also, for background information, please see Jonathan Kesselman and Finn Poschmann, *A New Option for Retirement Savings: Tax-Prepaid Savings Plans* (Toronto: C.D. Howe Institute, 2001), available at www.cdhowe.org/pdf/Kesselman_&_Poschmann.pdf.

39 There is an important stipulation about the avoidance of capital gains taxes within RRSPs. While individuals do not technically pay capital gains taxes nor any other tax on their earnings in an RRSP, income taxes are nonetheless assessed when earnings are withdrawn from RRSPs. The result of this arrangement is that while capital gains in an RRSP are not taxed, they are actually taxed at the higher personal income tax rate when

they are withdrawn from the accounts. This is actually a serious problem with the tax-based design of RRSPs that should be looked into in the future.

40 Capital gains taxes are estimated to account for less than 1 per cent (0.8 per cent) of total federal and provincial revenues, or approximately $4.1 billion in 2008–09. For more information, see Niels Veldhuis, Keith Godin, and Jason Clemens, *The Economic Costs of Capital Gains Taxes* (Vancouver: Fraser Institute, Studies in Entrepreneurship and Markets No. 4, 2007), available at www.fraserinstitute.org/commerce.web/product_files/EconomicCostsCapitalGainsTax.pdf.

41 A business organization, Tax Harmonization, has been established to promote provincial sales tax harmonization. A number of useful resources on this tax issue, including scholarly studies, are available at http://taxharmonization.on.ca.

42 For information on the Atlantic provinces' reforms and their results, please see Michael Smart, *Lessons in Harmony: What Experience in the Atlantic Provinces Shows About the Benefits of a Harmonized Sales Tax* (Toronto: C.D. Howe Institute, 2007), available at www.cdhowe.org/pdf/commentary_253.pdf. For a good overview of the study, please see David Shipley, "HST Was a Boon for Business, Study Finds," *Telegraph-Journal* (St. John, NB), July 28, 2007, available at www.aims.ca/publicfinances.asp?typeID=4&id=1824.

43 For information on the Quebec sales tax system, please see www.cra-arc.gc.ca/tx/bsnss/tpcs/gst-tps/menu-eng.html.

44 For a summary of the BC reforms, please see Niels Veldhuis and Charles Lammam, "Harmonizing Sales Taxes Is Smart Thinking," *Vancouver Sun*, July 28, 2009, available at www.fraserinstitute.org/newsandevents/commentaries/6815.aspx.

45 Please see Bev Dahlby, Michael Smart, and Benjamin Dachis, *New Housing and the Harmonized Sales Tax: Lessons from Ontario* (Toronto: C.D. Howe Institute, 2009), available at www.cdhowe.org/pdf/backgrounder_119.pdf; and Peter Dungan, Jack Mintz, Finn Poschmann, and Thomas Wilson, *Growth-Oriented Sales Tax Reform for Ontario: Replacing the Retail Sales Tax with a 7.5 Percent Value-Added Tax* (Toronto: C.D. Howe Institute, 2008), available at www.cdhowe.org/pdf/Commentary_273.pdf.

46 The accounting firm Deloitte recently established a webpage with resources on both the proposed BC and Ontario sales tax reforms at www.deloitte.com/view/en_CA/ca/article/d1cb0b8c56912210VgnVCM100000ba42f00aRCRD.htm.

47 Quite rightly, a number of economists have explained the benefits of introducing a provincial sales tax along the lines of a GST in Alberta while

simultaneously reducing personal and/or business income taxes in a revenue-neutral manner. In other words, economists have suggested changing the mix of revenues in Alberta but not the total amount collected in order to rely on more efficient consumption taxes and reduce the use of more costly income taxes. For example, please see Bev Dahlby, *Tax Reform and Economic Growth in Alberta* (Calgary, AB: Canada West Foundation, 2000), available at www.cwf.ca/V2/files/200015.pdf; and Kenneth J. McKenzie, *Replacing the Alberta Personal Income Tax with a Sales Tax: Not Heresy but Good Economic Sense* (Calgary, AB: Canada West Foundation, 2000), available at www.cwf.ca/V2/files/200014.pdf.

48 Since 2000–01, consolidated federal and provincial spending on health care has increased by an average of 7.1 per cent, from $70.4 billion in 2000–01 to $121.6 billion in 2008–09. See Statistics Canada, CANSIM Table 385-0001, 2009.

49 For international comparisons of spending and performance, see Nadeem Esmail and Michael Walker, *How Good is Canadian Health Care?* 2008 ed. (Vancouver: Fraser Institute, 2008), available at www.fraserinstitute.org/commerce.web/product_files/HowGoodisCanadianHealthCare2008.pdf.

50 Two of this book's authors have proposed deeper decentralization in other publications. However, the two proposals are not mutually exclusive, nor are they contradictory. Clemens and Veldhuis have simply recommended a deeper decentralization to the provinces from the federal government. For specific information, please see Jason Clemens, Niels Veldhuis, and Milagros Palacios, *Tax Efficiency: Not All Taxes Are Created Equal* (Vancouver: Fraser Institute, 2007), available at www.fraserinstitute.org/commerce.web/product_files/TaxEfficiency.pdf; and Clemens and Veldhuis, *Productivity, Prosperity, and Business Taxes* (Vancouver: Fraser Institute, 2006), available at www.fraserinstitute.org/commerce.web/product_files/ProductivityProsperityBusinessTaxes.pdf.

51 See, for example, the Kirby Report, named after Senator Michael Kirby, who chaired the report, *Fourteenth Report: Reforming Health Protection and Promotion in Canada: Time to Act* (Ottawa: Standing Senate Committee on Social Affairs, Science and Technology, 2003), available at www.parl.gc.ca/37/2/parlbus/commbus/senate/com-e/soci-e/rep-e/repfinnov03-e.htm.

52 For more detail, see Brian Lee Crowley, Brian Ferguson, David Zitner, and Brett Skinner, *Definitely Not the Romanow Report: Achieving Equity, Sustainability, Accountability, and Consumer Empowerment in Canadian Health Care* (Halifax, NS: Atlantic Institute for Market Studies, 2002), available at www.aims.ca/library/notromanow.pdf; and Cynthia Ramsay and Nadeem Esmail, *The Alberta Health Care Advantage: An Accessible,*

High-Quality, and Sustainable System (Vancouver: Fraser Institute, 2004), available at www.fraserinstitute.org/commerce.web/product_files/AlbertaHealthCare.pdf.

53 Wendy Dobson is generally credited with coining the term "The Big Idea." See, for instance, Wendy Dobson, *Shaping the Future of the North American Economic Space: A Framework for Action* (Toronto: C.D. Howe Institute, April 2002).

54 The latest Buy American provisions in the US stimulus package have served to illustrate the consequences of this legal vacuum. See Les Whittington, "'Buy American' Talks Bog Down: No Deal Yet in Sight to Help Canadian Firms Shut Out of U.S. Bidding," *Toronto Star*, October 24, 2009, A12; and Campbell Clark, "The Struggle to Bend an Ear in Washington," *Globe and Mail*, October 23, 2009, A4.

55 See Madhavi Acharya and Tom Yew, "Canada: Land of Opportunity," *Toronto Star*, June 6, 2009, B1; and Michael Kergin and Birgit Matthiesen, *A New Bridge for Old Allies* (Toronto: Canadian International Council, November 2008), p. 1.

56 See Someshwar Rao, *North American Economic Integration: Opportunities and Challenges for Canada* (Montreal: Institute for Research on Public Policy, Working Paper Series No. 2004-09a, 2004), pp. 1–14; and Michael Kergin and Brigit Matthiesen, *A New Bridge for Old Allies* (Toronto: Canadian International Council, November 2008).

57 Paul G. Bradley and G. Campbell Watkins, "Canada and the U.S.: A Seamless Energy Border?" *C.D. Howe Institute Commentary* No. 178 (April 2003): 1–35.

58 According to Michael Hart and Bill Dymond, "The typical automobile, for example, assembled in Canada and exported to the United States, is made up of inputs that may already have crossed the border up to five times as they wended their way up the value chain." See Hart and Dymond, *Policy Implications of a Canada-US Customs Union* (Ottawa: Policy Research Initiative discussion paper, June 2005), p. 6.

59 As Hart and Dymond put it, "There are fewer and fewer 'Canadian' products, even as Canadian integration into the global economy increases." See Michael Hart and Bill Dymond, "Navigating the New Trade Routes: The Rise of Value Chains and the Challenges for Canadian Trade Policy," *C.D. Howe Institute Commentary* No. 259 (March 2008): 2.

60 For more on Canadian electricity exports, see *Canadian Electricity: Exports and Imports* (Calgary, AB: National Energy Board, 2003).

61 Canada has been the largest oil supplier to the United States since 1999. In 2008 Canada sent 2.23 million barrels per day of crude oil and petroleum

products to the United States—1.928 million barrels per day of crude oil and 0.3 million barrels per day of petroleum products. Canadian supply represents 23 per cent of total US imports of 9.755 million barrels per day. For downloadable export data going back to 1973, see http://tonto.eia.doe.gov/dnav/pet/pet_move_neti_a_epco_IMN_mbblpd_a.htm.

62 Allan Gotlieb, "A Grand Bargain with the US," *National Post*, March 5, 2003, A14.

63 Colin Robertson, *The United States to 2020 and the Requirement for Canadian Initiative* (paper prepared for the Business Council of British Columbia's Outlook 2020 Project, June 2009), p. i.

64 See Juliet O'Neill, "McKenna Urges Missile Defence: Liberals Entreated to Drop Opposition," *National Post*, October 16, 2006, A1; and David Rudd, "Muddling Through on Missile Defence: The Politics of Indecision," *Policy Options* (May 2005): 29–34.

65 The IJC was established during the Laurier era in 1909 following the signing of the Boundary Waters Treaty. It has provided leadership on joint water and boundary issues ever since. For more on its history, see William R. Willoughby, *The St. Lawrence Waterway: A Study in Politics and Diplomacy* (Madison, WI: University of Wisconsin Press, 1961).

66 Former senior Canadian official and trade policy expert Derek Burney has long been of the view that Mexico used NAFTA to create a trilateral dynamic in North American economic relations that has not been helpful to Canada. He makes this case recently in his memoir. See Burney, *Getting it Done* (Montreal and Kingston: McGill-Queen's University Press, 2005), p. 159.

67 In 2009, while on a trilateral visit to Guadalajara, Prime Minister Harper said Canada would be investing up to $15 million to train Mexican police fighting the drug cartels. See Andrew Mayeda, "Amigos Get Ready for Work; Summit of Three NAFTA Allies Underway Today," *The Province* (Vancouver), August 10, 2009, A7.

68 Canada, House of Commons, *Debates* (March 7, 1911), pp. 4740–4824.

69 Jeffrey Simpson, "We Talk Boldly about Free Trade But Do Nothing to Achieve It," *Globe and Mail*, November 10, 2009, A23.

70 In October 2009 the government announced that it was launching free trade talks with the European Union. See Andrew Mayeda, "Canada Begins Talks with EU; But Trade Deal Could Take Years to Consummate," *Times Colonist* (Victoria), October 20, 2009, B4.

71 For more detail on the federal government's infrastructure plans, see www.buildingcanada-chantierscanada.gc.ca/index-eng.html. For a detailed analysis of why mobility is important, see Ted Balaker, *Why Mobility Matters* (Los Angeles, CA: Reason Foundation, Policy Brief No. 43. 2006), available

at http://reason.org/files/52551973a35d9e8d342b78197e6d31d9.pdf.

72 For example, please see David Hartgen, Claire Chadwick, and M. Gregory Fields, *Transportation Performance of the Canadian Provinces* (Vancouver: Fraser Institute, 2008), available at www.fraserinstitute.org/researchandpublications/publications/6266.aspx; and *Mind the Gap: Finding the Money to Upgrade Canada's Aging Public Infrastructure* (Toronto: TD Bank, TD Economics, 2004), available at www.td.com/economics/special/infra04.pdf. In addition, the Canada West Foundation (www.cwf.ca) has done a great deal of work on transportation and infrastructure-related projects over the years.

73 Richard M. Bird, *The Growth of Government Spending in Canada*, (Toronto: Canadian Tax Foundation, July 1970), p. 47.

bibliography

Government Publications

A New Framework for Economic Policy. Ottawa: Department of Finance, 1994, available at www.fin.gc.ca/Archive/NFrmrkEcPol_e.pdf.

Bliss, Michael. *The Evolution of Industrial Policies in Canada: An Historical Survey*. Ottawa: Economic Council of Canada, 1982.

Board of Trustees of the Federal Old-Age and Survivors Insurance and Federal Disability Insurance Trust Funds (2009). *2008 Annual Report of the Board of Trustees for the Federal Old-Age and Survivors Insurance and Federal Disability Insurance Trust Funds*. Washington, DC: Board of Trustees of the Federal Old-Age and Survivors Insurance and Federal Disability Insurance Trust Funds, 2008, available at www.ssa.gov/OACT/TR/2009/tr09.pdf.

Canadian Electricity: Exports and Imports. Calgary, AB: National Energy Board, 2003.

Canada. House of Commons, *Debates*. March 7, 1911, pp. 4740–4824.

Canada Revenue Agency. *Corporation Tax Rates*. 2008, available at www.cra-arc.gc.ca/tx/bsnss/tpcs/crprtns/rts-eng.html.

Canada Revenue Agency. What Are the Income Tax Rates in Canada for 2008? 2008, available at www.cra-arc.gc.ca/tx/ndvdls/fq/2008_rt-eng.html.

Chaoulli v. Quebec (Attorney General). [2005] SCC35, available at www.canlii.org/en/ca/scc/doc/2005/2005scc35/2005scc35.html.

Congressional Budget Office. *The Budget and Economic Outlook: An Update*. Washington, DC: Congressional Budget Office, August 2009, available at www.cbo.gov/doc.cfm?index=10521.

Congressional Budget Office. "The Long-Term Outlook for Social Security," *The Long-Term Budget Outlook*. Washington, DC: Congressional Budget Office, June 2009, Chapter 3, available at www.cbo.gov/ftpdocs/102xx/doc10297/06-25-LTBO.pdf.

Congressional Budget Office. *A Preliminary Analysis of the President's Budget and an Update of the CBO's Budget and Economic Outlook*. Washington, DC: Congressional Budget Office, March 2009, available at www.cbo.gov/doc.cfm?index=10014.

Congressional Budget Office (2009). *The Long-Term Budget Outlook*. Washington, DC: Congressional Budget Office, June 2009, p. vii, available at www.cbo.gov/ftpdocs/102xx/doc10297/06-25-LTBO.pdf.

Congressional Budget Office. *The Long-Term Economic Effects of Some Alternative Budget Policies.* Washington, DC: Congressional Budget Office, May 2008, p. 2, available at www.cbo.gov/ftpdocs/92xx/doc9216/05-19-LongtermBudget_Letter-to-Ryan.pdf.

Congressional Budget Office, *Data on the Distribution of Federal Taxes and Household Income,* April 2009, available at www.cbo.gov/publications/collections/taxdistribution.cfm.

Congressional Budget Office. *The Nation's Long-Term Fiscal Outlook.* Washington, DC: Government Accountability Office, April 2008, available at www.gao.gov/new.items/d08783r.pdf.

Congressional Budget Office. *Corporate Income Tax Rates: International Comparisons.* Washington, DC: Congressional Budget Office, 2005, available at www.cbo.gov/ftpdocs/69xx/doc6902/11-28-CorporateTax.pdf.

Council of Economic Advisers (www.whitehouse.gov/administration/eop/cea), 2009. *The Economic Case for Health Care Reform,* available at www.whitehouse.gov/administration/eop/cea/TheEconomicCasefor HealthCareReform.

Hon. Dinning, Jim. *Budget Speech.* Edmonton, AB: Ministry of Finance and Enterprise, 1993.

Finance Canada. *The Budget Plan 2006: Focusing on Priorities.* Ottawa: Department of Finance, 2006, available at www.fin.gc.ca/budtoc/2006/budlist-eng.asp.

Finance Canada. *The Budget Plan.* February 1995, available at www.fin.gc.ca/toc/1995/buddoclist95-eng.asp.

Finance Canada. *Economic and Fiscal Update.* October 1994.

Finance Canada. *The Budget Plan.* February 1994.

Finnie, Ross, Ian Irvine, and Roger Sceviour., *Social Assistance Use In Canada: National and Provincial Trends in Incidence, Entry and Exit.* Ottawa: Statistics Canada, Analytical Studies Research Paper No. 245, Catalogue No. F0019M1E, May 2005, available at www.statcan.gc.ca/pub/11f0019m/11f0019m2005246-eng.pdf.

Flaherty, James M. *The Budget Speech 2009.* Ottawa: Department of Finance, 2009, available at www.budget.gc.ca/2009/pdf/speech-discours-eng.pdf.

Fourteenth Report: Reforming Health Protection and Promotion in Canada: Time to Act. Ottawa: Standing Senate Committee on Social Affairs, Science and Technology, 2003, available at www.parl.gc.ca/37/2/parlbus/commbus/senate/com-e/soci-e/rep-e/repfinnov03-e.htm.

Government of Alberta. *2006 Annual Report,* available at www.finance.alberta.ca/publications/annual_repts/govt/ganrep06/execsumm.pdf.

Government of Alberta. *A Better Way: Budget '94.* Edmonton, AB: Ministry of Finance and Enterprise, 1994.

Government of Alberta. *Alberta Hansard*. February 24, 1994.
Government of Alberta. *Informing Albertans: Message from the Premier*. Edmonton, AB: Ministry of Finance and Enterprise, 1993.
Government of Alberta. *A Financial Plan for Alberta: Budget '93*. Edmonton, AB: Ministry of Finance and Enterprise, 1993.
Government of Canada. *White Paper on Tax Reform, 1987*. Ottawa: Minister of Finance, June 1987.
Government of Canada. *Fall Economic and Fiscal Statement*. Ottawa: Department of Finance, 2008, available at www.fin.gc.ca/ec2008/EC/ectoc-eng.html.
Government of Canada. *Update of Economic and Fiscal Projections*. Ottawa: Department of Finance, 2009, available at www.fin.gc.ca/ec2009/ec-eng.asp.
Government of Canada. *Canada's Economic Action Plan: Budget 2009*. Ottawa: Department of Finance, 2009, available at www.budget.gc.ca/2009/pdf/budget-planbugetaire-eng.pdf.
Government of Canada. *Public Accounts of Canada, 1997–98*. Ottawa: Ministry of Public Works and Government Services, 1999.
Government of Ontario. *Ontario Budget 1996*. Toronto: Ministry of Finance, 1996, available at www.fin.gov.on.ca/en/budget/ontariobudgets/1996.
Government of Ontario. *1995 Fiscal and Economic Statement*. Toronto: Ministry of Finance, 1995.
Harris, Mike. *Statement by Mike Harris*, premier of Ontario. 1995, available at www.fin.gov.on.ca/english/budget/fallstatement/1995.
Health Canada. *Canada Health Act*, see *Canada Health Act Annual Report 2007–2008*. Ottawa: Health Canada, 2008, available at www.hc-sc.gc.ca/hcs-sss/pubs/cha-lcs/2008-cha-lcs-ar-ra/index-eng.php.
Martin, Paul. *Budget Speech*. Ottawa: Department of Finance, 1995.
Martin, Paul. *Budget Speech*. Ottawa: Department of Finance, 1994.
McQuillan, Peter E. and E. Cal Cochrane. *Capital Tax Issues*. Ottawa: Department of Finance , Technical Committee on Business Taxation, Series 1996–8, available at http://www.collectionscanada.gc.ca/webarchives/20071205172430/http://www.fin.gc.ca/taxstudy/wp96-8e.pdf
OECD. *Economic Outlook*. December 1985 to June 2009.
OECD. *Revenue Statistics*. 1965–2007, available at www.oecd.org.
Office of Budget and Management. *Mid-Session Review: Budget of the U.S. Government*. Washington, DC: Office of Budget and Management, 2009, Table S1, p. 25, available at www.whitehouse.gov/omb/assets/fy2010_msr/10msr.pdf.
Office of the Superintendent of Financial Institutions Canada. *23rd Actuarial Report on the Canada Pension Plan*. Ottawa: Office of the Superintendent of Financial Institutions, Office of the Chief Actuary of the Superintendent,

2007, available at www.osfi-bsif.gc.ca/app/DocRepository/1/eng/oca/reports/CPP/cpp23_e.pdf.

Office of the Superintendent of Financial Institutions Canada. *Actuarial Report: Old Age Security*. December 31, 2006, at www.osfi-bsif.gc.ca/osfi/index_e.aspx?DetailID=500.

Office of the Superintendent of Financial Institutions Canada. *Canada Pension Plan Sixteenth Actuarial Report*. Ottawa: Office of the Superintendent of Financial Institutions, Office of the Chief Actuary, 1997, available at www.osfi-bsif.gc.ca/app/DocRepository/1/eng/oca/reports/cpp/cpp16_e.pdf.

Roy, F. *Social Assistance by Province, 1993–2003*. Ottawa: Statistics Canada, Catalogue No. 11-010, November 2004, available at www.statcan.gc.ca/pub/11-010-x/11-010-x2004011-eng.pdf.

Statement of Peter R. Orszag before the Committee of the Budget, U.S. House of Representatives, *Issues in Reinstating a Statutory Pay-As-You-Go Requirement*. Washington, DC: Congressional Budget Office, 2007, available at www.cbo.gov/ftpdocs/83xx/doc8385/07-24-PAYGO_Testimony.pdf.

Statistics Canada. CANSIM Table 385-0001, 2009.

Statistics Canada. *Provincial Economic Accounts Data Tables, 2009*, available at www.statcan.gc.ca/bsolc/olc-cel/olc-cel?catno=13-018-X&lang=eng.

Statistics Canada. *National Economic and Financial Accounts, 2009*, available at www.statcan.gc.ca/nea-cen/index-eng.htm.

Statistics Canada. *Income in Canada*, 2007, Catalogue No. 75-202-X . 2009, available at www.statcan.gc.ca/pub/75-202-x/75-202-x2007000-eng.pdf.

Statistics Canada. *Labour Force Historical Review 2008*, Catalogue No, 71F0004XCB.

Statistics Canada. *Income in Canada, 2006*, Catalogue No. 75-202-X. 2008, available at www.statcan.gc.ca/pub/75-202-x/75-202-x2006000-eng.pdf.

Statistics Canada, *Financial Management System*, Public Institutions Division, 2002.

Statistics Canada. National Economic and Financial Accounts, CANSIM Tables 380-0007 and 385-0014, available at http://cansim2.statcan.gc.ca.

Statistics Canada. Public Institutions Division, Financial Management System. Electronic data, 1998 and 1999.

Statistics Canada. *Canadian Economic Observer, Historical Statistical Supplement 1995/96*. Catalogue No. 11-210-XPB.

Statistics Canada. *National Economic and Financial Accounts*. CANSIM Tables 380-0007 and 385-0014, available at http://cansim2.statcan.gc.ca.

Tchorzewski, Ed. *Budget Address: Rebuilding Saskatchewan Together*. Regina: Saskatchewan Finance, 1992.

US Bureau of Economic Analysis. *National Income and Product Accounts Tables.* 2009, available at www.bea.gov.

U.S. Bureau of Economic Analysis. *National Income and Product Accounts Tables.* 2009, available at www.bea.gov.

US Department of Labor. *Bureau of Labor Statistics*, Regional and State Unemployment, 2008 Annual Averages. 2009, available at www.bls.gov/lau.

U.S. Government Accountability Office. *Social Security Reform: Answers to Key Questions.* Washington, DC: Government Accountability Office, 2005, available at www.gao.gov/new.items/d05193sp.pdf.

U.S. Government Accountability Office. *Tax Policy: Summary of Estimates of the Costs of the Federal Tax System.* Washington, DC: Government Accountability Office, 2005, available at www.gao.gov/products/GAO-05-878.

Newspapers And Magazines

Acharya, Madhavi and Tom Yew. "Canada: Land of Opportunity," *Toronto Star.* June 6, 2009, B1.

"America's Public Debt: Tomorrow's Burden," *The Economist.* October 22, 2009, available at www.economist.com/displaystory.cfm?story_id=14699754.

Andrews, Edmund L. "Wave of Debt Payments Facing U.S. Government," *New York Times.* November 22, 2009, available at www.nytimes.com/2009/11/23/business/23rates.html?_r=2&th&emc=th.

Azzi, Stephen. "Debating Free Trade," *National Post.* January 14, 2006, A18.

Beauchesne, Eric. "Reduce Debt Faster, Canada Told: Meeting Existing Target Is a Strict Minimum, OECD Warns," *Vancouver Sun.* December 6, 1994.

"Canada Bankrupt?" *Wall Street Journal.* January 12, 1995.

Clark, Campbell. "The Struggle to Bend an Ear in Washington," *Globe and Mail.* October 23, 2009, A4.

Crane, Agnes. "New German Minister Rules Out Balanced Budget Paper," Reuters. October 25, 2009, available at www.reuters.com/article/bonds News/idUSLP6829392009 1025.

Daniels, Mitch. "The Coming Reset in State Government," *Wall Street Journal.* September 4, 2009, A17, available at http://online.wsj.com/article/SB10001424052970204731804574390603114939642.html

Deibel, Linda. "Long Battle over Free Trade Coming to an End," *Toronto Star.* December 24, 1988, A1.

Frum, David. "Three Dangers and an Opportunity," *C2C Journal.* June 22, 2009.

Gotlieb, Allan. "A Grand Bargain with the US," *National Post.* March 5, 2003, A14.

Hilsenrath, Jon and Brian Blackstone. "Bernanke Urges Deficit Reduction, Sees Growth This Year," *Wall Street Journal.* June 4, 2009, A3, available at http://online.wsj.com/article/SB124403584900281215.html.

Holtz-Eakin, Douglas. "The Coming Deficit Disaster," *Wall Street Journal.* November 20, 2009, available at http://online.wsj.com/article_email/SB10001424052748704888404574547492725871998-lMyQjAxMDA5MDIwMjEyNDIyWj.html.

Hopkins, Kathryn. "Britain Cannot Afford Any Further Fiscal Stimulus, King Warns," *Guardian.* March 24, 2009, available at www.guardian.co.uk/business/2009/mar/24/bankofenglandgovernor-banking.

Johnson, William. "'Leap of Faith: Canada Must Act on Free Trade, Macdonald Says," *Globe and Mail.* November 19, 1984, A1.

Krugman, Paul. "Till Debt Does Its Part," *New York Times.* August 27, 2009, available at www.nytimes.com/2009/08/28/opinion/28krugman.html?_r=1.

Mayeda, Andrew. "Canada Begins Talks with EU; But Trade Deal Could Take Years to Consummate," *Times Colonist* (Victoria). October 20, 2009, B4.

Mayeda, Andrew. "Amigos Get Ready for Work; Summit of Three NAFTA Allies Underway Today," *The Province* (Vancouver). August 10, 2009, A7

Mintz, Jack. "Here's a Stimulus Plan: Fix the PST," *Financial Post.* February 20, 2009.

Mintz, Jack. "New Brunswick Rising: A Wide-Ranging Tax Revolution Is Set to Turn New Brunswick into a 'Have' Province, and a Tax Haven for Business," *National Post.* July 30, 2008, FP15.

Murray, Charles. "Tax Withholding Is Bad for Democracy," *Wall Street Journal.* August 13, 2009, available at http://online.wsj.com/article_email/SB10001424052970204313604574328273572673730-lMyQjAxMDA5MDEwMzExNDMyWj.html.

O'Neill, Juliet. "McKenna Urges Missile Defence: Liberals Entreated to Drop Opposition," *National Post.* October 16, 2006, A1.

Olson, Nina. United States; see "We Still Need a Simpler Tax Code," *Wall Street Journal.* April 10, 2009, A13, available at http://online.wsj.com/article/SB123933106888707793.html.

Rauch, Jonathan. "Demosclerosis," *National Journal.* September 5, 1992, available at www.jonathanrauch.com/jrauch_articles/demosclerosis_the_original_article.

Shipley, David. "HST Was a Boon for Business, Study Finds," *Telegraph-Journal* (St. John, NB). July 28, 2007, available at www.aims.ca/publicfinances.asp?typeID=4&id=1824.

Simpson, Jeffrey. "We Talk Boldly about Free Trade But Do Nothing to Achieve It," *Globe and Mail.* November 10, 2009, A23.

Simpson, Jeffrey. "A Very Scary PM: 'I Don't Believe Any Taxes Are Good Taxes," *Globe and Mail.* July 14, 2009, A13.

Veldhuis, Niels and Charles Lammam. "Harmonizing Sales Taxes Is Smart Thinking," *Vancouver Sun*. July 28, 2009, available at www.fraserinstitute.org/newsandevents/commentaries/6815.aspx.

Weisman, Jonathan and Deborah Solomon. "Decade of Debt: $9 Trillion.," *Wall Street Journal.* August 26, 2009, A1, available at http://online.wsj.com/article/SB125119686015756517.html.

Whittington, Les. "'Buy American' Talks Bog Down: No Deal Yet in Sight to Help Canadian Firms Shut Out of U.S. Bidding," *Toronto Star.* October 24, 2009, A12.

Woods, James. "Boom and Bust: Sask. Population Dipstirs Debate over Future," *Star-Phoenix* (Saskatoon). July 1, 2006, A1.

Research Institute Reports And Studies

Ahern, William. *Can Income Tax Hikes Close the Deficit?* Washington, DC: The Tax Foundation, No. 197, October 2009, available at www.taxfoundation.org/files/ff197.pdf.

Balaker, Ted. *Why Mobility Matters.* Reason Foundation, Policy Brief No. 43. 2006, available at http://reason.org/files/52551973a35d9e8d342b7819 7e6d31d9.pdf.

Bartlett, Bruce. "Remembering Reagan's Tax Cuts," *Human Events* 62. No. 27, August 14, 2006: 1–5.

Bird, Richard M. *The Growth of Government Spending in Canada.* Toronto: Canadian Tax Foundation, July 1970.

Boessenkool, Kenneth J. *Back to Work: Learning from the Alberta Welfare Reform Experience.* Toronto: C.D. Howe Institute, April 1997.

Bradley, Paul G. and G. Campbell Watkins, "Canada and the U.S.: A Seamless Energy Border?" *C.D. Howe Institute Commentary* No. 178. April 2003: 1–35.

Canadian Institute for Health Information. *Surgical Volume Trends, 2009: Within and Beyond Wait Time Priority Areas.* Ottawa: Canadian Institute for Health Information, 2009.

Canadian Institute for Health Information. *National Health Expenditure Trends: 1975–2008.* Ottawa: Canadian Institute for Health Information, 2008.

Canada West Foundation. *Welfare Reform in Alberta: A Survey of Former Recipients.* Calgary: Canada West Foundation, 1997, available at www.cwf.ca/V2/files/199713.pdf.

Card, Michalopoulos and Phillip Robins. *When Financial Incentives Pay for Themselves: Early Findings from the Self-Sufficiency Project's Applicant Study.* Ottawa: Social Research Demonstration Corp., 1999.

Carling, Robert. Fiscal Shock and Awe in the United States. St. Leonards, NSW, Australia: Centre for Independent Studies, Vol. 1, No. 118, October 2009, available at www.cis.org.au/issue_analysis/IA118/IA118.pdf.

Chamberlain, Andrew, Gerald Prante, and Scott A. Hodge. *Who Pays America's Tax Burden, and Who Gets the Most Government Spending?* Washington, DC: Tax Foundation, 2007, available at www.taxfoundation.org/files/sr151.pdf.

Chen, Duanjie and Jack Mintz. *The Path to Prosperity: Internationally Competitive Rates and a Level Playing Field.* Toronto: C.D. Howe Institute, 2009, available at www.cdhowe.org/pdf/commentary_295.pdf.

Chen, Duanjie and Jack Mintz. *Still a Wallflower: The 2008 Report on Canada's International Tax Competitiveness.* Toronto: C.D. Howe Institute, 2008, available at www.cdhowe.org/pdf/ebrief_63.pdf.

Clemens, Jason and Niels Veldhuis. *GST Harmonization: Not Sexy, But Smart.* Vancouver: Fraser Institute, 2008, available at www.fraserinstitute.org/Commerce.web/product_files/GSTHarmonization.pdf.

Clemens, Jason (ed). *The Impact and Cost of Taxation in Canada. Vancouver, BC*: Fraser Institute, 2008, available at www.fraserinstitute.org/researchandpublications/publications/5173.aspx.

Clemens, Jason, Niels Veldhuis, and Milagros Palacios. *Tax Efficiency: Not All Taxes Are Created Equal.* Vancouver: Fraser Institute, 2007, available at www.fraserinstitute.org/commerce.web/product_files/TaxEfficiency.pdf.

Clemens, Jason, Niels Veldhuis, and Keith Godin. *The Economic Costs of Capital Gains Taxes.* Vancouver: Fraser Institute, 2007, available at www.fraserinstitute.org/researchandpublications/publications/3193.aspx.

Clemens, Jason, Charles Lammam, Milagros Palacios, and Niels Veldhuis. *Government Failure in Canada, 2007 Report: A Review of the Auditor General's Reports, 1992–2006.* Vancouver: Fraser Institute, 2007.

Clemens, Jason and Niels Veldhuis. *GST Cut is the Least Beneficial.* Vancouver, Fraser Institute, 2006, available at www.fraseramerica.org/Commerce.web/article_details.aspx?pubID=3614.

Clemens, Jason and Niels Veldhuis. *Productivity, Prosperity, and Business Taxes.* Vancouver: Fraser Institute, 2006, available at www.fraserinstitute.org/commerce.web/product_files/ProductivityProsperityBusinessTaxes.pdf.

Clemens, Jason and Niels Veldhuis. *The CPP's Next Big Challenges.* Vancouver: Fraser Institute, 2005, available at www.fraserinstitute.org/researchandpublications/publications/3089.aspx.

Clemens, Jason, Todd Fox, Amela Karabegovi, Sylvia LeRoy, and Niels Veldhuis. *Tax and Expenditure Limitations: The Next Step in Fiscal Discipline.* Vancouver: Fraser Institute, October 2003, available at www.fraserinstitute.org/commerce.web/product_files/TaxandExpenditureLimitations.pdf.

Clemens, Jason, Joel Emes, and Rodger Scott. *The Corporate Capital Tax: Canada's Most Damaging Tax*. Vancouver: Fraser Institute, 2002, available at www.fraserinstitute.org/researchandpublications/publications/2651.aspx.

Clemens, Jason and Chris Schafer. *Welfare Reform in British Columbia: A Report Card*. Vancouver: Fraser Institute, 2002, available at www.fraserinstitute.org/commerce.web/product_files/WelfareReforminBC.pdf.

Clemens, Jason and Chris Schafer. *Welfare in Saskatchewan: A Critical Evaluation*. Vancouver: Fraser Institute, 2002, available at www.fraserinstitute.org/commerce.web/product_files/WelfareinSaskatchewan.pdf

Council of Canadian Academies. *Expert Panel on Business Innovation and Business Strategy: Why Canada Falls Short*. 2009, available at www.scienceadvice.ca/documents/(2009-06-11)%20Innovation%20Report.pdf.

Courchene, Thomas. "Tax Reform: Impact on Individuals," in E.A. Carmichael (ed.), *Tax Reform: Perspectives on the White Paper*. Toronto: C.D. Howe Institute, 1988, pp. 11–48.

Crowley, Brian Lee, Brian Ferguson, David Zitner, and Brett Skinner. *Definitely Not the Romanow Report: Achieving Equity, Sustainability, Accountability, and Consumer Empowerment in Canadian Health Care*. Halifax, NS: Atlantic Institute for Market Studies, 2002, available at www.aims.ca/library/notromanow.pdf.

Cyrenne, Philippe. *Private Health Care in the OECD: A Canadian Perspective*. Toronto: University of Toronto, Centre for Public Management, Monograph Series No. 13, 2004.

Dahlby, Bev, Michael Smart, and Benjamin Dachis. *New Housing and the Harmonized Sales Tax: Lessons from Ontario*. Toronto: C.D. Howe Institute, 2009, available at www.cdhowe.org/pdf/backgrounder_119.pdf.

Dhalby, Bev. *Tax Reform and Economic Growth in Alberta*. Calgary: Canada West Foundation, 2000, available at www.cwf.ca/V2/files/200015.pdf

Dobson, Wendy. *Shaping the Future of the North American Economic Space: A Framework for Action*. Toronto: C.D. Howe Institute, April 2002.

Drummond, Don. "The Economists' Manifesto for Curing Ailing Canadian Productivity," *International Productivity Monitor 13*. Fall 2006: 21–26.

Dungan, Peter, Jack Mintz, Finn Poschmann, and Thomas Wilson, *Growth-Oriented Sales Tax Reform for Ontario: Replacing the Retail Sales Tax with a 7.5 Percent Value-Added Tax*. Toronto: C.D. Howe Institute, 2008, available at www.cdhowe.org/pdf/Commentary_273.pdf.

Edwards, Chris. *Obama's Budget Builds on Bush Precedents*. Washington, DC: Cato Institute, Tax and Budget Bulletins No. 55, March 2009, available at www.cato.org/pubs/tbb/tbb_0311_55.pdf.

Edwards, Chris. *State and Local Government Debt Is Soaring*. Washington, DC: Cato Institute, Tax and Budget Bulletin No. 37, 2006, available at www.cato.org/pubs/tbb/tbb_0706-37.pdf.

Elton, David. *Where Are They Now? Assessing the Impact of Welfare Reform on Former Recipients, 1993–1996*. Calgary: Canada West Foundation, 1997.

Emery, Herbert and Ronald D. Kneebone. *Will It Be Déjà Vu All Over Again?* University of Calgary, School of Public Policy, SPP Briefing Papers 2, Issue 1, April 2009, available at http://policyschool.ucalgary.ca/files/publicpolicy/SPP%20Briefing%20Paper%20-%20Kneebone%20&%20Emery%20FINAL%20(Apr%2009).pdf.

Eriksson, Daniel and Arne Björnberg. *Euro-Canada Health Consumer Index 2009*. Winnipeg: Frontier Centre for Public Policy, Series No. 61, May 2009, available at www.fcpp.org/images/publications/61.%202009%20Euro-Canada%20Health%20Consumer%20Index.pdf.

Emes, Joel and Andrei Kreptul. *The Adequacy of Welfare Benefits in Canada*. Vancouver: Fraser Institute, 1999, available at http://oldfraser.lexi.net/publications/critical_issues/1999/welfare_benefits.

Esmail, Nadeem. *Waiting Your Turn: Hospital Waiting Lists in Canada, 19th ed.* Vancouver: Fraser Institute, 2009, available at www.fraserinstitute.org/commerce.web/product_files/WaitingYourTurn_2009.pdf.

Esmail, Nadeem and Michael Walker. *How Good is Canadian Health Care? 2008 ed.*Vancouver: Fraser Institute, available at www.fraserinstitute.org/commerce.web/product_files/HowGoodisCanadianHealthCare2008.pdf.

Esmail, Nadeem. *Canada's Physician Supply*. Vancouver: Fraser Institute, 2008, available at www.fraserinstitute.org/commerce.web/product_files/Fraser-Forum_November2008.pdf, pp 13–17.

Esmail, Nadeem. *Guaranteed Suffering*. Vancouver: Fraser Institute, May 2007.

Finnie, Ross and Ian Irvine. *The Welfare Enigma: Explaining the Dramatic Decline in Canadians' Use of Social Assistance, 1993–2005*. Toronto: C.D. Howe Institute, 2008, available at www.cdhowe.org/pdf/commentary_267.pdf.

Ford, Reuben, David Gyarmati, Kelly Foley, and Doug Tattrie. *Can Work Incentives Pay for Themselves? Final Report on the Self-Sufficiency Project for Welfare Applicants*. Ottawa: Social Research and Demonstration Corp., 2003.

Frenette, Marc and Garnett Picot. *Life After Welfare: The Economic Well Being of Welfare Leavers in Canada during the 1990s*. Ottawa: Statistics Canada, Business and Labour Market Analysis No. 192, 2003, available at www.statcan.gc.ca/pub/11f0019m/11f0019m2003192-eng.pdf.

Gabel, Todd, Jason Clemens, and Sylvia LeRoy. *Welfare Reform in Ontario: A Report Card*. Vancouver: Fraser Institute, 2004, available at www.fraserinstitute.org/COMMERCE.WEB/product_files/WelfareReformInOntario.pdf.

Gabel, Todd, Jason Clemens, Sylvia LeRoy, and Niels Veldhuis. *Staying the Course on Welfare Time Limits.* Vancouver: Fraser Institute, 2003, available at www.fraserinstitute.org/commerce.web/product_files/FraserForum_December2003.pdf.

Gabel, Todd and Sylvia LeRoy. *The Self-Sufficiency Project: No Solution for Welfare Dependency.* Vancouver: Fraser Institute, September 2003.

Gale, William and Alan J. Auerbach. *An Update on the Economic and Fiscal Crises: 2009 and Beyond.* Washington, DC: Brookings Institution, 2009, available at www.brookings.edu/papers/2009/06_fiscal_crisis_gale.aspx.

Graham, John R. "Why Consumer-Driven Health Care is Crashing on the Shoals of Medicare," *Health Policy Prescriptions 6, No. 4*, 2009, available at http://liberty.pacificresearch.org/docLib/20080408_HPPv6n4_0408.pdf.

Grubel Herbert (ed). *Unlocking Canadian Capital: The Case for Capital Gains Tax Reform.* Vancouver: Fraser Institute, 2000.

Hart, Michael and Bill Dymond. "Navigating the New Trade Routes: The Rise of Value Chains and the Challenges for Canadian Trade Policy," *C.D. Howe Institute Commentary No. 259*. March 2008.

Hart, Michael. Some Thoughts on Canada–United States Sectoral Free Trade. Montreal: Institute for Research on Public Policy, 1985.

Hart, Michael and Bill Dymond. *Policy Implications of a Canada-US Customs Union.* Ottawa: Policy Research Initiative discussion paper, June 2005.

Hartgen, David, Claire Chadwick, and M. Gregory Fields. *Transportation Performance of the Canadian Provinces.* Vancouver: Fraser Institute, 2008, available at www.fraserinstitute.org/researchandpublications/publications/6266.aspx.

Heritage Foundation. *Capital Gains Tax Cuts: Myths and Facts.* Heritage Foundation, WebMemo 47, 2001, available at www.heritage.org/Research/Taxes/wm47.cfm.

Hodge, Scott. "U.S. States Lead the World in High Corporate Taxes," available at www.taxfoundation.org/publications/show/22917.html.

Howe, Neil and Richard Jackson. *The Myth of the 2.2 Percent Solution.* Washington, DC: Cato Institute, 1997, available at www.cato.org/pubs/ssps/ssp11.html.

Hunter, Garson. *Social Assistance Caseload Impact of the Building Independence Program in Saskatchewan: A Time-Series Analysis. Regina: University of Regina*, Social Policy Research Unit, 2004, available at http://dspace.cc.uregina.ca/dspace/bitstream/10294/926/1/occasional_paper_15.pdf.

Johnson, Rachael M. and Jeffrey Rohaly. *The Distribution of Federal Taxes, 2009–12.* Washington, DC: Tax Policy Center, 2009, available at www.taxpolicycenter.org/UploadedPDF/411943_distribution_federal.pdf.

Kergin, Michael and Brigit Matthiesen. *A New Bridge for Old Allies.* Toronto: Canadian International Council, November 2008.

Kesselman, Jonathon and Finn Poschmann, *A New Option for Retirement Savings: Tax-Prepaid Savings Plans.* Toronto: C.D. Howe Institute, 2001, available at www.cdhowe.org/pdf/Kesselman_&_Poschmann.pdf.

Lawson, Robert and Michel Kelly-Gagnon. *The Scope of Government and the Wealth of Quebecers.* Economic Note, Montreal Economic Institute, February 2001.

Martin, Joe. *Irrational Exuberance: The Creation of the CNR, 1917–1919,*" Rotman School of Management case study, 2006.

McArthur, William, Cynthia Ramsay, and Michael Walker. *Healthy Incentives: Canadian Health Reform in an International Context.* Vancouver: Fraser Institute, 1996, available at www.fraserinstitute.org/commerce.web/product_files/Healthy_Incentives.pdf.

McCaleb, Thomas S. *Deficits and Taxes: Federal Budget and Fiscal Policy in the 1980s.* Washington, DC: Cato Institute, 1994, available at www.cato.org/pub_display.php?pub_id=911&full=1.

McKenzie, Kenneth J. *Replacing the Alberta Personal Income Tax with a Sales Tax: Not Heresy but Good Economic Sense.* Calgary: Canada West Foundation, 2000, available at www.cwf.ca/V2/files/200014.pdf.

Mintz, Jack. *Cutting the Effective Corporate Tax Rate.* Washington, DC: Cato Institute, Tax and Budget Bulletin No. 50, October 2008, available at www.cato.org/pubs/tbb/tbb_1008-50.pdf.

Mintz, Jack and Thomas Wilson. *Removing the Shackles: Deferring Capital Gains Taxes on Asset Rollovers.* Toronto: C.D. Howe Institute, 2006, available at www.cdhowe.org/pdf/backgrounder_94.pdf.

Mintz, Jack. *After 87 Years, It Is Time to Fix the Income Tax Act,* C.D. Howe Institute E-Brief. September 20, 2004.

Mintz, Jack and Duanjie Chen. *Ontario's Fiscal Competitiveness in 2004.* Toronto: Institute for Competitiveness and Prosperity, November 8, 2004.

Mitchell, Daniel. *Corporate Taxes: America is Falling Behind.* Washington, DC: Cato Institute, Tax and Budget Bulletin No. 48, July 2007, available at www.cato.org/pubs/tbb/tbb_0707_48.pdf.

Mitchell, Daniel. *The Impact of Government Spending on Economic Growth.* Washington, DC: Heritage Foundation, Backgrounder No. 1831, 2005, available at www.heritage.org/research/budget/upload/bg_1831.pdf.

Mitchell, William C. and Randy T. Simmons. *Beyond Politics.* Oakland, CA: Independent Institute, 1994.

Moore, Stephen and John Silvia. *The ABCs of the Capital Gains Tax.* Washington,

DC: Cato Institute, 1995, available at www.cato.org/pub_display.php?pub_id=1101.

Palacios, Milagros, Niels Veldhuis, and Kumi Harischandra. *Canadian Government Debt 2008: A Guide to the Indebtedness of Canada and the Provinces.* Vancouver: Fraser Institute, 2008, available at www.fraserinstitute.org/commerce.web/product_files/CanadianGovernmentDebt2008.pdf.

Palacios, Milagros, Niels Veldhuis, and Michael Walker. *Tax Facts 15.* Vancouver: Fraser Institute, 2008, available at www.fraserinstitute.org/researchandpublications/publications/5427.aspx.

Perry, David B. *Financing the Canadian Federation, 1867 to 1995: Setting the Stage for Change.* Toronto: Canadian Tax Foundation, 1997.

Pew Center for the States. *Beyond California: States in Fiscal Peril.* Washington, DC: Pew Center on the States, 2009, available at http://downloads.pewcenteronthestates.org/BeyondCalifornia.pdf; a summary and links are available at www.pewcenteronthestates.org/report_detail.aspx?id=56044.

Prante, Gerald. *Summary of Latest Federal Individual Income Tax Data,* Fiscal Fact No. 183, available at http://taxfoundation.org/publications/show/250.html.

Ramsey, Cynthia and Nadeem Esmail. *The Alberta Health Care Advantage: An Accessible, High-Quality, and Sustainable System.* Vancouver: Fraser Institute, 2004, available at www.fraserinstitute.org/commerce.web/product_files/AlbertaHealthCare.pdf.

Rao, Someshwar. *North American Economic Integration: Opportunities and Challenges for Canada.* Montreal: Institute for Research on Public Policy, Working Paper Series No. 2004-09a, 2004: pp. 1–14.

Richards, John. *Now That the Coat Fits the Cloth. . . .* Toronto: C.D. Howe Institute, Commentary No. 143, June 2000, available at www.cdhowe.org/pdf/rich-4.pdf.

Richards, John. *Retooling the Welfare State: What's Right, What's Wrong, What's to Be Done.* Toronto: C.D. Howe Institute, 1997.

Rivlin, Alice. "Why and How to Cut the Deficit," *Brookings Review,* 1984.

Robertson, Colin. *The United States to 2020 and the Requirement for Canadian Initiative.* Paper prepared for the Business Council of British Columbia's Outlook 2020 Project, June 2009.

Rodriguez, L. Jacob."Chile's Private Pension System at 18: Its Current State and Future Challenges," *Cato Project on Social Security Privatization No. 17.* July 30, 1999, available at www.socialsecurity.org/pubs/ssps/ssp-17es.html.

Rudd, David. "Muddling Through on Missile Defence: The Politics of Indecision," *Policy Options.* May 2005: 29–34.

Sabatini, E. (Rico). *Welfare—No Fair: A Critical Analysis of Ontario's Welfare System (1985–1994)*. Vancouver: Fraser Institute, 1996.

Sarlo, Chris. *Poverty in Canada: 2006 Update*. Vancouver: Fraser Institute, 2006, available at www.fraserinstitute.org/commerce.web/product_files/PovertyinCanada2006.pdf.

Schafer, Chris, Joel Emes, and Jason Clemens. *Surveying U.S. and Canadian Welfare Reform*. Vancouver: Fraser Institute, 2001, available at http://fraserinstitute.org.

Sharpe, Andrew. "Lessons for Canada from International Productivity Experience," *International Productivity Monitor 14*. Spring 2007: 1–18.

Sharpe, Andrew. *Three Policies to Improve Productivity Growth in Canada*. Ottawa: Centre for the Study of Living Standards, 2007, available at www.csls.ca/reports/csls2007-05.pdf.

Smart, Michael. "Lessons in Harmony: What Experiences in the Atlantic Provinces Show about the Benefits of a Harmonized Sales Tax," *C.D. Howe Institute Commentary No. 253*. July 2007: 1-28.

Tax Foundation. *Total Federal Income Tax Compliance Costs, 1990–2015*, available at www.taxfoundation.org/research/show/1962.html.

TD Economics. *The Coming Era of Fiscal Restraint*. October 20, 2009, available at www.td.com/economics/special/db1009_fiscal.pdf.

TD Economics. *5-Year Federal Fiscal Forecast*. June 2009, available at www.td.com/economics/special/db0609_fiscal.pdf.

TD Economics. *Government Budget Balances and Net Debt*. May 2009, available at www.td.com/economics/budgets/govt_budget_09.pdf.

TD Economics. *Capital Taxes in Canada: The Beginning of the End of an Era?* 2007, available at www.td.com/economics/special/pg0607_tax.pdf.

TD Economics. *In Search of Well Being: Are Canadians Slipping Down the Economic Ladder?* 2005, available at www.td.com/economics/topic/bc0105_wellbeing.pdf.

TD Economics. *Who's To Blame for Canada's Productivity Woes?* 2005, available at ww.td.com/economics/topic/cg0605_prod.pdf.

TD Economics. *Mind the Gap: Finding the Money to Upgrade Canada's Aging Public Infrastructure*. 2004, available at www.td.com/economics/special/infra04.pdf.

Teslik, Lee Hudson. "NAFTA's Economic Impact," *Council on Foreign Relations* backgrounder. July 7, 2009.

Treff, Karin and David B. Perry. *Finances of the Nation: A Review of Expenditures and Revenues of the Federal, Provincial, and Local Governments of Canada, multiple series, 1985–90*. Toronto: Canadian Tax Foundation, available at www.ctf.ca.

Tullock, Gordon, Arthur Seldon, and Gordon L. Brady. *Government Failure: A Primer in Public Choice.* Washington, DC: Cato Institute, 2002.

Veldhuis, Niels Keith Godin, and Jason Clemens. *The Economic Costs of Capital Gains Taxes.* Vancouver, BC: Fraser Institute, Studies in Entrepreneurship and Markets No. 4, 2007, available at www.fraserinstitute.org/commerce.web/product_files/EconomicCostsCapitalGainsTax.pdf.

Walker, Michael. "Wall Street Journal Sounds Warning," *Fraser Forum.* February 1995.

Watson, William, John Richards, and David Brown. *The Case for Change: Reinventing the Welfare State.* Toronto: C.D. Howe Institute, 1994.

Wonnacott, Paul. *The United States and Canada: The Quest for Free Trade: An Examination of Selected Issues.* Washington, DC: Institute for International Economics, 1987.

Periodicals

Afonso, Antonio, Ludger Schuknecht, and Vito Tanzi (2005) "Public Sector Efficiency: An International Comparison," *Public Choice* 123. 2005: 321–347.

Alesina, Alberto F. and Silvia Ardagna. "Large Changes in Fiscal Policy: Taxes Versus Spending," *National Bureau of Economic Research*, NBER Working Paper No. 15438, October 2009, available at www.nber.org/papers/w15438.

Alesina, Alberto, Silvia Ardagna, Roberto Perotti, and Fabio Schiantarelli. "Fiscal Policy, Profits, and Investment," *American Economic Review* 92, No. 3. 2002.

Alesina, Alberto and Roberto Perotti (1996), "Fiscal Adjustments in OECD Countries: Composition and Macroeconomic Effects," *National Bureau of Economic Research*, NBER Working Paper No. 5730, August 1996, available at www.nber.org/papers/w5730.

Alesina, Alberto, Roberto Perotti, Francesco Giavazzi, and Tryphon Kollintzas. "Fiscal Expansions and Fiscal Adjustment in OECD Countries," *Economic Policy 10*, No. 21. October 1995: 207–248.

Ballard, Charles L., John B. Shoven, and John Whalley. "General Equilibrium Computations of the Marginal Welfare Costs of Taxes in the United States," *American Economic Review* 75, No. 1. 1985: 128–138.

Beaulieu, Eugene and J.C. Herbert Emery. "Pork Packers, Reciprocity, and Laurier's Defeat in the 1911 Canadian General Election," *Journal of Economic History.* No. 4, December 2001: 1083–1101.

Bothwell, Robert. "Canadian-United States Relations: Options for the 1970s," *International Journal.* (Winter 2002-2003): 65-88.

Dion, Richard. "Interpreting Canada's Productivity Performance in the Past Decade: Lessons from Recent Research," *Bank of Canada Review.* Summer 2007: 19–32.

Feldstein, Martin. "The Effect of Taxes on Efficiency and Growth," *National Bureau of Economic Research*, NBER Working Paper No. 12201, 2006, available at www.nber.org/papers/w12201.

Green, David A and W. Craig Riddell. "The Economic Effects of Unemployment Insurance in Canada: An Empirical Analysis of UI Disentitlement," *Journal of Labor Economics.* No. 1, Part 2: U.S. and Canadian Income Maintenance Programs. January 1993: S96–S147.

Jorgensen, Dale W. and Yun Kun-Young. "The Excess Burden of Taxation in the United States," *Journal of Accounting and Finance* 6. 1991: 487–508.

Kotlikoff, Lawrence J. and Christian Hagist. "Who's Going Broke? Comparing Healthcare Costs in Ten OECD Countries," *National Bureau of Economic Research*, NBER Working Paper No. 11833, 2005.

Kuhn, Peter and Chris Riddell. "The Long-Term Effects of a Generous Income Support Program: Unemployment Insurance in New Brunswick and Maine, 1940–1991" *National Bureau of Economic Research*, NBER Working Paper No. 11932, January 2006.

Muirhead, Bruce. "From Special Relationship to Third Option: Canada, the U.S. and the Nixon Shock," *The American Review of Canadian Studies.* (Spring 2004): 439-462.

Rose, Joseph B., Gary N. Chaison, and Enrique de la Garza. "A Comparative Analysis of Public Sector Restructuring in the US, Canada, Mexico and the Caribbean," *Journal of Labor Research* 21, No. 4. Fall 2000: 601–625.

Schuknecht, Ludger and Vito Tanzi. "Public Sector Efficiency: An International Comparison," *Public Choice* 123: 321–347.

Sharp, Mitchell. "Canada-US Relations: Options for the Future," *International Perspectives Special Issue*, Autumn 1972: 1–24.

Tanzi, Vito. "The Economic Role of the State in the Twenty-First Century," *Cato Journal*, Vol. 25, No. 3. Fall 2005: 617–39.

Tanzi, Vito and Ludger Schuknecht. "Reconsidering the Fiscal Role of Government: The International Perspective," *American Economic Review* 87. 1997: 164–68.

Tanzi, Vito and Ludger Schuknecht. "Reforming Government: An Overview of the Recent Experience," *European Journal of Political Economy* 13. 1997: 395–417.

Winer, Stanley L. and J. Stephen Ferris. "Searching for Keynesianism," *European Journal of Political Economy* 24. 2008: 294–316.

Books And Pamphlets

Anastakis, Dimitry. *Auto Pact: Creating a Borderless North American Auto Industry, 1960–1971*. Toronto: University of Toronto Press, 2005.

Azzi, Stephen. *A Commentary: On Laurie Richie Dawson's The Evolution of Canadian FDI Policy in the Post-War Era*. April 2005, available at http://www.carleton.ca/ctpl/pdf/conferences/tradeinvestment_azzi_comments.pdf.

Azzi, Stephen. *Walter Gordon and The Rise of Canadian Nationalism*. Montreal and Kingston: McGill-Queen's University Press, 1999.

Baumol, William J., Robert E. Litan, and Carl J. Schramm. *Good Capitalism, Bad Capitalism, and the Economics of Growth and Prosperity*. New Haven, CT: Yale University Press, 2007.

Beito, David, Peter Gordon, and Alexander Tabarrok. *Voluntary City: Choice, Community, and Civil Society*. Ann Arbor: University of Michigan Press, 2002.

Beito, David. *From Mutual Aid to the Welfare State: Fraternal Societies and Social Services, 1890–1967*. Chapel Hill: University of North Carolina Press, 2000.

Bercuson, David (ed). *Canada and the Burden of Unity*. Toronto: Gage, 1980.

Berman, Dale, Morley Gunderson, and Douglas Hyatt (eds). *Public Sector Employment in a Time of Transition*. Madison, WI: Industrial Relations Research Centre, 1996.

Bliss, Michael. *Right Honourable Men: The Descent of Canadian Politics from Macdonald to Chrétien*. Toronto: HarperCollins Publishers, 2004.

Bliss, Michael. *Northern Enterprise: Five Centuries of Canadian Business*. Toronto: McClelland and Stewart, 1987.

Bothwell, Robert and J.L. Granatstein. *Our Century: Canadian Journey*. Toronto: McArthur and Company, 2000.

Bothwell, Robert, Ian Drummond, and John English. *Canada, 1900–1945*. Toronto: University of Toronto Press, 1987.

Bougrine, Hassan and Mario Seccareccia (eds). *Introducing Macroeconomic Analysis: Issues, Questions, and Competing Views*. Toronto: Emond Montgomery, 2009.

Brown, R.C. and Ramsay Cook. *Canada, 1896–1921: A Nation Transformed*. Toronto: McClelland and Stewart, 1974.

Bryden, P.E. *Planners and Politicians: Liberal Politics and Social Policy 1957–1968*. Montreal and Kingston: McGill-Queen's University Press, 1997.

Burney, Derek. *Getting it Done*. Montreal and Kingston: McGill-Queen's University Press, 2005.

Campbell, Robert M. *Grand Illusions: The Politics of the Keynesian Experience in Canada, 1945–1975*. Peterborough, ON: Broadview Press, 1987.

Canto, Victor A., Douglas H. Jones, and Arthur B. Laffer. *Foundations of Supply-Side Economics—Theory and Evidence*. New York: Academic Press, 1982.

Cohen, Andrew and J.L. Granatstein (eds). *Trudeau's Shadow: The Life and Legacy of Pierre Elliott Trudeau*. Toronto: Vintage Canada, 1999.

Creighton, Donald. *The Forked Road: Canada, 1939–1957*. Toronto: McClelland and Stewart, 1976.

Crowley, Brian Lee. *Fearful Symmetry: The Fall and Rise of Canada's Founding Values*. Toronto: Key Porter Books, 2009.

Cook, Ramsay and Réal Bélanger. *Canada's Prime Ministers, Macdonald to Trudeau: Portraits from the Dictionary of Canadian Biography*. Toronto: University of Toronto Press, 2007.

de Tocqueville, Alexis. *Democracy in America*. Chicago: University of Chicago Press, 2002.

Dafoe, J.W. *Laurier: A Study in Canadian Politics*. Toronto: McClelland and Stewart, 1963.

Doern, Bruce and Brian Tomlin. *Faith and Fear*. Toronto: Stoddart, 1991.

Easterbrook, W.T. and Hugh G.J. Aitken. Canadian Economic History. Toronto: University of Toronto Press, 1990.

Edwardson, Ryan. *Canadian Content: Culture and the Quest for Nationhood*. Toronto: University of Toronto Press, 2008.

Fayerweather, John. *Foreign Investment in Canada: Prospects for a National Policy*. Toronto: Oxford University Press, 1974.

Ferguson, Barry. *Remaking Liberalism: The Intellectual Legacy of Adam Shortt, O.D. Skelton, and W.A. Mackintosh, 1890–1925*. Montreal and Kingston: McGill-Queen's University Press, 1993.

Forster, Ben. *A Conjunction of Interests: Business, Politics, and Tariffs, 1825–1879*. Toronto: University of Toronto Press, 1986.

Frizzell, Alan, Jon H. Pammett, and Anthony Westell (eds). *The Canadian General Election of 1988*. Ottawa: Carleton University Press, 1989.

Frum, David. *How We Got Here: The '70s*. New York: Basic Books, 2000.

Gillespie, Irwin W. *Tax, Borrow and Spend: Financing Federal Spending in Canada, 1867–1990*. Ottawa: Carleton University Press, 1991.

Gordon, Scott H. "A Twenty Year Perspective: Some Reflections on the Keynesian Revolution in Canada," in *Canadian Economic Policy since the War: A Series of Six Public Lectures in Commemoration of the Twentieth Anniversary of the 'White Paper' on Employment and Income of 1945*. Ottawa: Carleton University Press, 1965: 23-46.

Gratzer, David. *Code Blue: Reviving Canada's Health Care System*. Toronto: ECW Press, 1999.

Guest, Denis. *The Emergence of Social Security in Canada*. Vancouver: University of British Columbia Press, 1985.

Hart, Michael. *A Trading Nation: Canadian Trade Policy from Colonialism to Globalization*. Vancouver: UBC Press, 2002.

Hillmer, Norman (ed). *Partners Nevertheless: Canadian-American Relations in the Twentieth Century*. Toronto: Copp Clark Pitman Ltd., 1989.

Hillmer, Norman and J.L. Granatstein. *Empire to Umpire*. Toronto: Irwin, 2000.

Iacovetta, Franca (ed). *A Nation of Immigrants: Women, Workers, and Communities in Canadian History, 1840s–1960s*. Toronto: University of Toronto Press, 1998.

Johnson, Harry. *The Canadian Quandary: Economic Problems and Policies*. Toronto: McClelland & Stewart Limited, 1977.

Johnson, Paul. *The Birth of the Modern: World Society 1815-1830*. New York: Harper Perennial, 1999.

Laxer, Gordon. *Open for Business: The Roots of Foreign Ownership in Canada*. Toronto: Oxford University Press, 1989.

Levitt, Kari. *Silent Surrender: The Multinational Corporation in Canada*. Montreal and Kingston: McGill-Queen's University Press, 2002.

MacKay, Donald. *The People's Railway, A History of Canadian National*. Vancouver: Douglas and McIntyre, 1992.

Mackintosh, W.A. *The Economic Background of Dominion-Provincial Relations*. Ottawa: Royal Commission on Dominion-Provincial Relations, first published in 1939.

McCalla, Douglas (ed). *The Development of Canadian Capitalism: Essays in Business History*. Toronto: Copp Clark Pitman, 1990.

Morris, Edmund. *The Rise of Theodore Roosevelt*. New York: Modern Library, 2001.

Morton, W.L. *The Critical Years: The Union of British North America, 1857–1873*. Toronto: McClelland and Stewart, 1968.

Mueller, David. *Public Choice Approach to Politics*. Northampton, MA: Edward Elgar, 1993.

Muirhead, Bruce. *The Development of Postwar Canadian Trade Policy: The Failure of the Anglo-European Option*. Montreal and Kingston: McGill-Queen's University Press, 1993.

Murphy, Rae. *Canadian History since 1867: The Post-Confederation Nation*. Piscataway, NJ: Research and Education Association, 1993.

Nelles, H.V. *Politics of Development: Forests, Mines, and Hydro-Electric Power in Ontario, 1849–1941*, 2nd ed. Montreal and Kingston: McGill-Queen's University Press, 2005.

Newman, Peter C. *The Secret Mulroney Tapes: Unguarded Confessions of a Prime Minister*. Toronto: Vintage Canada, 2006.

Norrie, Kenneth and Doug Owram. *A History of the Canadian Economy*. Toronto: Harcourt, Brace and Jovanovich, 1991.

North, Douglass. *The Role of Institutions in Economic Development—Gunnar Myrdal Lecture.* New York: United Nations, 2003.

North, Douglass. *Institutions, Institutional Change, and Economic Performance.* Cambridge: Cambridge University Press, 1990.

Olson, Mancur. *The Rise and Decline of Nations: Economic Growth, Stagflation, and Social Rigidities.* New Haven, CT: Yale University Press, 1992.

Owram, Douglas. *The Government Generation: Canadian Intellectuals and the State, 1900–1945.* Toronto: University of Toronto Press, 1986.

Pomfret, Richard. *Economic Development of Canada.* Toronto: Routledge Press, 2006.

Rosenberg, Nathan and L.E. Birdzell Jr. *How the West Grew Rich: The Economic Transformation of the Industrial World.* New York: Basic Books, 1986.

Savoie, Donald J. *Governing from the Centre: The Concentration of Power in Canadian Politics.* Toronto: University of Toronto Press, 1999.

Sawler, Harvey. *Frank McKenna: Beyond Politics.* Douglas and McIntyre, 2009.

Schull, Joseph. *Laurier: The First Canadian.* Toronto: Macmillan, 1965.

Shoven John B. and John Whalley. *Canada–U.S. Tax Comparisons.* Chicago and London: University of Chicago Press, 1992.

Solimano, Andres (ed). *Social Inequality.* Ann Arbor: University of Michigan Press, 1998.

Speer, Sean C. *J.J. Deutsch: A Keynesian in Canada, 1911–1976.* Unpublished Ph.D. thesis, University of Ottawa, forthcoming in 2011.

Stevens, G.R. *History of the Canadian National Railways.* New York: Macmillan, 1973.

Thompson, John Herd and Stephen J. Randall. *Canada and the United States: Ambivalent Allies.* Athens: University of Georgia Press, 1994.

Thompson, John Herd and Allen Seager. *Canada, 1922–1939: Decades of Discord.* Toronto: McClelland and Stewart, 1985.

Waite, P.B. *Canada, 1874–1896: Arduous Destiny.* Toronto: McClelland and Stewart, 1971.

Watson, William. *Globalization and the Meaning of Canadian Life.* Toronto: University of Toronto Press, 1998.

Whitaker, Reg. *Canadian Immigration Policy Since Confederation.* Ottawa: Canadian Historical Association, 1991.

Willoughby, William R. *The St. Lawrence Waterway: A Study in Politics and Diplomacy.* Madison: University of Wisconsin Press, 1961.

Yergin, Daniel, and Joseph Stanislaw. *The Commanding Heights: The Battle for the World Economy.* New York: Simon & Schuster, 2002.